The Decline and Fall
of the Liberal Republicans

The Decline and Fall
of the Liberal Republicans
From 1952 to the Present

NICOL C. RAE

New York   Oxford
OXFORD UNIVERSITY PRESS
1989

Oxford University Press

*JK 2356
R 24
1989*

Oxford New York Toronto
Delhi Bombay Calcutta Madras Karachi
Petaling Jaya Singapore Hong Kong Tokyo
Nairobi Dar es Salaam Cape Town
Melbourne Auckland
and associated companies in
Berlin Ibadan

Published by Oxford University Press, Inc.
200 Madison Avenue, New York, New York 10016

Oxford is a registered trademark of Oxford University Press

Library of Congress
Library of Congress Cataloging-in-Publication Data
Rae, Nicol C.
  The decline and fall of the liberal Republicans :
from 1952 to the present / Nicol C. Rae.
    p.   cm.
  Revision of the author's thesis (doctoral).
  Bibliography: p.
  Includes index.
  ISBN 0-19-505605-1,
  1. Republican Party (U.S. : 1854-   ) 2. Liberalism—United States.
3. United States—Politics and government—1945-   I. Title.
JK2356.R24   1989   88-18790
324.2734'09—dc19   *CIP*

10 9 8 7 6 5 4 3 2 1

Printed in the United States of America
on acid-free paper

*For my parents
to whom I owe everything*

Preface

This book is about the decline and fall of a once-dominant faction within a major U.S. political party. As such, it attempts to provide an extended discussion of three subjects which have been largely ignored by scholars of contemporary American politics: the Republican party, the decline of the "eastern establishment," and party factionalism.

The remarkable neglect of the Republican party in American political science has led to an extremely one-sided account of the transformation of the American party system in recent decades. Even more neglected is the rapid and extraordinary disappearance of what was once popularly known as the Republicans' "liberal wing" in presidential politics. Liberal Republicans have been America's closest analogue to a political and social "establishment" in the European sense. Their eclipse as a significant political force thus demands greater attention from those who wish to understand developments in American politics and society over the last quarter-century. The final objective of this study is to make some contribution to the other greatly neglected area of party factionalism in modern American politics.

The book began as a doctoral thesis at Oxford University where the fellows, staff, and students of Nuffield College, Oxford provided a congenial academic environment for my studies. In the United States, Yale University and the Brookings Institution were ideal bases for my research. The Economic and Social Research Council of Great Britain and Nuffield College have also been generous in their financial support.

My work could not have proceeded without the inspiration and encouragement of the late Philip Williams of Nuffield College, to whom all students of American government in the U.K. owe an immense debt. I am also particularly grateful to my doctoral supervisors, Gillian Peele and Byron Shafer, for patiently reading and revising the text and for their invariably sound advice as the book progressed. Thesis examiners David Goldey and Professor Anthony King are to be thanked for their helpful and constructive criticism, and I am grateful to Michael Brock, formerly Warden of Nuffield College, for his consistent and generous support of the project. I am greatly indebted to Elaine Herman who introduced me to the intricacies of the word processor and whose skills have subsequently rescued me from many actual and potential crises in the preparation of this book.

In the United States, I have been assisted by many persons, but particular mention should be made of Professor David Mayhew of Yale University, for his wise advice and unrivaled knowledge of the American party system. Lawrence DeNardis of New Haven and James Reichley of the Brookings Institution provided encouragement for the project and I benefited considerably from their wide knowledge and experience of Republican party politics. I am also grateful to Richard Neustadt for his interest in my travails and promotion of my work. Special thanks are due to two good friends, Andrew Robertson and Michael Lind, for many stimulating discussions on liberal Republicans and other related topics, and to their families for their extraordinary hospitality during my time in the United States.

I would like to take this opportunity to thank all those who agreed to be interviewed for the project (their names and the dates of the interviews are listed at the end of this book), since it could certainly not have been written without their generous assistance.

At Oxford University Press, Henry Hardy in Oxford and Valerie Aubry in New York showed great patience in dealing with my relentless queries and the delayed arrival of my manuscripts.

Finally, thanks are due most of all to my parents, John and Lily Rae, for their patience, understanding, and moral and material support during the writing of this book and at all other times.

All the facts set down in this book are accurate to the best of my knowledge, although subsequent scholarship will no doubt reveal deficiencies in many areas. If nothing else, I hope the book will at least go some way to remedy the neglect of Republican party affairs in recent American political science and historical scholarship. Should it succeed in stimulating debate and further study on this subject, it will have fulfilled its purpose.

Oxford   N. C. R.
February 1988

Contents

Tables

*The Decline and Fall
of the Liberal Republicans*

INTRODUCTION

Liberal Republicans and American Party Factionalism

The transformation of the party system is *the* critical factor under-lying recent developments in American politics. Those who view this transformation as having ultimately strengthened or renewed the parties, as opposed to having fostered their decomposition, nevertheless do not deny that the traditional model of the non-ideological, state- and local-based, pluralist American political party needs to be substantially modified in the light of recent developments.

One particularly significant aspect of this revised model is the greater emphasis on ideology in partisan debate. The traditional American party was almost defined by its peculiarly nonideologi-cal character: both leaders and followers were motivated more by pragmatic considerations of electoral victory and patronage, and divided from their opponents more by (often symbolic) ethnocultural factors, than great issues of philosophical principle. This nondogmatic character made possible the remarkable social pluralism within American party coalitions, allowing apparently alien groups (for example, northern Jews and southern white Protestants) to co-exist under the same party label. In the new world of American politics, however, the Democratic party has become a more consistently liberal party, and the Republican party more consistently conservative, than has been the case in any previous period of American history. And as the parties have become more narrowly defined in terms of ideology, the centrist or incongruous elements in both parties have declined in influence. In modern American politics liberal Republicans and conservative Democrats appear to be mavericks or misfits, rather than natural elements of their respective party coalitions.

A major problem with the scholarly analysis of the new American party system is that it has been mainly confined to study of the Democratic party. As a consequence there has been a tendency to consider the Republican party as being of secondary importance, and to assume that changes in the Democratic party have been exactly paralleled in the GOP with similar effects. The Democratic party is seen as the dynamic actor in the process, following a thesis of partisan change in America resembling that of Samuel Lubell:

> Our political solar system, in short, has been characterized not by two equally competing suns, but by a sun and a moon. It is within the majority party that the issues of any particular period are fought out; while the minority party shines in reflected radiance of the heat thus generated.[1]

The following pages should demonstrate that this view is incorrect, and that in recent American political history, the "moon" party has generally been more indicative of change in the party system that the "sun." It was within the minority party's ranks that ideological, or purist, politics first came to the fore, with the growth of the Conservative movement during the 1950s and the nomination of Barry Goldwater, a self-proclaimed conservative ideologue, for president in 1964. Nevertheless, the Republicans also had a long-standing progressive or liberal wing which had sought to broaden the party's electoral base by making some accommodation with the public philosophy of the New Deal. In alliance with Republican party regulars, oriented primarily toward victory at the polls, this wing was generally successful in Republican presidential politics in the 1932–60 period. Since 1964, however, the liberal wing has been more or less eliminated from the Republican party at the presidential level.

This book views developments in American politics in the second half of this century from the perspective of the liberal wing of the Republican party, and shows the extent to which its decline has been symptomatic of the advent of the "new politics" in the

United States. The decline of the liberal Republicans is frequently cited as evidence of the dissolution of traditional American party politics and the concomitant development of ideologically homogeneous parties in the United States. Underlying trends in the political system, such as the breakup of the popular consensus around the New Deal public philosophy, the changing demographics of Republican electoral support, and the loss of influence on the part of party regulars and officeholders over candidate selection at all levels, were all decisive factors in this process. Yet the extent of the liberal Republican decline was also exacerbated by the foibles of the liberal Republican leadership in the 1960–80 period. In the Democratic party, conservative Democrats were able to maintain their position through maintaining a regional base in the South and West. On the Republican side, centrist Republicans adapted to the new politics in many instances, at the subpresidential level, and ensured their survival. At the national level, however, tactical ineptitude, indiscipline, lack of foresight, and failure to construct the type of political organization required by the reformed nominating process led the liberal Republicans from a weakened position in presidential politics to virtual extinction by 1980.

Before proceeding further, it is necessary to make some general points here about the troublesome concept of factionalism as applied to American parties and also to elucidate some terminological difficulties.

American party factions have characteristically been *ad hoc,* amorphous, and indisciplined; centered around particular personalities; and rooted in sectional divisions.[2] Richard Rose, writing on British parties, introduced a distinction between factions and tendencies, defining the former as "self-consciously organised as a body with a measure of discipline and cohesion," and defining tendencies as

> a stable set of attitudes rather than a stable group of politicians. . . .
> Adherents are often not self-consciously organised in support of a
> single policy and they do not expect, nor are expected, to continue
> as a group supporting the same tendency for a long period of time.[3]

American parties lack the disciplined, intraparty blocs characteristic of party factions in West European systems, and "tendencies" would appear to be the more apposite term to apply in this case, although Howard Reiter is correct in arguing that American tendencies probably have a greater continuity of personnel than Rose's term implies.[4]

Within the Republican party in this century, it is possible to discern three different bases of intraparty division. The first is the old sectional division, which has been prevalent since the founding of the party. At different times this has taken the form of a straight East-West division; the two coasts against the middle; and, in its most recent manifestation, Frostbelt against Sunbelt.

It would be too crude, however, to describe Republican intraparty cleavages exclusively in terms of diverging regional interests. The sectional division is frequently reinforced by an ideological dimension, reflecting differences in the fundamental direction of policy. Since the New Deal, the ideological cleavage within the Republican party has been between conservative Republicans based in the midwestern states, who have usually predominated within the Republican ranks in Congress, and liberal Republicans based in the urban Northeast, and to some extent on the Pacific Coast, who have been predominant among Republican state governors. Conservative Republicans have been traditionally isolationist or militantly anti-Soviet in foreign policy, and vehemently opposed to federal government regulation of the American economy. Liberal Republicans have been more prepared to countenance interventionism at home and abroad, and have been more conscious of the Republicans' Lincolnian heritage on civil rights questions.

While the sectional and ideological divisions within the GOP have tended to reinforce each other, the third major division in Republican ranks between purists and professionals has tended to cut across lines of cleavage on substantive policy.[5] According to Gary Orren, this division is less ideological than concerned with whether or not to emphasize ideology:

> Note that what is referred to here is not the substance or direction of ideology, but rather the decision of whether or not to emphasize it and make it a central element in one's political arsenal. There are liberal and conservative ideologues, just as there are coalition-oriented politicians on both sides of the spectrum.[6]

Thus Robert Taft, while undoubtedly a conservative Republican in terms of ideology, was also a professional in his orientation toward the Republican party, while liberals such as Wendell Willkie and John V. Lindsay established their political careers by indicating their hostility toward partisan politics and the regular Republican organization.

For most of its history, power in the Republican party lay with state and local party leaders, who controlled state delegations to the Republican National Convention and nominations for lower offices in states where the party organization was strong. Regardless of their personal ideological preferences, their primary orientation was toward winning office and keeping the party united. Although most Republican regulars were probably inclined toward conservatism in terms of ideology, they were prepared to support presidential candidates from the liberal camp such as Dewey, Willkie, and Eisenhower in order to win the presidency for the party. This regular group lost most of its power within the party during the upheaval in the American party system from 1960 to 1980. The reformed presidential nominating process placed a greater priority on a politics of style, principle, and independence from party, and thereby gave decisive advantages to those elements within the Republican party with a more purist orientation toward politics.

So as to more clearly define the terms that will be used to designate the various elements of the Republican party in this work, Figure 1 shows, in diagrammatic form, the ideological division within the Republican party during the 1960–80 period, and the stylistic cleavage that cuts across the ideological divide. The subdivisions within the two main ideological tendencies are based on style and attitude toward politics in general, rather than ideological considerations. The terms used to label the four subdivisions—progressives, moderates, stalwarts, fundamentalists—are those used by Reichley in his analysis of Republicans in Congress during the Nixon and Ford administrations.[7]

American parties are amorphous, complex, and heterogeneous bodies, and their kaleidoscopic nature entails that the student of intraparty affairs can legitimately be accused of some superficiality and imprecision in employing such terminology. On the other

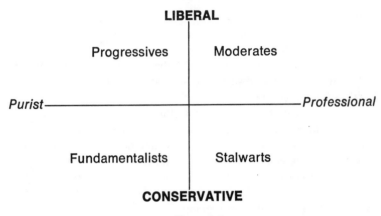

FIGURE 1

hand, the diagram does convey the essential cross-cutting cleavages within the Republican party in recent times, and these divisions in ideology and style are crucial to understanding the collapse of the liberal Republicans after 1964 and the continuing tensions within the conservative wing of the party. As the liberals have declined, Reiter's model of the Republican party as composed of three clusters—fundamentalist realigners, stalwart regulars, and a dwindling band of liberal misfits—now more accurately represents Republican reality.[8] This work deals with events within the Republican party from a time in which Reiter's labels were less appropriate, and the term liberal Republicans is used to describe moderates and progressives together, while conservative Republicans is used to cover stalwarts and fundamentalists. While discussing stylistic divisions within the two major ideological wings, Reichley's terminology is used.

National party politics in the United States revolves around the office of the presidency. American parties developed around the direct election of the president, and the quadrennial national nominating convention is the most visible manifestation of the existence of national parties. As this analysis is concerned primarily with intraparty conflict at the national level, it will focus mainly on developments in the Republican presidential nominating process from 1960 to 1980. In the absence of much serious academic treatment of the modern Republican party, I have relied to a large extent on journalistic accounts of variable quality. In 1983–84, however, I conducted numerous interviews with key actors in past and present Republican party politics, which yielded valuable insights into the ideology and tactics of the various participants in Republican intraparty conflict.

The structure of the book is as follows. Chapter 1 provides background on the liberal-conservative conflict within the Republican party. It sketches the development of the GOP from 1854 to 1960, the last presidential election year in which the liberal and conservative wings were roughly co-equal in strength within the national party. Chapters 2 and 3 focus on the bitter Republican nomination battles of 1964 and 1968 and the rise of the Republican Right. The effects on the Republican party of changes in the presidential nominating process are discussed in Chapter 4, together with the responses of leading Republicans to the new politics. In Chapter 5 the relationship between the congressional and presidential Republican parties is considered, and I account for the less drastic decline of the liberal Republicans at the congressional level. In order to assess the influence of liberal Republicans within the Republican party in recent years, the activities of liberal Republicans in Congress during the conservative administration of Ronald Reagan are also examined. Finally, in Chapter 6, some conclusions are reached regarding the reasons for the decline of the liberal Republicans as well as their future prospects in American party politics.

I

The Liberal Republican Tradition

This chapter describes the origins and development of liberal Republicanism, the rise of the Progressive movement from the periphery of Republican politics to control of the party at the turn of the century, and the influence of progressivism over the national party from 1896 to 1960. To understand fully the roots of Republican liberalism, however, it is first necessary to discuss the formative years of the Republican party from 1854 to 1896.

The Early Republican Party, 1854 to 1896

The Republican party was formed in reaction to the Kansas-Nebraska Act of 1854, which shattered the strained Whig-Democrat party alignment and acted as the catalyst for the formation of a new political party in the northern and western states. According to Milton Viorst:

> The early Republican party was, most of all, the embodiment of the Yankee middle-class. Its chief partisans were those struggling for fortune and status in business, whether in shops, on farms or in mills. They were white, Calvinist and Anglo-Saxon. Most were descendants of the colonial settlers.[1]

Malcolm Moos indicated the importance of capitalist ideology in the Republicans' formative period:

The slavery issue galvanized the party into action, but we should be doing serious disservice to the facts if we overlooked the significance of liberal capitalism as a cohesive force in bringing together the elements that formed the Republican party and giving it the staying power to last out more than one or two political engagements.[2]

Yet even in the early years of unity against the expansion of slavery, there were tensions between two major components of the party: the aspiring industrialists of the urban Northeast, and the small farmers and traders of the West. One of the most important pieces of legislation initiated by the Republicans was the 1862 Homestead Act, which guaranteed free land to settlers moving into the western territories and thereby cemented the allegiance of the western farmers to the party.[3] But the Republicans also drew support from the remnants of the Whig party in the Northeast, and these proponents of Henry Clay's "American System" were more concerned with the constraints that the slave system placed on America's industrial development.[4] The conflict between the Republicans' eastern-industrial and western-agrarian wings would prevade the history of the party from the Civil War to the New Deal.

From the election of Ulysses S. Grant in 1868 to that of Grover Cleveland in 1892, America enjoyed its somewhat ironically named Gilded Age, as the establishment of the banking system during the war and the introduction of a high protective tariff facilitated the rapid growth of American industry. The Republicans were increasingly identified with the new class of American plutocrats who profited from their policies of high tariffs, gold-based currency, and laisser faire economics, and Republican presidents elected during this era—Grant, Hayes, Garfield, Arthur, and Harrison—were content to permit eastern industrial and financial interests to dictate the course of national and party policy.

In national politics Republicans and Democrats were evenly matched in this period. The Republicans won more presidential elections during the later half of the nineteenth century, but the national results were invariably close, and congressional control oscillated between the parties.[5] The Republicans were the party of New England, the Upper Midwest, and the Plains states (see Table 1–1). After the end of Reconstruction in 1876, the Democrats could rely on the Solid South and the Border states. The

TABLE 1-1. Mean Republican Vote in Presidential Elections, 1856–1982

Region	Safe Republican (≥60%)	Mainly Republican (55–59%)	Leaning Republican (50–54%)	Leaning Democrat (45–49%)	Mainly Democrat (40–44%)	Safe Democrat (<40%)
Northeast	Vermont[a] Massachusetts Rhode Island	Maine	New Hampshire Pennsylvania West Virginia Connecticut New York	New Jersey		Delware Maryland
Midwest	Kansas	Minnesota Iowa	Michigan Wisconsin Illinois Ohio South Dakota	North Dakota	Missouri	
West			Nevada Wyoming Colorado Oregon	California	Idaho Montana	
South[b]						Kentucky

[a] The states are grouped within each region on the basis of Republican strength (e.g., Vermont was the most Republican of the northeastern states).

[b] The eleven confederate states are excluded from this analysis because of the distortions caused by the Civil War, Reconstruction, and black disenfranchisement.

Sources: Congressional Quarterly, Inc., Presidential Elections Since 1879 (Washington, DC: CQ Press, 1975); Paul T. David, Party Strength in the United States, 1872–1970 (Charlottesville, VA: University Press of Virginia, 1972).

major eastern industrial states were competitive. Civil War allegiances were the major determinants of partisan choice during the
Gilded Age, and the Republicans had no hesitation in waving the
"bloody shirt."[6] But the electoral cleavage based on the war was
reinforced by strong cultural differences between the two parties.
The Republicans remained the party of northern Anglo-Saxon
Protestantism, and their strongest bastions of support lay on the
trail of Yankee settlement from Portland, Maine to Portland,
Oregon. As a consequence, when moral or cultural issues such as
anti-Catholicism and Prohibition appeared, they tended to find
most of their adherents within the Republican ranks. The party's
attitude toward its opponents is accurately summarized in the
famous (or infamous) description of the Democratic party by the
Reverend Samuel Burchard in 1884, as the party of "Rum, Ro-
manism, and Rebellion."

During the Gilded Age the tension between the requirements of
eastern industry and western agriculture was a constant feature of
Republican politics. The high protective tariffs sought by industry
were a perennial item in Republican platforms, but the party also
needed the support of the small farmers of the Midwest and West,
who sold on a world market, who were dependent on eastern
credit for their mortgages and machinery, and who relied upon
eastern-controlled railroads to transport their produce. The obvious economic conflict of interest between the homesteaders and
the business and professional classes of the East was manifested
in the growth of the agrarian protest movement during the depres-
sions of the 1870s and 1880s. Sundquist describes the conflict in
the following terms:

> The battle for influence within the Republican party was a never-
> ending one, for the railroads and their allies sought also to make the
> party their political instrument. Prominent in the Republican party
> in every state were the railroad representatives, and they were lavish
> with their contributions, beginning with the free passes. At best, the
> farmers could only share power in the party with their enemies the
> railroads; they could not control it. The party, confronting a cross-
> cutting issue, could not cope with it decisively, and this situation
> could only continue unless the agrarian zealots could somehow re-
> align the party system.[7]

In addition to the sectional cleavage, there was already an important difference of opinion within the eastern wing of the party. The scandals and excesses of the Grant administration provoked a response in the form of the movement for civil service reform. When Grant ran for re-election in 1872, a group led by Senator Carl Schurz of Missouri advocated a fusion of civil service reformers, lower-tariff advocates, and critics of President Grant's harsh Reconstruction policies, and took the designation of Liberal Republicans so as to distinguish themselves from the so-called Radicals.[8] Finding little response within Republican ranks, the dissidents held their own convention, which nominated the veteran abolitionist Horace Greeley for President (Greeley was also the Democratic nominee). Unfortunately the Liberal Republicans were buried in the anti-Greeley landslide in the fall, and all of their supporters in the U.S. House lost their seats.[9]

The reform impulse did not die with the Liberals. The issue of civil service reform remained potent, as an important section of Republican opinion became increasingly concerned about the widespread corruption that pervaded American government in the Gilded Age. These concerns were echoed in the leading intellectual journals of the time, particularly *The North American Review,* edited by Charles Eliot Norton; E. L. Godkin's *The Nation;* and *Harper's Weekly,* edited by George William Curtis.[10]

Reform was also the rallying cry of the celebrated Mugwump reformers of New York.[11] These consisted mainly of Republicans who had inherited their wealth and social position and were appalled by the low ethical standards of the capitalist nouveaux riches and the concomitant corruption in public life. They congregated around the civil service reform clubs in New York City, making the case for "good, clean, government" based on an ethic of public service as opposed to the patronage, bribery, and electoral horse-trading characteristic of New York politics in the 1870–90 period. Some Mugwumps supported the Liberal Republicans in 1872, and in 1884 such Mugwump bastions as the Civil Service Reform Club, the Knickerbocker Club, and the Union Club bolted the Republican party in disgust at the nomination of James G. Blaine and helped deliver a close election to the Democrat Grover Cleveland. (Two Mugwumps who were to have an important influence over the future of the national Republican party—Theodore Roosevelt and Henry Cabot Lodge—did not join the bolt.) The Mugwumps sought to return the Republican party to what they regarded as the ideals of its founders: a national party committed to honest and effective government, fired by idealism, and morally superior to its political opponents. Richard Hofstadter describes their ideology as follows:

> Their conception of statecraft was set by the high example of the Founding Fathers, or by the great debating statesmen of the Silver Age, Webster, Sumner, Everett, Clay and Calhoun. Their ideal leader was a well-to-do, well-educated, high-minded citizen, rich enough to be free from motives of what they often called "crass materialism" whose family roots were deep not only in American history, but in his local community. Such a person, they thought, would be just the sort to put the national interest, as well as the interests of civic improvement, above personal motives or political opportunism. And such a person was just the sort, as Henry Adams never tired of complaining, for whom American political life was least likely to find a place.[12]

Although the Republican party in the Gilded Age was acting as the political vehicle for the interests of industrial, eastern, corporate America, there were two dissident streams within the party, with different bases of support, contending for national influence. Ultimately these merged to form the Progressive movement, but the two streams of progressivism nevertheless remained distinct. The election of 1896, although ostensibly a resounding endorsement of the high-tariff, sound-money, laisser faire policies of the Republican Old Guard, provided the discontented Republicans with their opportunity.

The Rise and Decline of Progressive Republicanism, 1896 to 1932

The Republicans' tenuous hold on the institutions of American government during the Gilded Age was consolidated by their victory in the presidential election of 1896. Economic depression and the takeover of the Democratic party by southwestern populists delivered a comfortable victory to the Republican candidate,

William McKinley, that ensured Republican dominance of American government at virtually all levels (outside the South) for the next thirty-five years. From 1896 to 1932 the Republicans won a series of landslide victories in presidential elections broken only by Wilson's victories in 1912 and 1916. They also controlled both houses of Congress from 1896 to 1930, save for the Democratic interregnum between 1910 and 1918.

The key to the Republicans' electoral success was their dominance in the growing urban centers of the industrial North, where the party was particularly successful in wooing northern labor.[13] Pressure from industrialists terrified by Bryanite radicalism was partly responsible, but the Democrats were also blamed for the severe economic depression during the second Cleveland administration. Bryan's free silverism and low-tariff policy appeared to constitute a further threat to the continued prosperity of eastern industry and the livelihood of the urban laborer. And finally, the evangelical fervor of Bryan and his agrarian followers alienated Roman Catholic immigrants in the North. Following the return to prosperity under McKinley, the urban centers of the northeastern metropole remained predominantly Republican in presidential elections until 1928. According to Sundquist,

> The Republican campaign of 1896 and the events on which it was based undoubtedly painted in the minds of many urban voters a new image of the Democratic party. Bryan enthusiasts may denounce the campaign as built on "scare" tactics that drastically distorted the facts. Be that as it may, the campaign succeeded. Many voters were in fact scared. To the image of the Democrats as the party of Rum, Romanism, Rebellion, and economic recession was added another R—radicalism.[14]

By contrast the Republicans became the Grand Old Party of prosperity and, after the Spanish-American War of 1898, of nationalism and Manifest Destiny. Tensions remained within the Republican coalition, however. The settlers of the Northwest had maintained their Civil War loyalties against the southwestern populists in 1896, but they still had a fundamental incompatibility of interests with eastern industry and commerce.[15] The eastern manufacturing and financial interests that controlled the national party believed that they had been vindicated by the triumph of

1896, but in addition to the western agrarians they also had to cope with eastern progressives who distrusted the political judgment of the "captains of industry," and felt uncomfortable about the appalling social conditions of the urban working class.

Theodore Roosevelt embodied the spirit of eastern progressivism. Scion of an old, established, New York family, Roosevelt despised the corrupt businessmen and politicians of the Republican party machines in the East (although he was not averse to cooperating with them in order to advance his own political career). His progressivism was fundamentally conservative in its inspiration: worried by the excesses of the business trusts and monopoly capital, Roosevelt feared a violent upheaval among the growing urban masses. In the words of one biographer,

> He [Roosevelt] did not expect wealth to continue to corrupt American life, because he had faith that men of character would understand the responsibility of power. Where such character was lacking, where the power of wealth was misdirected, Roosevelt was prepared to have the government intercede. Roosevelt was never radical, but, while resisting what seemed to him to be revolution, he welcomed change. From his rudimentary beginnings in the movements for civil service reform and for slum clearance, enlightened alike by the reformers he fought and reformers he helped, he developed increasing concern over the abuses of great wealth, increasing inclination to listen, at least, to the demands of organized labor, and increasing determination to invest the state with the authority to control the powerful and assist the weak.[16]

Thus Roosevelt's primary motive was not to undermine American free enterprise, but to safeguard and promote it through necessary reforms. In foreign policy, he continued the aggressive interventionism of the McKinley era.[17] Roosevelt's program was essentially one of selective government intervention in domestic and international affairs to assert his conception of the interests of the nation as a whole. The concept of a national interest, which it was the duty of the federal government to promote against the multifarious sectional interests, was central both to Roosevelt's personal thought and to the ideology of eastern progressivism.

The base of support for the Rooseveltian brand of progressivism lay among the urban, middle, and professional classes of the

TABLE 1-2. Mean Republican Vote in Presidential Elections, 1896–1928[a]

Region	Safe Republican (≥60%)	Mainly Republican (55–59%)	Leaning Republican (50–54%)	Leaning Democrat (45–49%)	Mainly Democrat (40–44%)	Safe Democrat (<40%)
Northeast	Vermont Maine Pennsylvania Massachussetts New Hampshire New Jersey	Connecticut Rhode Island Delaware New York	West Virginia Maryland			
Midwest	North Dakota Michigan Minnesota Iowa Wisconsin South Dakota	Kansas Ohio Nebraska	Indiana Illinois Missouri			
West	Wyoming	California Oregon Washington Idaho	New Mexico Arizona Colorado Utah Montana	Nevada		

South	Kentucky	Tennessee Oklahoma	North Carolina	Arkansas Texas Florida Georgia Louisiana Mississippi South Carolina

[a] To avoid distorting the overall pattern of Republican electoral strength during this period, the Republican and Progressive party totals of 1912 and 1924 have been added together.

Sources: CQ Inc., *Presidential Elections Since 1789;* David, *Party Strength in the United States, 1872–1970.*

Northeast, who shared Roosevelt's suspicion of big business, supported social reformers such as Jane Addams, and read the muckraking magazines that attacked the urban political machines and the "malefactors of great wealth."[18] They sought to replace the patronage and graft of machine politics in the major cities with clean, effective, urban government, based on the new management techniques that had proven to be successful in many business firms. Herbert Croly's *Promise of American Life* became the intellectual bible of the movement and Croly established a progressive base of support among young eastern intellectuals in the Ivy League colleges, such as Walter Lippmann. Government, according to Croly, was a positive force for moral and social good:

> In order to be true to their past, the increasing comfort and economic independence of an ever increasing proportion of the population must be secured, and it must be secured by a combination of individual effort and proper political organization. Above all, however, this economic and political system must be made to secure results of economic and social value. It is the seeking of such results which converts Democracy from a political system into a constructive social ideal; and the more the ideal significance of the American national promise is asserted and emphasized, the greater will become the importance of securing these moral and social benefits.[19]

Yet despite the radical ideas of the social reformers, the political motivation of the eastern progressive leadership remained conservative. As Henry Stimson wrote to Theodore Roosevelt in 1910,

> To me it seems vitally important that the Republican party which contains, generally speaking, the richer and more intelligent citizens of the country, should take the lead in reform and not drift into a reactionary position. If instead, the leadership should fall into the hands of either an independent party, or a party composed like the Democrats, largely of foreign elements and the classes which will immediately benefit from the reform, and if the solid business Republicans should drift into new obstruction, I fear the necessary changes could hardly be accomplished without much excitement and possible violence.[20]

If a fundamental conservatism inspired the more patrician progressives of the East, this was certainly not shared by their western brethren. Western progressivism, embodied in the figures of Robert LaFollette in Wisconsin, George Norris in Nebraska, and Hiram Johnson in California, was a genuinely radical movement, reflecting its populist antecedents and the continuing economic plight of the western and farm states.[21] While the eastern reformers sought to alleviate the social conditions of the poor, and mitigate the excesses of big business and the machines, the westerners launched an assault on the entire political structure in their states and on the vested interests—notably the railroad companies—that had previously controlled that party structure.[22] In pursuit of the extirpation of business influence from politics, the western progressives instituted the direct primary for all public offices, abolished all forms of political patronage, introduced nonpartisan elections and the city-manager system at the local level, and established the initiative, referendum, and recall procedures. In the western and plains states, with their large numbers of discontented small farmers and small businessmen, this assault on corporate control of the political process aroused enthusiastic electoral support. While the western radicals and the urban progressives of the East had a common desire to improve living conditions and curb the excesses of big business and the political machines, the eastern progressives were highly suspicious of agrarianism and the fervor of the radicals' attacks on the eastern corporate and intellectual elite.[23] Both sections of the movement nevertheless united in exasperation with the Taft administration (1909–1913). Although President William Howard Taft had been Roosevelt's designated successor, progressives never forgave him for his alliance with the Old Guard Republican leadership in Congress in raising tariff rates, after he had pledged to reduce them in the 1908 campaign. The initial challenge to Taft's renomination in 1912 came from LaFollette, but his radicalism was regarded with unease by the more sedate progressives of the East, who succeeded in persuading Theodore Roosevelt to enter the race in the hope of disposing of the ineffectual Taft while simultaneously defusing the threat from the West.

Roosevelt's campaign aroused great moral and electoral fervor. Adopting a more radical tone in order to secure the western progressive vote, he swept through the primary election, winning 236 delegates in the primary states to 41 for LaFollette and 34 for Taft.[24] Yet Taft retained control of the Republican National Committee and used his considerable patronage powers as president to defeat Roosevelt in the credentials contests over the rump southern convention delegations. The end of Reconstruction and the advent of black disfranchisement in the South had gradually eliminated most vestiges of Republican electoral support from that region, save for some Appalachian redoubts. According to Moos,

> Virtually driven out of the South in 1876, the southern wing of the Republican party was now just a holdover organization functioning only for the power it could wield in national conventions. It survived on whatever federal patronage was thrown its way, delivering no votes for the national ticket, nor any support in the federal legislature. Thus the end of Reconstruction brought a new problem for Republican National Conventions—the beginning of the "demoralizing influence" that went with the shameful scramble for the votes of southern delegates.[25]

With the help of the southern delegations Taft was able to secure renomination (see Table 1-4). The Roosevelt delegates bolted and formed their own Progressive convention where Roosevelt and Hiram Johnson were nominated. The schism in Chicago doomed Republican hopes of victory, and this was confirmed when the Democrats nominated Woodrow Wilson, who had impeccable progressive credentials and thus cut into Roosevelt's eastern middle-class support. In November Roosevelt secured the bastions of progressive radicalism: Minnesota, South Dakota, and Washington, plus Michigan and Pennsylvania, but his 27.5% of the popular vote was far behind Wilson's 42%.

The schism of 1912 marked both the end of Roosevelt's political career and the high point of progressive influence within the Republican party. Roosevelt himself encouraged the reunification of the party in 1916 behind the candidacy of the moderate progressive Charles Evans Hughes, but as many eastern progressives drifted toward Wilson's New Freedom, the machines of the large eastern and midwestern states regained their dominance within the GOP. In 1920 the Republican presidential nomination went to a conservative party regular from Ohio, Warren G. Harding. The impetus for social reform was spent, and the accession of Harding to the presidency illustrated the pervasive desire for a "return to normalcy" after the turmoil of the preceding decades.

While Harding and his successor Calvin Coolidge presided indolently over America in the 1920s, the western progressives remained as a perpetual irritant to conservative stalwarts in the Republican party leadership. A bloc of radical Republicans (derisively dubbed "the Sons of the Wild Jackass" by their Republican opponents) used the U.S. Senate as a platform to rail against the iniquities of eastern capital and internationalism, the leading members being the veteran progressives George Norris, of Nebraska; Robert LaFollette, of Wisconsin (later succeeded by his son Robert LaFollette, Jr.); Hiram Johnson, of California; and William Borah, of Idaho.[26] Because of the persistent agricultural crisis in the West, many of these senators were also prominent members of the bipartisan Senate farm bloc, which agitated consistently for federal government relief to agriculture throughout the 1920s.[27] Although they had adopted the Progressive label, the generally agrarian outlook of the Senate radicals bore little relation to the paternalist, urban, upper middle-class progressivism of Roosevelt and Herbert Croly.[28]

Another issue that divided the western progressives from the heritage of Roosevelt was their vehement isolationism. Senators from states with large German-American populations, such as Wisconsin and South Dakota, were adamantly opposed to American involvement in European affairs.[29] The unprincipled financiers of the East had, they believed, maneuvered America into an unnecessary war, and thereby contaminated her with decadent colonialism. Thus LaFollette, Johnson, Borah, and their progressive allies devoted a great deal of their energies to the task of keeping America's international entanglements at a minimum. This, of course, was in stark contrast to the pugnacious "big stick" diplomacy of Roosevelt and the eastern reformers, which had been heavily oriented toward Europe. As Mayer observed,

> What they [Roosevelt and Lodge] had in mind was a new international order ruled by the English-speaking people, with help from the French. They were fully prepared for America to redraw the map of Europe in pursuit of this objective. They also favored a postwar international organization to uphold the settlement. Yet the sort of League they envisioned was not an organization including all states, but a permanent alliance of the "good" powers to keep the "bad" ones in their place.[30]

Despite the fulminations of the radicals, it was the conservative (or stalwart) Republicans who controlled the party at the national level during the 1920s. Based in the smaller cities and rural areas of the Midwest, the stalwarts adhered to the virtues of William McKinley and late nineteenth-century America: hard work, free enterprise, self-reliance, and Protestantism. Warren Harding and Calvin Coolidge were the perfect representatives of this world of Main Street. Disdaining the activist presidential style of Theodore Roosevelt and Woodrow Wilson, they spurned legislative initiatives and allowed big business to manage the economy unhindered by federal government interference. In international affairs they felt uncomfortable with the more radical isolationists, but remained secure in their expectation that America would avoid involvement in any ensuing European conflict.

The Republicans' reversion to the laisser faire attitudes of the Gilded Age during the 1920s emasculated the executive branch of the federal government and left them helpless in the face of the economic crisis of 1929–33. In the 1928 election, the mobilization of the Catholic immigrant vote behind the presidential candidacy of Al Smith increased Democratic support in the urban centers of the East and Midwest, but Republican Herbert Hoover was still able to win an overwhelming victory through mobilizing the Protestant prohibitionist vote (which enabled him to break into the Solid South).[31] Being a moderately progressive businessman, Hoover sought to apply the skills of effective corporate management to public service, but the Crash of 1929 and the Great Depression overwhelmed him.[32] Although his administration instituted the Reconstruction Finance Corporation (RFC) and federal relief for agriculture, Hoover's profound distaste for federal government intervention in the economy made him appear impervious to the sufferings of the unemployed and destitute. The electoral repudiation of Hoover and the Republican party in 1932 marked the end of seventy years of Republican ascendancy in American politics. As defeat followed defeat for the Republicans in the 1930s, it appeared that their only means of revival at the polls lay in a rebirth of the eastern, progressive element, which had become virtually moribund during the previous decade.

Progressive Rebirth: The Post–New Deal Republican Party

Under Franklin Roosevelt the Democrats constructed a majority coalition of the South, Labor, Roman Catholics, blacks, and poor farmers, leaving the Republicans with their rural redoubts in the Northeast and Midwest. The impact of Roosevelt's landslide victories in 1932 and 1936 left the Republicans in a state of disarray (the extent of the electoral weakness of the party in the New Deal era is illustrated in Table 1-3), and during the 1930s the party's two major tendencies—western progressive and eastern and midwestern conservative—both appeared unable to cope with the advent of the New Deal. By the end of the Roosevelt era, western progressivism was virtually extinct and the stalwarts had lost control over the GOP to a revived liberal wing based on the East Coast, more specifically, in New York State.

Of the twenty-five Republicans in the Senate after the 1934 elections, ten, including the Senate Minority Leader Charles Mc-Nary of Oregon, were western progressives. In accordance with their populist agrarian heritage, the radicals supported Roosevelt on the major New Deal measures which came before Congress in 1932–36 (indeed Johnson, Norris, and LaFollette, Jr. endorsed FDR against Hoover in 1932), but their relationship with the president was uneasy. The western Republicans' antimonopolistic, individualistic, liberalism did not accord with the bureaucratizing tendencies of the New Deal, and they maintained their dogmatic isolationism (most notably in the Senate's Nye Committee Report of 1935, which blamed eastern financiers and armaments manufacturers for maneuvering America into the First World War).[33] According to Ronald Feinman,

> As promoters of greater federal involvement in the economic and social affairs of the farmer, worker and consumer, they [the western Republicans] welcomed strong presidential leadership, but they did not intend a vast centralization of power in the hands of the chief executive at the expense of the legislative branch. As firm supporters of political isolationism from international power politics, they were determined to keep America out of foreign wars at all cost, convinced that otherwise the nation could not remain democratic and virtuous.[34]

TABLE 1-3. Mean Republican Vote in Presidential Elections, 1932–1960

Region	Safe Republican (≥60%)	Mainly Republican (55–59%)	Leaning Republican (50–54%)	Leaning Democrat (45–49%)	Mainly Democrat (40–44%)	Safe Democrat (<40%)
Northeast	Vermont	Maine	New Hampshire New Jersey Connecticut	Pennsylvania Delaware New York Massachusetts Maryland West Virginia	Rhode Island	
Midwest		Kansas Nebraska	South Dakota Iowa Indiana North Dakota Ohio	Illinois Michigan Wisconsin Missouri		
West			Alaska Colorado Hawaii Wyoming	Idaho Oregon Utah New Mexico Montana Nevada California	Arizona Washington	

South	Kentucky	Oklahoma	Florida
		Virginia	North Carolina
		Tennessee	Texas
			Arkansas
			Louisiana
			Alabama
			Georgia
			Mississippi
			South Carolina

Source: David, *Party Strength in the United States, 1872–1970.*

After 1937 the influence of the westerners within the Republican party began to wane. Borah's campaign for the Republican presidential nomination in 1936 attracted little support, and three leading members of the progressive bloc (Senators Cutting, of New Mexico, Norbeck, of South Dakota, and Couzens, of Michigan) either died or failed to be renominated in 1935–36. After the 1936 elections, which reduced the number of Republicans in Congress to 89 Representatives and 17 Senators, the two most outstanding leaders of the farm bloc, Senators Norris and LaFollette, Jr., renounced the Republican label (becoming Independent and Progressive, respectively) and drew ever closer to FDR. The remaining western progressives turned vehemently against Roosevelt after the 1937–38 "court-packing" fracas, and adopted increasingly extreme isolationist positions in the face of the Nazi threat in Europe in the late 1930s. Pearl Harbor, and the entry of America into World War II, were thus fatal to western progressive Republicanism.

The radical populist heritage remained a constant factor in western politics, but after 1945 its vehicle would be the post–New Deal Democratic party rather than the GOP. Liberal Republicans in the West resisted this trend longest on the Pacific Coast, and some vestiges of the tradition persist in Oregon and Washington to this day. In California, the state's peculiar practice of cross-filing in party primaries assisted the political careers of progressives such as Governors Earl Warren and Goodwin Knight and Senator Thomas Kuchel, who were prepared to adopt the Republican label in national politics.[35] The end of cross-filing in 1958 completely transformed the nature of California politics, as will be shown in the next chapter.

With the western wing of the party either veering toward the Democrats or to the extreme right, the midwestern stalwarts became even more dominant within the national party in the 1930s. Patterson describes the stalwart Republicans of the 1930s as follows:

> They had been reared in, and then represented, rural areas so conservative that even Roosevelt's great electoral strength was not enough to displace them. They sought to recreate Jefferson's vision of America: a rural nation of independent yeomen, a small govern-

ment which left people alone. Whether this form of society had existed in the twentieth century, or even in their lifetimes, did not matter: these men thought it had. Glum about the New World they confronted, they were nonetheless the great optimists of the era, for they sought to live in an irretrievable, idyllic land and believed it could be created simply by leaving things alone.[36]

The shock of defeat and the national economic crisis prompted most of the Republican Old Guard to vote for Roosevelt's emergency measures in 1932–34.[37] After another bad year at the polls in 1934, however, they launched severe attacks on the New Deal, with the support of ex-President Hoover and the anti-Roosevelt American Liberty League. The main theme of their diatribes was that the Roosevelt administration, through excessive intervention in the domestic economy, was leading America toward a centralization and concentration of power characteristic of fascism or communism. The virulence of the stalwarts' attacks on the New Deal contributed to the disastrous 1936 election, with Republican presidential candidate Alfred M. Landon carrying only Maine and Vermont, and the GOP being reduced to a rump in Congress. Demoralized by their defeat, the Republican congressional leadership adopted a quieter approach. Their first real chance to embarrass FDR came when the president submitted his controversial proposals for reform of the Supreme Court in 1937. Congressional opposition united the conservative Republicans, most of the western mavericks, and the conservative southern Democrats, who ultimately defeated the proposals. In the 1938 midterm elections the Republicans also capitalized on the sudden economic downturn, winning 6 Senate and 80 House seats.

Among the new Republican Senators elected in 1938 was Robert A. Taft of Ohio, the leading representative of stalwart Republicanism until his death in 1953. Reared in the Republican bastion of Cincinnati, Taft epitomized conservative midwestern Republicanism in his ferocious loyalty to his party and distrust of the eastern financial establishment, which he suspected of collaboration with the New Deal and encouragement of intervention overseas. Taft further feared that the New Deal's centralization of government and intervention in economic affairs would stifle America's exceptional "individualism."[38] Although he supported welfare legislation and introduced the first public housing bill to Congress,

Taft's public image as a small-town, isolationist reactionary persisted, perhaps because of the Senator's fanatical following among stalwart Republicans. As a consequence, his three attempts to secure the presidential nomination of his party were all unsuccessful.

The stalwart Republicans' association in the public mind with big business and laisser faire was too strong to enable them to challenge Roosevelt and the Democrats effectively. Thus it was almost inevitable that, sooner or later, urban Republican progressivism would re-emerge. Henry Cabot Lodge, Jr., of Massachusetts, elected to the Senate in the 1930s, represented the New England patrician tradition of public service which still lingered within the GOP.

> In becoming a Republican, I thought I was joining something affirmative, evolutionary and idealistic, which demanded sacrifice and generosity, not a party which said no to all proposals for change.[39]

Similar considerations motivated John Hay Whitney, another scion of a distinguished family, to become involved in Republican party politics:

> Born himself into a carefree way of life that was on the whole impregnable, he was persistently nagged by a sense of owing some debt to society, by a search for the true dimensions of that obligation, and above all, for a constant pursuit of what, for want of a better word, could be called excellence.[40]

Big business also mitigated its bitter opposition to government intervention. With important overseas investments at stake, the business and financial communities could ill afford to adhere rigidly to the splendid isolation beloved of the stalwarts and the western radicals. This more amicable relationship between government and big business was consolidated by the war years, when the federal government granted generous contracts to many large manufacturing firms.[41] From the late 1930s onward, eastern business influence was an important factor in turning the Republican party in a more activist direction in both foreign and domestic policy, this trend being exemplified by Roosevelt's inviting two impeccable representatives of the Republican business establishment, Henry Stimson and Colonel Frank Knox, into his Cabinet as Secretaries of War and of the Navy, respectively, in 1940.[42]

The first national political figure who embodied the progressive Republican resurgence, however, was the Indiana-born Wall Street lawyer Wendell Willkie. Willkie made his name representing the Commonwealth and Southern Utility Corporation against the federal government in court battles over the Tennessee Valley Authority. He gained further national attention with a series of speeches and articles attacking the New Deal and extolling the virtues of private enterprise, while at the same time stressing his commitment to welfare and the Allied cause in Europe. Willkie, an active Democrat until 1938, remained a rank outsider for the Republican nomination, the principal contenders being Senator Taft, New York District Attorney Thomas E. Dewey, and Senator Arthur Vandenberg of Michigan. Nevertheless, anxiety concerning the European situation in early 1940 and unease over the isolationism of Taft and Vandenberg and the inexperience of Dewey led many leading members of the Republicans' eastern establishment to consider the unlikely figure of Willkie as a presidential nominee.

The Willkie movement relied on the support of two main groups: "Willkie for President" clubs organized by Orren Root (a young Wall Street lawyer) among nonpartisan amateurs, and publishers, financiers, and media magnates—particularly Henry Luce of *Time,* Roy Howard of the Scripps-Howard chain of newspapers, and Ogden Reid of the *New York Herald Tribune* (the mouthpiece of eastern establishment Republicanism)—who undertook a massive public relations campaign on Willkie's behalf.[43] These supporters bombarded Republicans around the country with letters, telegrams, and petitions urging support for Willkie, and by the time the Republican convention opened in Philadelphia, the carefully orchestrated Willkie boom had reached its height. At this point Willkie's support from Wall Street became crucial, as its major law firms and banks were exerting pressure on Republicans throughout the country.[44] Yet the decisive factor in Willkie's nomination was the fall of France to Hitler a week prior to the opening of the convention, which raised further doubts over the isolationist positions of his opponents. With the latter unable or unwilling to cooperate to stop him, Willkie secured the nomination on the fifth ballot. Taft's support in the Midwest and South remained firm, but Willkie forged a winning coalition of the Atlantic Seaboard states and the progressive states of the West. This pat-

TABLE 1-4.   Regional Patterns of Support for Republican Presidential
Nominees, 1856–1952

Year	Winning candidate	% From Northeast		% From Midwest		% From South		% From West	
1856	Fremont	62	(62)	35	(35)	1	(1)	2	(2)
1860	Lincoln	40	(51)	41	(35)	15	(11)	3	(3)
1876	Hayes	37	(34)	30	(31)	29	(28)	4	(6)
1880	Garfield	39	(34)	41	(31)	14	(28)	6	(6)
1884	Blaine	31	(34)	48	(33)	14	(29)	8	(6)
1888	Harrison	43	(31)	24	(33)	22	(29)	10	(6)
1892	Harrison	25	(30)	34	(32)	35	(28)	7	(10)
1896	McKinley	16	(31)	42	(31)	33	(28)	9	(10)
1912	Taft	26	(30)	16	(31)	43	(28)	16	(11)
1916	Hughes[a]	38	(32)	20	(33)	25	(22)	16	(12)
1920	Harding[b]	33	(32)	33	(34)	30	(22)	5	(12)
1940	Willkie[c]	56	(32)	28	(32)	14	(21)	14	(4)
1948	Dewey[d]	46	(30)	22	(32)	17	(21)	15	(16)
1952	Eisenhower	50	(31)	19	(29)	17	(19)	13	(19)

[a] Third ballot.
[b] Tenth ballot.
[c] Sixth ballot.
[d] Second ballot.

Source: Richard C. Bain and Judith H. Parris, Convention Decisions and Voting Records (Washington, DC: Brookings Institution, 1973).

tern of the two coasts voting against the conservative "middle" persisted in Republican conventions up to 1960, and the importance of northeastern support to the winners of the Republican nomination is illustrated in Table 1-4.

Willkie moved his party away from isolationism and revived the liberal element in the GOP. He made it respectable once more for Republicans to espouse the goals of social reform and attracted a new generation of urban, middle-class activists into Republican party politics. After his defeat by FDR in November, however, Willkie, a plausible Republican candidate in the peculiar circumstances of 1940, became overly committed to internationalism and was utterly repudiated in his campaign for renomination in 1944. Nevertheless, the tentative endorsement of a post-war world role for the United States by Vandenberg, Dewey, and even Taft at the

1943 Mackinac Island Conference was a mark of the Indiana maverick's legacy to his party.

The task of consolidating the resurgence of Republican liberalism that Willkie had engendered devolved upon the more substantial figure of Thomas E. Dewey. Dewey achieved national acclaim as the "racket-busting D.A." of New York City in the 1930s. After a narrow failure to win the New York governorship in 1938 against the popular Democratic incumbent Herbert Lehman, he immediately became a presidential contender. The international crisis of 1940 exposed Dewey's inexperience in foreign affairs, and his hopes were buried in the Willkie boom; but having won the New York governorship in 1942, Dewey consolidated his control over the decrepit Republican party in New York State and began to extend his influence over the national party.[45] He also introduced figures such as Irving Ives, William Rogers, Herbert Brownell, F. Clifton White, and Hugh Scott into New York and national politics. Senator Scott acknowledges the liberal Republicans' debt to Dewey:

> The rise of the moderates in the party was due as much to Dewey in New York as to any other factor. He was a young man with new ideas, who had proven that he alone among Republicans could command a heavy vote in the urban, Democratic areas of his state. Dewey's influence and alliances led to a strengthening of moderate forces in other states, for example, Kuchel in California, and Hatfield in Oregon. Most of the new moderates in the party took their cues from Dewey in New York.[46]

Dewey succeeded in the Empire State and in the country at large because, like Theodore Roosevelt, he appealed to that section of the American professional middle-class that supported an internationalist foreign policy and political and social reform at home, but felt ill at ease with the Democratic party because of its racist southern wing, its ethnic urban machines, and its anti-business elements—particularly organized labor. The young lawyer Jacob J. Javits exemplified the attitudes of these Republican reformers:

> Even had I not been repelled by the corruption of Tammany politics in New York City, I doubt that I could have allied myself with

the party whose national power depended to a great extent on a regional political and social system that kept black citizens in a state of subservience and often fear. As I saw it then, northern Democrats who castigated southern racism while reaping political benefits (such as congressional committee chairmanships) from the Democratic majorities provided by the Solid South, were not entitled to the mantle of liberalism they claimed as their right.[47]

Influenced by Willkie, Dewey, and New York City's maverick reform Mayor Fiorello LaGuardia, these types were attracted back into involvement in Republican party affairs, and, as before, provided the electoral base of support for Republican liberalism in state and national politics.

In national politics, Dewey quickly learned the lessons of his failure in 1940. By 1944 he had ceased to equivocate and had become a firm internationalist, committed to an American role in a post-war international organization. With the help of a formidable national political operation directed by his aide, Herbert Brownell, and with his business and legal connections in New York, Dewey obtained the Republican presidential nominations in 1944 and 1948 with relative ease. In the 1940s he was by far the dominant figure in his party, and his defeat by Truman in 1948 was a grievous blow to the post–New Deal Republican revival. After the Republican victory in the congressional elections of 1946, leadership in Congress had passed to the Republican stalwarts, most notably Senator Taft, Chairman of the Senate Republican Policy Committee, and House Speaker Joseph Martin of Massachusetts. While the record of that Congress was not as reactionary as Truman led the public to believe in the 1948 campaign, the image of reaction and intransigence purveyed by Taft undoubtedly contributed to Dewey's defeat. Truman did not hesitate to exploit the contrast between the stalwart anti–New Deal attitudes of Taft and the progressive platform adopted by the Republican convention in 1948. According to Herbert Brownell, Dewey's campaign manager in that year,

> The Eightieth Congress defeated Dewey, not the Democrats. We adopted a reasonable, progressive platform. Truman called the Congress into special session, and challenged them to implement the Republican platform. I was sent by Dewey to consult with the Republi-

can congressional leadership in Washington, in order to get them in line with the party platform. They refused to do so. For years they had opposed the New Deal on the basis of a very conservative alternative. I proposed two pieces of legislation that they should initiate to show good faith in their willingness to carry out the platform, one of which was a bill to liberalize immigration quotas. They turned them both down. The committee chairmen had opposed such legislation for too long to adopt it now, and Taft wouldn't overrule the committee chairmen. We refused to publicize this since it would have demonstrated that Truman was right, and that there was a split in the party. The congressional leadership deserves credit for the 1948 Republican defeat.[48]

Senator Taft and his partisans did not, of course, accept this explanation of the Republican defeat. His biographer records the Ohio Senator stating to friends,

> I could have won the election if nominated. I am absolutely certain that Dewey could have won if he had put up any kind of fight at all and dealt with the issues before the people.[49]

These differing interpretations of the 1948 defeat illustrate the dichotomy within the Republican party in the late 1940s. Under Dewey's leadership, Republican liberalism had been revived as part of the party's attempt to challenge the New Deal, and thanks to the Dewey organization the resurgent liberals had come to exercise the predominant influence at Republican nominating conventions.[50] Yet the stalwarts controlled the Republican party in Congress, and they had little time for the Dewey strategy. The basis of their criticism was that the Dewey wing of the party, instead of attempting to challenge the fundamental premises of the New Deal, was advocating little more than an opportunistic "me-tooism." As the stalwarts saw it, the liberals were sacrificing cherished Republican principles of individualism and free enterprise in an attempt to outdo the Democrats at their own game, interventionism and centralized government.

The debate between these factions was further polarized over foreign policy. During the Eightieth Congress, Taft had left the direction of Republican foreign policy to Senator Arthur Vandenberg. The war and its aftermath had converted the formerly isolationist Michigan senator into a zealous internationalist, and his policy of cooperation with the Truman administration on foreign affairs helped the president pass through a skeptical Congress emergency aid for Greece and Turkey, as well as the Marshall Plan. Bipartisanship could not, however, survive the fall of China to Mao Tse-tung's Communists, the outbreak of the Korean War, and Vandenberg's death in 1950. Strong traces of pre-war isolationism remained in Taft's foreign policy positions. While the Ohio senator was highly suspicious of the NATO treaty and American intervention in the affairs of the Old World, he, in common with many of his Old Guard colleagues, regarded the Pacific and the Far East as legitimate spheres of American influence. Hence the fall of Chiang Kai-shek and the Korean stalemate were particularly traumatic events for the Republican right, and their ally, General Douglas MacArthur, who, after his dismissal by Truman in 1951, became something of a martyr for their cause. The basic position of Taft, MacArthur, and other "Asia-Firsters" was that America was neglecting its vital interests in the Far East in order to appease Western Europe, which was of less strategic importance.

Another stream of Republican opinion was more concerned about the global advance of communism, whether in Europe or Asia. The "new nationalism" adopted by Vandenberg, John Foster Dulles, and Senator Richard Nixon held that Soviet expansionism had to be challenged worldwide, although, like the Old Guard, the new nationalists generally repudiated the use of U.S. ground forces overseas and were more eager to use air power and the threat of atomic weaponry to achieve America's aims. By these means, they believed, Soviet communism could be defeated, American lives saved, and the increasingly heavy defense budget curtailed. Miles accurately describes the new nationalists' position within the Republican party in the early 1950s:

> In many ways the new nationalists were the most militant rightists and nationalists and yet at the same time they could occupy a strategic center position in the Republican party, and draw the political leverage therefrom, because of the dispute between the old nationalists and internationalists. Here was the wave of the future within the party.[51]

Many from the liberal eastern wing of the party, who might have had some reservations about the obsession of some new nationalists with domestic communist subversion, supported their positions on foreign and defense policy. This was especially true of Dewey and his principal foreign policy advisor Dulles. The eastern wing of the party, whether liberal or conservative, had always been more oriented toward Europe because of its closer personal and financial ties to the Old World. The Asia-First policies of Taft, MacArthur, and the China lobby filled them with foreboding, but they were no more congenial toward Soviet communism than were the new nationalists. As a consequence, they had little hesitation in adding their voices to the general clamor against the foreign policy of Truman and Acheson. Although many felt that Senator Joseph McCarthy's virulent anti-communism was rather crass, from an internationalist perspective, at least, it had forced most of the Republican right to revise its conception of America's role in the world.

The isolationist-internationalist debate was a critical factor in the battle for the Republican nomination in 1952. Dewey had been discredited by the 1948 defeat, but was nevertheless determined to prevent the quasi-isolationist Taft from getting the nomination. The eastern wing of the party thus began increasingly to consider General Dwight D. Eisenhower, who possessed impeccable internationalist credentials and, as a national hero, was untainted by association with the section of the party blamed for the 1948 defeat, as a likely presidential contender. Dewey was alleged to have stated, "I owe a lot to the Republican party and I'm going to pay my debt by helping to make Dwight Eisenhower President."[52] Senator Lodge was duly dispatched to sound out the general concerning his possible candidacy. According to Eisenhower's memoirs,

> The Republican party, Cabot said, must now seek to nominate one who, supporting basic Republican convictions—which had come down to us from Lincoln and Theodore Roosevelt—could be elected, and achieve at least a partial reversal of the trend towards centralisation in government, irresponsible spending, and catering to pressure groups, and at the same time avoid the crucial error of isolationism.[53]

It was probably the last-mentioned consideration that most influenced Eisenhower's decision to run in 1952. Like Lodge, he was

particularly determined to prevent the Republicans' falling back
into isolationism under Taft's leadership.[54] Eisenhower had considerable advantages in the 1952 campaign: his war record, his
congenial public image, and the support of the still formidable
Dewey-Brownell organization; but success was not easily achieved.
Taft possessed a devoted following among grass roots Republicans
in the Midwest and considerable support among the "patronage"
Republicans of the South. Yet many of his southern delegates were
vulnerable to credentials challenges and the Eisenhower forces
duly challenged the Taft delegations from Texas, Louisiana, Florida, and Georgia. Herbert Brownell then devised his master stroke.
Acting on his advice, Dewey persuaded twenty-three of the twenty-
five Republican governors meeting in Houston to support a reso-
lution that demanded fair play with regard to the contested southern delegations. By "fair play" they meant that the contested Taft
delegates should not vote in contests concerning their own credentials. Goldman, Bain, and Moos concluded that

> the Eisenhower strategy sought to enlist the support of the majority
> of the Republican Governors—an extremely important group since
> Governors more often than Congressmen and Senators control their
> state party organizations. Seeking soft spots in the armor of the Taft
> organizations where they could find them, the Eisenhower man-
> agers also exploited quite a few in an area that heretofore had been
> considered a safe preserve for hunting Taft delegates—the South.[55]

The Governors' Manifesto brought national attention to the fair
play issue, and the adverse publicity it created for Taft finally destroyed his chances of success. With Taft's southern delegates being supplanted by Eisenhower supporters, the general was able to
prevail by a narrow margin.

Taft was defeated by the usual coalition: the New England
states, the Mid-Atlantic states, the Pacific Coast, and the more
progressively inclined states of the Midwest, Michigan and Minnesota (see Tables 2-2 and 2-4). Once again the Republican governors and party managers of the Eastern and Western Seaboard
states succeeded in holding their delegations in line for the progressive candidate. According to Patterson,

> As in 1940 and 1948, he [Taft] had collided with a keystone of
> political demography. At Convention time, it was often the impor-

tant eastern states that ruled the Republican party. . . . the real
problem was that coastal Republicans had long distrusted Taft's
views, especially on foreign policy, and his voting record since 1948
had done nothing to set their minds at rest.[56]

The coalition that nominated Eisenhower was not composed exclusively of eastern progressives. Richard Nixon, chosen as Eisenhower's running mate, represented the new nationalism, and several
stalwarts, such as former Senator Darby of Kansas, supported the
general. Eisenhower himself did not fit easily into the liberal Republican mold. His Republicanism was grounded in the mores of
his small-town Kansas boyhood, with internationalism grafted on
top.[57] Although he did not attack the foundations of the New Deal
welfare system, Eisenhower encouraged Republicans in Congress
to restrain domestic spending. His views on domestic matters were
governed by the traditional Republican precepts of fiscal conservatism and a balanced federal budget. According to Reichard,

> Very conservative in fiscal affairs and devoted to the principle of
> local responsibility in power and resource development, President
> Eisenhower acquiesced in certain New Deal programs, but did noth-
> ing to expand them, and he remained philosophically opposed to
> much of the spirit of both the New and Fair Deals. His acquies-
> cence in programs like social security and limited public housing
> reflected political inevitability by the 50s, not the triumph of a
> "moderate" or "liberal" wing within the Republican party.[58]

The general was highly unsympathetic toward Taftite foreign
and defense policies, however, and was more influenced by new
nationalist thinking. This was evident in his rapid disengagement
of American ground forces from Korea; his New Look defense
policy, which sought to cut the defense budget through reliance on
air power and nuclear weaponry to deter Soviet aggression; and
Secretary of State Dulles's concomitant foreign policy doctrine of
"massive retaliation."

Overall, the Eisenhower administration was guided by traditional Republican doctrine in domestic affairs and by new nationalism in foreign policy. It was to be more liberal in rhetoric
than in practice.

The Eisenhower Legacy and the Election of 1960

Traditional interpretations of the Eisenhower administration portrayed Eisenhower as a rather innocent and indolent leader who disliked partisan politics and neglected Republican party affairs during his presidency.[59] In recent years this view has been challenged by a revisionist school of historians and political scientists which has sought to depict Eisenhower as a more active and skillful chief executive.[60] One member of this school, Cornelius Cotter, has applied the revisionist thesis to Eisenhower's role as party leader:

> The record reads that as President, Eisenhower exerted considerable influence over the Republican party and pursued a well-informed and sustained program to strengthen it. Arguably, he was the most constructive and consistent intervener in party organization matters of any President after Franklin D. Roosevelt.[61]

Despite this argument, it appears, from Cotter's own evidence, that Eisenhower's involvement in party affairs did not extend beyond striving for unity in the ranks and improving the party's national organization (as in the establishment of Operation Dixie under National Chairman Meade Alcorn for the purpose of attracting southerners to the GOP).

The president certainly made little attempt to reorganize the national party around the modern Republican principles he claimed to espouse. Following his landslide re-election in 1956, Eisenhower made the following statement:

> I think that modern Republicanism had now proved itself, and America has approved of modern Republicanism. As we look ahead, let us remember that this political party deserves the approbation of America only as it represents the ideals, the aspirations and hopes of Americans.[62]

But Eisenhower had also resolved to maintain unity in the Republican party at all costs, and this tempered his efforts to popularize the modern Republican creed. According to Reinhard,

> Proclaimed in the ecstasy of his 1956 victory, modern Republicanism was a blunder for a number of reasons. It was first of all a

hazy concept that left Republicans and pundits alike arguing about its true meaning. Modern Republicanism amounted to little more than a *smorgasbord* of liberal and conservative offerings. It lacked philosophical backbone. Nor did Ike make any real effort to build up modern Republicanism or attend to state and local political affairs in order to bring about such a change in his political party.[63]

Perhaps given the highly decentralized structure of American political parties and the unfortunate precedent of Franklin Roosevelt's involvement in intraparty strife in 1938, it was unlikely that Eisenhower could have done a great deal more than he did to promote the liberal Republican cause within the GOP.

In 1960, with Eisenhower ineligible for a third term because of the Twenty-second Amendment, Vice-President Richard M. Nixon was able to win the Republican nomination with considerable ease. Nixon's impeccable anti-communist credentials (earned in the Alger Hiss case) endeared him to the right, while his modern Republican outlook on domestic matters made him acceptable to more liberal easterners, such as National Chairman Len Hall and Senator Hugh Scott of Pennsylvania. Among Republican regulars in the state party organizations, Nixon was held in high esteem for his tireless campaigning for Republican candidates throughout the Eisenhower administration. According to Stewart Alsop, one of the most commonly heard comments at any gathering of the Republican faithful in the late 1950s was, "Dick Nixon is our kind of guy."[64]

Nixon's otherwise smooth path to the nomination was impeded by one factor: Nelson Rockefeller's landslide victory in the New York gubernatorial election of 1958 (achieved in a year of heavy Republican losses) immediately thrust him into the presidential race. Rockefeller had earlier resigned from the administration in impatience with the cautious tenor of Eisenhower's policies on defense, social reform, and civil rights, and, in the fall of 1959, he undertook preliminary soundings of Republican organizations around the country to assess whether he could mount a viable challenge to Nixon for the 1960 nomination. The regulars were solidly behind Nixon, however, and the campaign was abandoned.[65] After the shooting down of the U-2 spy plane and the failure of the Paris summit in May 1960, Rockefeller revived speculation about his presidential intentions by announcing that he was open to a draft by the convention.[66] On June 8, 1960 he issued the following statement:

> I am deeply convinced and deeply concerned that those now assuming control of the Republican party have failed to make clear where this party is heading and where it proposes to lead the nation.[67]

Rockefeller never had a serious chance of loosening Nixon's hold on the nomination, however, and the dispute between them was confined to the subject of the party platform. Rockefeller sought to strengthen the plank on civil rights, and also to commit the Republicans to spending an additional $3 billion on defense in order to meet the "crisis" in American security.[68] Nixon could not afford a confrontation between Rockefeller and the Republican conservatives over the platform, so he decided to compromise. The result was the so-called Treaty of Fifth Avenue, agreed upon by Nixon and Rockefeller at the latter's New York apartment, where Nixon more or less acceded to Rockefeller's demands.[69] Once again, it appeared that Republican principles had been compromised to satisfy the demands of the party's eastern liberals, and Nixon's "surrender" to Rockefeller in 1960 had far-reaching implications for developments in the Republicans' conservative wing in the following four years.

By trying to appease both Rockefeller and the conservatives, Nixon succeeded in displeasing both. For most of the fall campaign he was on the defensive, adopting vague and vacillating positions on the major issues (particularly civil rights). The enmity between the party's ideological factions continued throughout the campaign. The liberals urged Nixon to direct his appeal toward the metropolitan vote of the Northeast. The conservatives wanted a more explicit appeal to conservative voters, southern whites in particular. As a consequence, Nixon, through fear of offending either wing, found himself immobilized on the issues.[70] The Republican performance in 1960—losing the presidency by a very narrow margin and holding their strength in Congress and the states—was by no means disastrous for a minority party. Nevertheless, the mismanagement of the Nixon campaign left a residue of hostility toward the candidate among prominent Republicans. The ideological and sectional dichotomy within the GOP remained as intractable as it had ever been, and the efforts by Eisenhower and Nixon to reconcile the divergent streams of Republican ideology only succeeded in concealing, rather than resolving, the continuing conflict between the factions. The stage was set for a dramatic confrontation between the liberals and the conservatives for the soul of the party in 1964.

Summary

In concluding this survey of Republican party history from 1854 to 1960, it is useful to isolate the factors that will have some bearing on the analysis to be presented in future chapters.

First, the Republican party has usually been an arena of sectional conflict, with regional factions bearing ideological labels struggling for control and influence. The East and the Midwest struggled for the party's presidential nomination, competing for the allegiance of the maverick Republicans of the West and the derisory Republican state parties in the South. The eastern section usually had the upper hand in this struggle because of its greater population, the influence of the governors and party bosses of the larger states, and the power of the business community. The eastern wing of the party has always been more oriented toward Europe in foreign affairs. Midwesterners and westerners have either been militant isolationists or have regarded the Far East as America's legitimate sphere of influence.

Since the late nineteenth century, the party has possessed an eastern, urban, liberal element, conservative in the sense of seeking reform to avoid social conflict, but often radical in its desire to exorcise corruption from government and to promote effective and well-managed public services. These eastern reformers enjoyed two periods of dominance within the Republican party: from 1901 to 1916 and from 1940 to 1960. In each case this came about because the reformers were able to produce a national leader with acute political skills (Roosevelt and Dewey) whose opinions were in harmony with the popular mood of the time. The Republican party has had another element, sometimes labeled radical or progressive, but distinct from, and only intermittently allied with, the eastern reformers. This group was more preoccupied with agrarian issues; it was suspicious of international commitments and hostile toward large business corporations. Its roots lay in populism and the agrarian revolt of the 1890s, rather than in urban social and political reform. The westerners stressed political independence and, although still nominally Republican, harbored a strong dislike of organized political parties per se. This section of the GOP was destroyed as an effective political force by the New Deal and then divided between the Republican and Democratic parties. But traces of western progressivism lingered in the Yankee- and Scandinavian-settled states of the Pacific Northwest, and to some extent in California. The Yankee cultural heritage in those states made them allies of the second wave of Republican liberalism, from 1940 to 1952.

In normal times the Republican party relied for its base of electoral support on the so-called stalwart or Old Guard Republicans of the Midwest and the rural Northeast. This element generally supported business interests, although its main preoccupation was with small business, individualism, free enterprise, and Protestant ethics. It was dubious about American involvements overseas, but its isolationism was rarely as vehement as that of the westerners. Its position regarding most political questions was to cling to the Republican past and stand as firmly as possible against all change. The stalwarts' leading political representatives in Republican history had been McKinley, Harding, Coolidge, and Robert Taft. They were distrustful of Federal government activism and disliked large government expenditures for any purpose. The stalwart wing also usually predominated within the congressional branch of the Republican party.

Finally, throughout most of the party's history, its southern section had been moribund, consisting only of Appalachian enclaves and "post office" Republicans. The southern delegations remained an important presence at Republican national conventions, however, and were invariably for sale to the highest bidder in terms of federal patronage. These delegations were also subject to perennial credentials challenges.

Republican party conflict in the twentieth century has been characterized by liberal and stalwart battles for the soul of the party. In times of normalcy and prosperity, the stalwart wing has usually prevailed. In times of social unrest at home and international crisis such as the 1900s and 1940s, the liberals have generally had the upper hand. In 1948 the liberals lost a possible opportunity to consolidate their dominance when Dewey was defeated. Eisenhower won the Republican nomination and the presidency in 1952, in large part because of the Dewey-Brownell organization and enthusiastic liberal Republican support, but fundamentally, he was more at home with the stalwart Republican tradition on economic and social policy, and during his presidency he made little attempt to recast the Republican party in a liberal form. Although the liberal Republicans still had a slight advantage in the factional battle of the early 1950s, their hold on the party was tenuous and vulnerable. The Eisenhower administration, with its amalgam of progressive rhetoric and stalwart policy, merely postponed the fundamental decision on the direction in which the GOP would move in the 1960s and 1970s.

2

The Impact
of the Goldwater Campaign

The presidential campaign of 1964 was a most critical event, dramatically illustrating the changing balance of power between the major Republican tendencies. The latent tensions within the Republican coalition, which had been contained during the Eisenhower era, came to the fore in the internecine strife that characterized the 1964 campaign for the Republican nomination. After Barry Goldwater was nominated in San Francisco, the liberal wing would not again control the presidential Republican party. The events of 1964 further demonstrated the emergence of a new genus of Republican conservatism based on the rapidly expanding southern and western regions of the United States. The Taftite regulars of the Midwest, who traditionally acted as the guardians of Republican orthodoxy, formed an alliance with the more populist conservatives of the Sunbelt, leaving the liberals of the Eastern Seaboard an isolated minority, with limited influence over the future course of the Republican party.

This chapter demonstrates how the conservative Goldwater movement was able to take control of the national Republican party in 1964, and why the supposedly all-powerful eastern Republican establishment collapsed in the face of this assault.

The Changing Nature of Republican Conservatism

The defeat of Nixon in 1960 gave encouragement to the forces within the Republican party that had never accepted the New

Deal's system of government, but that had been temporarily quiescent during the Eisenhower years. These elements were gaining additional strength from a combination of demographic trends and the changing pattern of Republican electoral support—most obviously through the emergence of more organized Republican state parties in the southern and Border states. Nevertheless, the conservatism of the Goldwater movement was different in kind from that of the midwestern party regulars who had rallied behind Taft in the 1940s and 1950s. The Taftites had been regular Republicans from Ohio and the neighboring states in the traditional Republican heartland. Although these stalwarts were devoted to Taft and generally loathed internationalism and the New Deal, they were the most loyal of Republicans and were generally prepared to compromise with the dominant eastern wing to secure power at the national level. Senator Taft himself was a party loyalist above all else, and gave wholehearted support to the Eisenhower administration until his death.[1] The Goldwater movement included some elements of the old Taft constituency, but its base of support was generally made up of elements that had not previously been closely associated with the Republican coalition. As Richard Rovere observed,

> Taft drew much of his support from Middle-Western industrialists and bankers who had some understanding of the imperatives of an industrial society; they didn't spend much time denouncing the graduated income tax or social security. Goldwater's support comes largely from southwestern speculators and promoters whose economic views and practices are largely pre-industrial. They have no tradition of Republicanism; many of them are former Democrats, and their loyalty is not to the Republican party, but to Goldwater and Goldwaterism.[2]

As late as 1948, most of the southern, Border, and western states had voted for Democrat Harry S. Truman, while Dewey's base of support had lain in the traditional Republican strongholds of the Northeast and the Upper Midwest. The Eisenhower breakthrough in the South in 1952 (when he carried Tennessee, Florida, Texas, and Virginia for the GOP) and in 1956 (when he carried the same four states plus Louisiana) created the basis for something more than "post office" Republican state parties in that region. With the national Democratic party becoming ever more liberal on the issue of civil rights and more oriented toward the interests of the urban Northeast, Republican conservatism had an obvious potential appeal to disenchanted conservative southern Democrats. The political effects of migration and industrialization—particularly on the states of the southern rim—further aided the Republican cause in presidential elections (see Table 2-1).[3] At the congressional level, the proportion of southern House seats held by Republicans rose from 2% in 1948 to 32% by 1972, and the proportion of Senate seats from 0% to 32% over the same period (see Table 5-2).

The surge in electoral support for the Republicans in the South was not the sole source of right-wing support tapped by the Goldwater conservatives. As the Republican party declined as an electoral force in the 1950s, with little sense of direction from the White House, groups of disenchanted conservatives and former followers of Senator Joseph McCarthy began to organize outside the Republican party apparatus.[4] In so doing American conservatives were seeking to rid themselves of their Protestant, nativist image and to reach out to groups outside the historical Republican coalition, which were thought to have been attracted by the strident anti-communism of Senator McCarthy.[5] A particular target group was upwardly mobile Catholic ethnics, whose conservatism was based on social and cultural themes such as family, religion and social order, rather than on the traditional conservative Republican shibboleths of free enterprise and political individualism. In 1950, the New York Roman Catholic millionaire, William F. Buckley, Jr., established the *National Review* as an organ of opposition to the consensus politics of the Eisenhower regime. Between 1960 and 1969 the circulation of the *National Review* increased (from 30,000 to 100,000) and Buckley's syndicated column, *On the Right,* was circulated in over 300 newspapers.[6] Buckley was given a program on nationwide network television, *Firing Line,* and he controlled Arlington House Publishers, in addition to the commercial radio venture Starr Broadcasting. He also helped establish the conservative Intercollegiate Studies Institute in 1953, and in 1960 the Young Americans for Freedom (YAF).[7] All these conservative organizations were to play a crucial role in the Goldwater campaign. Operating outside the official Republican organization, Buckley and his associates, such as William Rusher, M. Stanton Evans, and James J. Kilpatrick, had established a national network of conservative political organizations that could be mobilized for a national campaign.[8]

During the Eisenhower years, the social effects of industrialization and rapid economic growth further contributed to the emergence of the radical right as a significant political force in the southwestern United States. Industrial development in the Southwest was accompanied by rapid population growth, especially in the new metropolitan centers of San Diego, Los Angeles, Phoenix, Tucson, Houston, and Dallas–Fort Worth. Many of those who migrated (particularly in southern California) were small-town midwesterners who took their conservative politics with them to the Southwest. Others were attracted to right-wing politics because of changes in their socioeconomic status. Given that most of the South and Southwest was unorganized by trade unions, and that low labor costs were a major incentive in attracting industrial investment to these areas, the nascent Sunbelt business class found conservative economics very congenial to its aspirations. Sunbelt nouveaux riches were also suspicious of established eastern wealth, fearing that the federal government was directing an excessive amount of its resources toward the industries and cities of the Northeast at the expense of their own region. The free-enterprise ethos of conservative Republicanism thus attracted considerable business support in the Sunbelt states, providing new sources of funds, organization, and electoral support for conservative candidates.

One other factor in the economic development of the southwestern states also corresponded with the ideology of the new conservative strain in the Republican party. The southern part of California was the area most identified with the so-called "military-industrial complex." Lockheed, Northrop, McDonnell Douglas, and Hughes were all based there. Military-aerospace expenditures concentrated in Los Angeles, San Diego, Orange and Santa Clara Counties generated 83% of the new manufacturing jobs in California from 1950 to 1962, and 62% of the net influx of new residents:[9]

TABLE 2-1. Mean Republican Vote in Presidential Elections, 1956–1980

Region	Safe Republican (≧60%)	Mainly Republican (55–59%)	Leaning Republican (50–54%)	Leaning Democrat (45–49%)	Mainly Democrat (40–44%)	Safe Democrat (<40%)
Northeast			Vermont Maine New Jersey	Connecticut Delaware Pennsylvania Maryland New York West Virginia	Massachusetts Rhode Island	District of Columbia
Midwest	Nebraska	Kansas North Dakota Indiana	South Dakota Iowa Illinois Ohio Wisconsin	Missouri Michigan Minnesota		
West	Utah	Idaho Arizona Wyoming	Colorado Nevada Montana New Mexico Alaska California	Oregon Washington Hawaii		

South				
	Oklahoma	Florida	Kentucky	Georgia
		Virginia	North Carolina	
		Texas	Tennessee	
			South Carolina	
			Alabama	
			Louisiana	
			Mississippi	
			Arkansas	

Source: Richard M. Scammon and Alice V. McGillivray, *America Votes 14* (Washington, DC: Congressional Quarterly, 1981).

This military-aerospace complex dovetailed nicely with the political style of the new Republican right. Republican foreign policy was traditionally Pacific-oriented, while its strategic doctrine was slanted toward air-power. The new nationalism was overriding old-guard inhibitions about military might.[10]

The margins for Barry Goldwater in Los Angeles, Orange, and San Diego Counties were decisive in his 1964 California primary triumph, the victory that virtually guaranteed his nomination. California had been a bastion of western progressivism under Hiram Johnson, Earl Warren, and Goodwin Knight, but the weak and fluid nature of the California party system created by the progressives permitted issue-oriented appeals, volunteer activism, and mass media campaigns directed by campaign-management firms to play a much more important role in California elections than in states with strong party organizations. This system began to work to the disadvantage of liberal Republicans in the early 1960s. The disastrous defeats of Goodwin Knight and William Knowland in 1958, added to the growing electoral weight of immigrant-swollen southern California in statewide races and the end of cross-filing in primary elections (which had been so crucial to the political career of Earl Warren), had the cumulative effect of leaving the liberal Republicans in the state isolated and vulnerable, and facilitated the takeover of the state Republican party by the militant right. In 1962, Richard Nixon, a conservative hero a decade previously, was forced to fight hard to secure his party's nomination for California governor against conservative Joseph Shell, who was vigorously supported by the notorious John Birch Society.[11] The Los Angeles County Republican Committee (once a Nixon preserve) supported Shell, and Nixon was repudiated by the California Young Republican organization, which had come under a strong right-wing influence.[12] Nixon's difficulty in defeating Shell (who won 33% of the primary vote) demonstrated the extent to which the California GOP was moving to the right, and when Nixon spurned the Birchers and attacked "extremism," many conservatives refused to work for him in the general election against the Democratic incumbent Pat Brown. (Nixon would not make the same mistake again.) The militant conservatives' takeover of the volunteer organizations, so important in California politics, was illustrated by the case of the California Republican Assembly (CRA), created by Earl Warren as a liberal Republican citizens' organization. By 1965, five of the CRA's sixteen key leaders were members of the John Birch Society.[13]

The net effect of all these changes in the nature of Republican conservatism was ominous for the liberal wing of the party. New sources of conservative electoral support, generated by economic and social developments, had emerged in the South and West, and when added to the old stalwart base in the Midwest, gave a conservative Republican coalition the potential to wrest power in the national GOP away from the distrusted eastern establishment. The proliferation of conservative journals and volunteer organizations had created the possibility of establishing a national conservative political movement independent of the existing party structure, with its own loyal battalions of activists and independent sources of finance. The Goldwater movement would reveal the political power of the "new" conservatism.

The Goldwater Movement

The "Draft Goldwater" movement was established in 1961 to concentrate the resources of the various conservative organizations that supported the candidacy of Senator Barry M. Goldwater for the 1964 Republican presidential nomination. Under the direction of F. Clifton White (a former member of Dewey's staff), a national organization was formed without the assistance of the candidate himself. Other leading figures in the early days included William Rusher (Chairman of the Young Republicans and publisher of the *National Review*) and John Grenier of Alabama and Peter O'Donnell of Texas, both southern Republican state chairmen who represented the strong southern interest in a Goldwater nomination. These men were not former Taft followers (indeed, Rusher and White had been Eisenhower backers in 1952) but young conservative politicians seeking to use the GOP as a national vehicle for their cause.[14]

While he did not discourage his followers from promoting his cause, Goldwater was ambivalent about running for the White House. First elected to the Senate in 1952, he had become the leading national spokesman for conservatism through an unrelenting schedule of public appearances at Republican party functions around the United States. According to Kessel,

> The Senator had spent the better part of a decade befriending the party activists and the Goldwater field organization was set up to translate friendship into votes.[15]

The message that party workers heard from Goldwater was one of undiluted southwestern conservatism. The Arizona senator had strong laisser faire views on economic matters; believed that the welfare state and the permissive society were threatening public morals; and thought that the Soviet Union would have to be met with unmitigated hostility in the international arena. These opinions were aggregated in Goldwater's 1960 volume *The Conscience of a Conservative,* which had a profound impact on the American right.[16]

Despite his extreme views, Goldwater maintained a reputation as a loyal Republican. He described the Eisenhower administration as a "dime-store New Deal" and the Rockefeller-Nixon compromise of 1960 as the "sellout of Fifth Avenue," but in his speech declining nomination at the 1960 convention, Goldwater had called for Republican unity[17]:

> We are conservatives. This great Republican party is our historical house. This is our home. Now some of us don't agree with every statement in the official platform of our party, but I might remind you that is always true in every platform of an American political party.[18]

During the 1960 campaign, however, Goldwater became increasingly irritated by Nixon's equivocation and vacillation:

> He [Nixon] appeared to be equivocating, anxious to please everyone, determined not to say anything which might alienate any ideologically united subgrouping within the party.[19]

Thus, notwithstanding his reluctance to enter the presidential arena through fear of compromising his positions, Goldwater was the obvious leader of a campaign to secure the party's 1964 nomination in the name of his conservative principles.

The initial strategy of the Draft Goldwater organization was to use the conservative network to encourage conservatives to stand for precinct, county, and state party positions, which had little public visibility but would enable the organization to get conservative delegates selected for the 1964 convention.[20] This was where Goldwater's hard work for the party was an immense asset. The system of indirect elections used to select most of the convention delegates involved elections from precinct caucuses to congressional district conventions to the state convention, where the national convention delegates were chosen. This elaborate and tortuous process was ideally suited to the White group's purposes. At the lowest level, the precinct caucuses, only the most committed, and therefore most conservative, activists were likely to participate. The Goldwater organization directed by White and using regional directors such as John Grenier for the South and Stephen Shadegg for the West was successful in mobilizing local supporters for the precinct meetings, thereby ensuring the selection of delegates favorable to Goldwater for the county conventions. This process was followed through all its stages up to the state convention, with the aim of preparing committed slates of Goldwater delegates for the national convention. White succeeded, moreover, in getting Goldwater supporters elected to the convention's important Rules and Credentials committees. Theodore White described the efforts of F. Clifton White and his Goldwater volunteers as follows:

> Their planning was more useful, more determined, and earlier begun than that of any previous presidential campaign; it was a masterpiece of politics.[21]

Of the 25 national convention delegates selected in state conventions or by state committees between January and April 1964, Goldwater secured 130, which put him far ahead of the other contenders and illustrated the effectiveness of the activist-oriented campaign conducted by White and his associates at the Republican grass roots.[22]

The South was an area of particular attention. The young southern Republican leaders—O'Donnell, of Texas, Yeager, of Mississippi, Grenier, of Alabama, and Stagg, of Louisiana—were able to organize their delegations for Goldwater, whose states' rights position on the race issue conformed with southern white sentiments.[23] These leaders of the incipient southern Republican state parties were no longer placated by offers of federal patronage from the eastern wing of the party. According to F. Clinton White,

> We organized the South. I first got involved in the South for Eisenhower in 1952. In that year the only Republican organization in the South was the Young Republicans. The oldsters had been holding conventions in phone booths. By 1964 we had a bunch of young kids in the South who couldn't be bought.[24]

Southern Republican feeling regarding the 1964 nomination was summarized by Tom Stagg, Jr. of Louisiana:

> I just hope to God that for once my party has the guts to say the hell with carrying New York. I hope that for once we have the guts to say to hell with those eastern liberals.[25]

The emphasis on the southern base paid handsome dividends for Goldwater. At San Francisco in 1964, he would win 271 of the 278 southern delegates. More important, because of the Republicans' delegate-allocation formula (which allocated delegates to states of the basis of Republican performance in the immediately preceding presidential election), the South's growing population, and Eisenhower and Nixon's successes in the region, the proportion of Republican convention delegates from the South had risen from 19% in 1952 to 25% in 1964 (see Table 2-3). This growth in southern delegate strength was a critical factor in moving the center of power in the Republican party away from the liberals of the Northeast and toward the southwestern conservatives.

By the beginning of June 1964, Goldwater had secured some 300 delegates from the caucus states and his southwestern base—far more than his nearest rival. To be sure of the nomination, however, Goldwater needed to win the support of the large midwestern delegations, particularly those of Ohio and Illinois. As Reinhard points out,

> The Goldwater nomination struggle had pitted the burgeoning power centers of the South and West against the eastern seaboard, with the Midwest now representing the crucial balance of power.[26]

These states had strong Republican state organizations that were not so easily penetrated by radical conservative activists. Although the Midwest was the heartland of Republican orthodoxy, sectional prejudice and the instincts of party professionals (such as Ohio State Chairman Ray Bliss) to look for a candidate who could win the general election meant that Goldwater could not rely on the solid support of the old Taft constituency. His delegate strength had come from uncontested primaries and caucus states. To be sure of nomination, Goldwater had to demonstrate that he could win a contested primary in a state heavy with electoral college votes. In the prenomination campaign, Goldwater's outstanding success in the caucus states was not reflected in the primaries. In New Hampshire he was defeated by non-candidate Henry Cabot Lodge, and in Oregon by Nelson Rockefeller. Even his superficially impressive triumphs in Illinois, Indiana, and Nebraska were achieved against very lackluster opposition from inactive candidates Margaret Chase Smith, Harold Stassen, Richard Nixon, and Lodge.[27] The crucial contest for the 86 delegates in California's "winner take all" primary was between Goldwater and Rockefeller. If Goldwater won, he was likely to sweep the remaining caucus and convention states, and his bandwagon would be unstoppable. A Rockefeller victory, on the other hand, might allow the party moderates to regroup and block Goldwater's nomination.

The Goldwater organization in California displayed all the strengths of the conservative network in grass roots politics. The conservative volunteer organizations—the John Birch Society, the YAF, and the California Young Republicans (YRs), led by Robert Gaston—all campaigned assiduously. In Los Angeles County (which contained 36% of the state's population), 8,000 volunteers canvased 600,000 homes and compiled lists of 300,000 Goldwater voters.[28] In other counties, such as Orange, San Bernadino, and Santa Barbara, Gaston controlled his own volunteer organization, independent of the official Goldwater campaign. In contrast to this well-organized effort, Rockefeller had only 2,000 volunteers and had to rely on an expensive television campaign rather than on personal contact with the Republican voters.[29] Goldwater finally won the primary by 51.6% to 48.4%, thanks largely to the work of his volunteer army. Rockefeller carried 54 of the state's 58 counties, but Goldwater's sweeping pluralities in Los Angeles, Orange, and San Diego Counties saw him through to victory. As Kessel observed,

Goldwater won the election because he was at least close enough to be within striking distance, because many potential Goldwater supporters were more intense in their attitudes and so more likely to vote and because Goldwater groups in Los Angeles and Orange counties had enough volunteers to reach the pro-Goldwater voters who needed to be reminded.[30]

In spite of the desperate effort by the Republican moderates in the weeks leading up to the convention, Goldwater's California triumph virtually assured him of nomination.

The strength of the Goldwater organization, operating independently of the national party machinery, was not the sole revolutionary aspect of the Goldwater movement. The influence of Wall Street and eastern money over Republican fund-raising had been eroded by the proliferation of new financial and industrial centers in Houston, Dallas, Miami, Denver, and Los Angeles. Goldwater was able to raise $5.5 million in pursuit of the nomination, with California alone accounting for $2 million.[31] In the 1964 general election the eastern financial interests generally supported Lyndon Johnson, but Goldwater did not suffer through lack of funds. In 1952, 88% of Republican money had come in gifts of over $500; in 1964, only 28% of Republican campaign funds were accounted for by sums in excess of that figure.[32] The Goldwater prenomination and general election campaigns were able to raise large amounts of money from small donors through direct mail (using mailing lists compiled by conservative volunteer organizations) and television appeals. Approximately 650,000 people gave sums of $100 or less to the Goldwater campaign in 1964.[33] According to Hess and Broder,

> The continued increase in the numbers of small contributors in response to direct mail solicitations and the success of the televised appeals during presidential campaigns frees the party from any veto power over a nominee by a specific number of contributors.[34]

In subsequent presidential elections, the diffusion of managerial talent, the rise of campaign consultants whose services were available for hire to any candidate with the necessary finances, and the revolution in fund-raising typified by the Goldwater campaign would all contribute to the rise of the candidate organization over the national party as the dominant actor in presidential election campaigns. These newfound sources of finance and organization for campaigning liberated candidates from an important incentive to modify their ideological stances at the party convention or in the general election, since the moderating influence of senior party leaders and financiers was considerably reduced. Moreover, many of the foot soldiers of the Goldwater movement had no roots inside the Republican party and felt little compulsion to reach an accommodation with Republican liberals, who represented everything that they had been striving against for years. Describing the attitude of the Goldwater delegates at San Francisco, Richard Rovere concluded that

> the spirit of compromise and accommodation was wholly alien to them. They did not come to San Francisco merely to nominate their man and then rally his former opponents behind them. They came for a total ideological victory and the total destruction of their critics.[35]

The conservatives were thus able to take over the Republican party in 1964, using newfound bases of electoral support, astute campaign management, effective grass roots organization, and an ever expanding network of conservative volunteers. In the next section it will be shown how their victory was expedited by the errors of their ideological opponents.

The Failure of the Republican Moderates

The Republican liberals did not stand idly by while Goldwater walked off with the nomination. However, they were not awakened to the danger until it was too late to prevent the conservative takeover of the party. The moderate Republican leaders' refusal to confront Goldwater openly followed from their faith in the traditional mechanisms of Republican nominating politics, which they thought would ensure the emergence of a more viable candidate, as in 1940 and 1952. Yet the complacent liberal Republicans of 1964 were deceived by the myth of the Republican establishment as effectively as the conservatives had been in previous years. Eastern establishment figures, such as Dewey, Brownell, Henry Luce, and the Rockefellers, Mellons, and Scrantons, had exerted some influence within the national Republican party, but the Republican establishment had never been the monolithic institution that its reputation implied, and its political and financial power within the Republican party was rapidly diminishing as these resources became less concentrated on the East Coast. The liberals had possessed a superb campaign organization, constructed by Dewey and Herbert Brownell, but even they had great difficulty in defeating Taft in 1952 with a national hero as their candidate. By the early 1960s, Dewey, Brownell, and the other major figures in the Eisenhower campaign organization had retired from active politics, and the machinery had atrophied. The revolution in campaign technology, and the increasing threat from the right, demanded that liberal Republicans create a new national campaign organization and a network of volunteer activists to challenge the conservatives at the base of the party. However, the failure of the Republican liberals to comprehend the changes that were taking place precluded their adapting their campaign strategy to the new electoral environment. The lessons of 1964 were never effectively learned by the liberal wing of the party, resulting in an ever-diminishing influence for the liberal wing over the selection of Republican presidential candidates.

Ideological coherence had been a consistent problem for Republican liberals since the New Deal. In one sense, it appeared that they had learned the lessons of the 1930s too well. In their eagerness to adapt themselves to the New Deal, Dewey, Willkie, and Eisenhower exposed themselves to allegations of opportunism, or "me-tooism." This failure to define a cogent liberal Republican philosophy seemed to legitimize the claim of the conservatives that they stood as the loyal guardians of the Republican faith, representing a politics of principle as opposed to the "shameless expediency" practiced by the eastern moderates.

During the Eisenhower era, several Republicans did attempt to formulate a theoretical justification for liberal Republicanism. The most serious attempt to refashion Republican doctrine in a manner relevant to the concerns of the post–New Deal era was made by Eisenhower's Under Secretary of Labor Arthur Larson in his book *A Republican Looks at His Party,* published in 1956. Larson advocated a new Republicanism based on the style and policies of the Eisenhower administration. This Republicanism would be conservative in a genuinely American sense, since it would seek to conserve the American liberal tradition in government. Securing individual rights and the maintenance of the free-enterprise system should be the permanent objectives of the Republican party, but government should also take responsibility for providing relief to the less fortunate members of society and for defending the right of workers to improve their lot through labor unions and collective bargaining:

> Now we have as much government activity as is necessary, but not enough to stifle the normal motivations of private enterprise. And we have a higher degree of government concern for the needs of people than ever before in our history, while at the same time pursuing a policy of maximum restoration of responsibility to individuals and private groups. This balance, together with a gradual restoration of a better balance between federal and state governments, is allowing all these elements in society to make their maximum contribution to the common good.[36]

The overall theme of Larson's work was an emphasis on consensus politics. He saw Eisenhower as representing the broad middle ground of American politics, between Democratic liberals and dogmatic conservatives. This cautious and moderate approach to government would be the key to future Republican electoral success.

The liberal Republican standard-beaders of 1964—Rockefeller, Romney, Lodge, and Scranton—all eschewed ideological appeals and oriented their campaigns around personality and their reputations as pragmatic, problem-solving reformers who approached problems with an open mind and in an ad hoc manner. Their failure to articulate any coherent set of beliefs for which the GOP was supposed to stand cost the liberals dearly. Goldwater and the conservatives were allowed to win the intellectual argument by default because their principles were not effectively challenged by their moderate opponents who attacked the Arizona senator for his extremism and unelectability, but never attempted to formulate an intellectual alternative to the "true Republicanism" that Goldwater claimed to preach.

However, it was not lack of ideology, but the personal and political problems of the leading liberal candidate, Nelson Rockefeller, that initiated the liberal Republicans' collapse in 1964. Rockefeller had far greater electoral appeal than any other prospective Republican candidate for 1964, but his actions at the 1960 convention did not endear him to hard-line conservatives or to more moderate party regulars, who perceived him as an irresponsible party wrecker for his insistence on amending the party platform to accord with his wishes. The fact that the Rockefeller name evoked images of excessive wealth and eastern establishment power, in addition to his reputation for disloyalty, led his campaign managers to try to present a conciliatory impression of the New York governor in the hope of avoiding an open battle with Goldwater for the nomination. The Rockefeller campaign was thus initially low-key and oriented around the theme of Republican unity.[37] New York national committee member George Hinman (who enjoyed good personal relationships with many conservative Republicans in the heartland states) was dispatched as Rockefeller's goodwill emissary to the Republican state parties. For a time the strategy appeared to be working. Republican state party leaders who might have been ideologically inclined toward Goldwater were nevertheless impressed by Rockeller's poll ratings. Even Goldwater came to look more kindly on the New York governor as compared with other possible candidates, such as Nixon or Romney.[38]

For all his efforts, Rockefeller aroused little genuine enthusiasm among regular Republicans, and his strength in that sector rested on very tenuous foundations: his electoral popularity as evinced by public opinion polls. When Rockefeller's controversial second marriage to "Happy" Murphy was announced in June 1963, the outcry in the Republican ranks was such that the tacit support for his nomination that Hinman had carefully nurtured among state party leaders for the previous two years collapsed overnight.[39] The party regulars were freed from supporting a candidate with whom they felt philosophically uncomfortable, and, by September 1963, according to Gallup, Goldwater was leading Rockefeller by 59% to 41% among Republicans.[40] In desperation, Rockefeller rejected the conciliation strategy and adopted the more confrontational stance toward Republican conservatives advocated by New York State Chairman L. Judson Morhouse.

This merely infuriated the conservatives even more, shattered Rockefeller's personal rapprochement with Goldwater, and aggravated those Republican leaders who sought to unify the party. Rockefeller was once again cast in the role of the candidate who seemed intent on destroying the GOP.

Liberal Republicans had placed all their hopes for 1964 on Rockefeller, and with his elimination from the race an alternative challenger had to be found. After his defeat in the California gubernatorial election of 1962, Richard Nixon's chances were discounted, although he remained a possible compromise choice in the event of a stalemate at the convention. Nixon's 1960 running mate, Henry Cabot Lodge, was disliked by other party leaders and was preoccupied as the Kennedy adminstration's Ambassador to Saigon. Former President Eisenhower could have played a pivotal role had he been willing to throw his influence behind a compromise candidate, but although he gave encouragement to several potential candidates, the former president refused to lend his public support to any particular candidacy.[41] This left only two possible contenders, both of them relatively inexperienced first-term governors: George Romney of Michigan and William Scranton of Pennsylvania.

In 1962 Romney had been elected the first Republican governor in Michigan in fourteen years, and had considerable popular appeal as a pragmatic reformer in the progressive tradition. However, Romney was not a "regular" Republican, and his calls for the GOP to become a "citizens' " party sounded too reminiscent of Eisenhower and Willkie to conservative ears. In addition, the Michigan Republicans, having been out of power for so long, were eager to keep Romney at the top of their state ticket, and the governor had already made a commitment not to run for President in 1964 during the 1962 gubernatorial campaign.

Scranton had won a huge victory in Pennsylvania in 1962, which also thrust him into the presidential limelight. The Pennsylvania governor came from an eminent Republican dynasty, and although relatively liberal in his political outlook, had succeeded in ingratiating himself with conservative regulars. Like Romney, Scranton was very reluctant to enter the presidential race, but his aides, James Reichley and Pennsylvania State Chairman Craig

Truax, believed Scranton could fill the vacuum left by Rockefeller's demise, and they encouraged speculation about the governor's intentions.[42]

Apart from the discredited Rockefeller, none of the various liberal candidates were willing to risk their reputations within the party by openly confronting Goldwater. This anxiety to maintain party unity precluded their establishing a counterorganization to challenge Goldwater in earnest. In the crucial contest between Goldwater and Rockefeller in California, the New York governor could call on only 2,000 volunteers, compared to the 10,000 working for Goldwater in Los Angeles County alone. Even more important in that decisive primary was that only the young volunteers who had put together Henry Cabot Lodge's primary organization (without the cooperation of their candidate, who remained in Saigon) rallied behind Rockefeller in order to block Goldwater. Nixon, Romney, Scranton, and Eisenhower all repudiated Rockefeller's efforts to obtain endorsements, as they did not want to antagonize the conservatives within the party by confronting Goldwater at this stage. By so doing, they more or less ensured Goldwater's nomination and eliminated whatever prospects they might have had of getting nominated themselves. They failed to appreciate the impact of the new activist politics and continued to believe that the Republican establishment would work its hidden hand to save the party. Senator Hugh Scott's assessment of the situation was typical:

> Before the summer ended, I was assured, the professionals in the big industrial states that generally supply the votes and the money to elect Republican Presidents would have reached a collective judgement to rally behind a candidate with less restricted appeal than Goldwater's.[43]

Another of the liberals' more costly mistakes was to permit the conservatives' total capture of the nascent southern Republican state parties. Southern Republicans could no longer be bought off with federal patronage, and the Republican organizations in the South were no longer the "rotten boroughs" that could provide a pretext for credentials challenges by the eastern liberals at the national convention. This fact went apparently unnoticed by the liberal Republican leaders, and no serious effort was made by a liberal candidate to try and loosen the conservative grip on the emerging southern Republican party.[44] Once again, through their failure to comprehend the changing environment in which the Republican factional competition was taking place, the moderates and liberals lost out. According to Richard Rovere,

> In a most peculiar sense Goldwater owes his success to the widespread belief that the system was a machine constructed to produce a result opposite to the one about to be produced in San Francisco. All the Republican leaders of the era that has now closed—with the possible exception of Nelson Rockefeller—thought Goldwater's elimination inevitable. Their behavior, from Eisenhower's early commitment to neutrality to Scranton's belated campaign—can only be explained in terms of their ideas of how the system should work. Because they thought it could not happen, it is happening.[45]

The events at the June 1964 National Governors' Conference in Cleveland, Ohio, held directly after the California primary, provided the most dramatic illustration of the Republican liberals' ineptitude and disarray in the face of the Goldwater challenge. In 1952, Dewey had used the governors' conference in Houston to effectively destroy Taft's prospects of nomination. There had been thirty-two Republican governors in 1952, but in 1964 there were only sixteen, and although they were nearly all from the liberal wing of the party, many had only been in office for little over a year and lacked experience in national Republican politics. There was also no Dewey to play a leadership role in rallying the GOP governors against Goldwater, and no strategy had been worked out by any of the governors prior to arrival in Cleveland. Perhaps the most significant contrast with 1952 was that, while Eisenhower and Taft had been so closely matched that the governors' influence could play a decisive part in the final outcome, in 1964 Goldwater, in the wake of his California triumph, already could rely on some 600 of the 655 delegates required to win in San Francisco.

The 1964 Republican governors faced the further problem that none of the prospective challengers to Goldwater were prepared to forfeit their jealously guarded neutrality. Scranton was nevertheless emerging as the most likely choice, and in a private meeting with Eisenhower was led to believe that the general would endorse him for the nomination. At the Governors' Conference, however, the anti-Goldwater forces failed to agree on a candidate or a campaign strategy, although they showed no hesitation in attacking Goldwater and his policies. When Eisenhower began to back away from his endorsement of Scranton, the Pennsylvania governor made a disastrous television appearance in which he vacillated and failed to announce his candidacy. Some liberals (such as Oregon Governor Mark Hatfield) believed that further activity was useless, and an embittered Rockefeller also conceded the nomination to Goldwater and attacked his moderate allies. The Cleveland conference ended in confusion and vituperation and the humiliation of the Republican liberals seemed complete.[46]

Scranton, embarrassed by the events at Cleveland and aghast at Goldwater's vote against the 1964 Civil Rights Bill, finally announced his candidacy on June 12, 1964. His chances were meager from the outset. According to Novak,

> Goldwater outnumbered, outorganized and outmaneuvered Scranton. The Goldwater camp was resolute, disciplined and monolithic. The Scranton camp was divided, vague and disorganized. The issue was never in doubt.[47]

Scranton's only hope was to break Goldwater's hold on the delegations of key heartland states, such as Illinois and Ohio, by convincing the delegates through opinion poll data that Goldwater was bound to lose in the general election, while he, Scranton, could win. It was an appeal to party professionals using the old argument of electability that had triumphed so frequently in the past, and it was backed up by polls that showed Scranton leading Goldwater 55% to 34% at the end of June.[48] Midwestern leaders such as Senator Everett Dirksen of Illinois and Ohio Governor James Rhodes were nevertheless disinclined to risk further division within the party, and both of them leaned toward acceptance of Goldwater's nomination. The superb Goldwater delegate operation managed by F. Clifton White succeeded in holding the midwestern delegates firmly in line, and it became clear that Goldwater's support was impregnable. Scranton's polls showed Johnson defeating Goldwater by 78% to 14%, but this carried little weight with Republican delegates, when the same polls showed Johnson polling over 70% against Scranton as well. As long as defeat in November seemed inevitable in any case, most of the Goldwater delegates calculated that they might as well lose with the candidate they really wanted.[49] This argument did not, of course, take into account the disastrous effects a Goldwater candidacy might have on other Republicans further down the party ticket, but an attempt to block Goldwater that would further demonstrate the divisions in the party might have had even more disastrous consequences. In any event, the final roll at the convention read: Goldwater, 883; Scranton, 214; Rockefeller, 114; Romney, 41; Margaret Chase Smith, 27—testimony to the rout of the Republican liberals in 1964.

None of the various initiatives undertaken by the Republican liberals in order to revitalize their strength within the party after Eisenhower's retirement was of any consequence in the 1964 campaign. After the 1960 defeat, New York Senator Kenneth Keating suggested a Republican summit conference involving the most important Republican leaders to chart the future direction of the party. Eisenhower supported this initiative, and the conference duly took place at his Gettysburg farm in June 1962. National Chairman William E. Miller was wary about the entire enterprise, and both conservatives and liberals suspected that it was part of an Eisenhower plan to impose Nixon or Romney on the party in 1964.[50]

The Gettysburg conference did nevertheless produce a proposal for a Republican Citizens' Committee, organized by Walter N. Thayer (publisher of the *New York Herald Tribune* and a close friend of Eisenhower) as an association to attract the allegiance of volunteers who preferred to work outside the regular party organization. In theory, this kind of grouping might have provided the activist volunteer base that the Republican liberals lacked. Goldwater and Miller both disliked the notion of an autonomous volunteer organization within the official party machinery, and to placate Goldwater, Miller made sure that the Citizens' Committee followed the example of the RNC and stressed organizational rather than ideological matters. A year after the Gettysburg conference, the Citizens' Committee took up the task of policy research in a Critical Issues Council (CIC) under Dr. Milton Eisenhower (the brother of the ex-president); this produced a series of position papers covering major issues such as NATO, foreign aid, and the balance of payments. Yet in their limited roles as policy and research groups, the Citizens' Committee and the CIC could play no part in the faction battle within the party.[51]

Meanwhile, plans had also been laid for a conference of Republican governors. The predominantly liberal Republican governors apparently sought to extend their influence over national party policy through a permanent forum in which they could jointly discuss national issues. Their chairman, Robert Smylie of Idaho, wanted a permanent staff for this conference, which would liaise with Republicans in Congress and, it was hoped, exert influence on the national party's activities in the pre-convention period. This suggestion met with little response from the conservative-dominated national committee, which jealously guarded its prerogatives as the sole national coordinating agency in the Republican party. The governors ultimately accepted Miller's good offices as liaison between their conference and other national Republican organizations, and had to rely on the RNC for staffing. Miller thereby succeeded in checking another potential instrument of liberal influence within the national party, and, as we have seen, the resultant impact of the Republican governors on the events of 1964 was minimal.[52]

Both of these initiatives were thwarted by the intransigence of the RNC and its chairman, and by the reluctance of the proponents of these measures to pursue any course of action that would offend the RNC, antagonize the conservatives, and divide the party. It was apparent that the conservative domination of the Republican National Committee, the sole manifestation of the national Republican party between elections, lay at the heart of the problem. Seats on the RNC were allocated on the basis of two members for each state, plus one bonus member for states that had voted Republican in the last presidential election, had a Republican governor or a Republican majority in its congressional delegation. This formula overrepresented small and mainly conservative western states at the expense of the liberal heartland in the metropolitan Northeast. As a result, the RNC was permanently controlled by conservative Republicans.

In 1961 the national committee had selected Representative William E. Miller of New York, a neutral figure acceptable to all the major elements in the party, as chairman. Miller was a rather lethargic chairman, preoccupied with the appearance of unity and fearful of giving offense. He poured RNC resources into Operation Dixie (the RNC operation to expand the party's support in the South), and Goldwater, as Chairman of the Republican Senatorial Campaign Committee in 1962, concentrated a great deal of attention on races in South Carolina and Alabama, with the full encouragement of Miller's national committee.[53] This so-called "southern strategy" could only improve the position of the right over the long term in the intraparty struggle. The national chairman did nothing, moreover, to counter the ultraconservative domination of the party's youth organization, the Young Republicans.[54]

Miller was not a willing servant of the Goldwater cause, although his efforts to conciliate Goldwater and his stifling of the various liberal initiatives assisted the conservatives. In this respect, however, the liberals themselves were no less culpable, for most of them were also preoccupied with maintaining the facade of party unity and were all too willing to accept Miller's arguments against effective countermobilization. For instance, few liberals paid much attention to New York State Chairman Judson Morhouse's proposals for radical reform of the system of election to the national committee.[55] Morhouse sought to break the conservative hold on the committee by ending the system of representation for all states and reallocating committee seats on a strict population basis. Aware that the conservative majority on the RNC would not willingly relinquish their own power, Morhouse urged Republicans from metropolitan states to boycott the committee and establish their own liberal national committee. No leading liberal candidate was prepared to endorse such a drastic challenge to a major center of right-wing power within the party, and the fate of the Morhouse proposals serves as yet another illustration of the liberals' reluctance to risk overt confrontation with conservative power during the 1960–64 period.

The rapidity with which the liberal Republican cause disintegrated in the wake of Rockefeller's remarriage exposed the fragile foundations on which it was built. The traditional kingmakers of Wall Street and the eastern establishment could not redeem the situation in 1964, although many moderates and liberals deluded themselves into believing that these insubstantial forces could still deliver victory to their cause. The liberals' cautious approach in the years leading up to 1964 and their reluctance to risk dividing the party produced tactical errors such as the failure to unite behind Rockefeller in California, and the farce of the Cleveland Governors' Conference. On the other hand, a more aggressive approach, culminating in a nomination won after bitter intraparty strife, might have been worth very little to the prevailing candidate, particularly when defeat in the general election appeared likely in any case. The key to the liberal failure in 1964 was primarily the reluctance to appreciate the shift in the pattern of Republican electoral support and the transformation of the candidate selection process, which now demanded volunteer activists, candidate organizations, and small-donor fund-raising rather than the mobilization of support among state party leaders. This failure to comprehend the changing rules of the nomination game allowed the conservatives to take the initiative in the delegate hunt through their assiduous cultivation of grass roots support.[56] Finally, the liberals also neglected the emerging southern Republican party and thereby assisted the consolidation of conservative strength in that region.

Had the Republican liberals appreciated these developments, they might have avoided the capitulation to the right that occurred in 1964. However, the senior figures in the party, who might have been expected to aid their cause, had either retired from active politics or were reluctant to get involved in factional strife. Remaining was a group of relatively inexperienced politicians who looked back to the lessons of the Dewey-Brownell era, rather than reorienting themselves toward the new terrain of battle within the GOP.

Implications of the 1964 Election

The conservative triumph at the 1964 convention marked the end of a long period of frustration during which the conservatives had been consistently outwitted by the eastern, liberal wing of the party. Although Goldwater and his followers differed from the Taftites in many respects, their geographical pattern of support was similar (as can be seen from Table 2-2). Goldwater gained the support of the contested delegations that had lost the nomination for Taft in 1952: Texas, Louisiana, and Georgia. He held the delegations in all the Mountain and Pacific states, with the exception of Oregon, where Rockefeller won the primary. The South and Border states were solidly behind him, as they had never been for Taft; and Goldwater picked up the heartland states that Taft had failed to carry in 1952—Iowa, Kansas, and Missouri—while keeping the Taftite bastions of Ohio and Illinois in line.

Liberal strength was reduced to the New England states, the northeastern industrial states—New York, New Jersey, and Pennsylvania—and Michigan, increasingly suburban Maryland, and the surviving liberal strongholds in the West—Minnesota and Oregon. One common characteristic of the remaining liberal states was that

TABLE 2-2. Non-Conservative States at Republican National Conventions 1940–1964

Region	State	Taft, 1940 (5th ballot)	Taft, 1948 (2d ballot)	Taft, 1952 (1st ballot)	Goldwater, 1964 (1st ballot)
South	Alabama		x[a]		
	Arkansas		sp[a]	x	
	Florida	x	x		
	Georgia	sp	x	x	
	Kentucky		x		
	Louisiana			x	
	Mississippi				
	North Carolina	x	x		
	Oklahoma		x	x	
	South Carolina	x			
	Tennessee	sp			
	Texas			x	
	Virginia	x	x		
West	Alaska[b]	—	—	—	x
	Arizona	x	sp		
	California	x	x	x	
	Colorado	x	x	x	
	Hawaii[b]	—	—	—	sp

TABLE 2-2. *(Continued)*

Region	State	Taft, 1940 (5th ballot)	Taft, 1948 (2d ballot)	Taft, 1952 (1st ballot)	Goldwater, 1964 (1st ballot)
	Idaho		x		
	Montana	sp	x		
	Nevada	x	x		
	New Mexico	x	x		
	Oregon	x	x	x	x
	Utah	x	x		
	Washington		x	x	
	Wyoming	sp	s	sp	
Midwest	Illinois				
	Indiana	x	x		
	Iowa		x	x	
	Kansas		x	x	
	Michigan	x	x	x	x
	Minnesota		x	x	x
	Missouri	x	x	x	
	North Dakota	sp	x		sp
	Nebraska		x		
	Ohio				
	South Dakota		x		
	Wisconsin	x	x		
Northeast	Connecticut	x	x	x	x
	Delaware	x	x	x	
	Maine	x	x	x	x
	Maryland	x	x	x	x
	Massachusetts	x	x	x	x
	New Hampshire	x	x	x	x
	New Jersey	x	x	x	sp
	New York	x	x	x	x
	Pennsylvania	x	x	x	x
	Rhode Island	sp	x	x	x
	Vermont	x	x	x	x
	West Virginia		x		

a X = A majority of the state delegation voted against the conservative candidate; sp = the delegation was split evenly between conservatives and others.
b The votes of Alaska and Hawaii prior to their becoming states in 1959 have been discounted.

Source: Bain and Parris, *Convention Decisions and Voting Records.*

TABLE 2-3.   Regional Voting Strengths at Republican
Conventions, 1940–1964

Year	Percentage of Total Convention Vote			
	South	*West*	*Midwest*	*Northeast*
1940	21.3	13.6	32.2	32.2
1944	20.7	15.1	31.5	31.7
1948	21.4	15.7	31.5	30.3
1952	19.0	19.0	29.0	30.8
1956	24.6	18.0	28.8	26.9
1960	24.6	17.5	27.9	28.4
1964	24.8	18.6	27.8	26.6
Difference 1940–64	+3.5	+5.0	−4.4	−5.6

Source: Bain and Parris, *Convention Decisions and Voting Records.*

they were, in the main, states in which overall Republican electoral
strength was declining, whereas the Goldwater bastions in the
Southwest were gaining in Republican support. When added to the
fact that the conservative Southwest was also experiencing the highest economic and population growth within the country, it was
clear that demographic trends and the changing electoral geography of the Republican coalition were not on the liberals' side.
(The declining voting strength of the liberals' northeastern base
at Republican conventions is illustrated in Table 2–3.)

Those liberals who hoped that Goldwater and his supporters
would seek a reconciliation with a view to a united effort in the
fall campaign were to be disappointed. The Republican Platform
Committee, controlled by Goldwater adherents, drew up a platform based on Goldwater's issue positions, including the adoption
of a states' rights position on civil rights. This was utterly at odds
with the Lincolnian tradition within the GOP, and liberals such
as Rockefeller, Scranton, Romney, and Jacob Javits were duly
horrified. When the liberals, led by Romney and Rockefeller, proposed platform amendments on civil rights, the use of nuclear
weaponry, and extremism in the party, Rockefeller was jeered by
Goldwater supporters in the galleries, and the Goldwater managers
made sure that all three amendments were defeated.[57] According
to Kessel,

In the weeks after the California primary, liberal leaders had made three serious attempts to come to terms with the Goldwater coalition: the request for a meeting between Goldwater and the Republican governors at Cleveland, the relatively mild civil rights and anti-extremism platform amendments proposed by Governor Romney, and Governor Scranton's offer of full support in the fall campaign. Each time the moderate leaders had been rebuffed or ignored. The Goldwater coalition was determined to act as it saw fit.[58]

This determination also helps to explain the refusal on the part of Goldwater to balance his ticket with a Republican liberal. The Arizona Senator preferred ideological compatibility, and he selected William E. Miller as the vice-presidential candidate. The final insult was the nominee's famous (or infamous) acceptance speech, with its ringing peroration, which repudiated any compromise on Goldwater's conservative principles and virtually invited his opponents to quit the party:

> Anyone who joins us in sincerity we welcome. Those who do not care for our cause, we do not expect to enter our ranks in any case. . . . And let our Republicanism, so focused and so dedicated, not be made fuzzy and futile by unthinking and stupid labels. Let me remind you: *Extremism in the defense of liberty is no vice!* . . . *Moderation in the pursuit of justice is no virtue.*[59]

The speech typified the Goldwater movement's adherence to "principle" rather than electability, and Goldwater's oration was, of course, rapturously received by his followers at the convention. Their feelings toward the candidate and their concern with principle and integrity rather than traditional partisan considerations are illustrated in these remarks, quoted by Aaron Wildavsky:

> This the first time a campaign will be on issues; I think it's wonderful.
> We didn't want a blurred image, we've been a me-too party for too long. We want to take a clear position.
> He [Goldwater] doesn't talk from both sides of his mouth.[60]

Rigid adherence to principle was also the central theme of Goldwater's general election campaign. His supporters countered the unelectability argument, in part, by maintaining that the presence on the November ballot of a true conservative candidate who epitomized personal and political integrity would bring out all those "hidden" conservative voters who, frustrated since 1936 by the lack of a conservative option, would sweep Goldwater to victory.[61] The campaign was directed by Dennison Kitchel and other loyal Goldwater aides from Arizona, not party professionals, and another of Goldwater's Arizona acolytes, Dean Burch (who had never even served as a Republican county chairman), was installed as head of the RNC.[62] Most Republican liberals were excluded from the Goldwater operation and had no influence over the course of the campaign. Some progressives, such as Scranton and Charles Percy (the Republican gubernatorial candidate in Illinois), loyally endorsed the ticket. Others, such as Jacob Javits, Kenneth Keating, George Romney, and Nelson Rockefeller, dissociated themselves from their party's presidential candidate at every available opportunity. Even some conservatives, such as North Dakota Senator Milton Young, refused to appear on the same platform with Goldwater. The defection of formed Dixiecrat presidential candidate Strom Thurmond to the Republicans during the campaign further symbolized the impact of the Goldwater revolution on traditional party allegiances. As the results came in on election night, telling the story of a landslide defeat, Goldwater's reaction was typical of the movement he headed. He appeared to regard his 38.5% of the popular vote as a victory for conservatism and a solid base on which conservatives could build. He omitted to note that he had dragged dozens of Republican candidates down to defeat with him.[63]

The 1964 election results made grim reading for Republicans. The Goldwater-Miller ticket was beaten 61% to 38.5% in the popular vote, and 486 to 52 in the electoral college. Goldwater carried only his home state of Arizona and the five Deep South states of Alabama, Mississippi, Louisiana, Georgia, and South Carolina, four of which had not voted Republican in a presidential election since Reconstruction. The Republicans suffered a loss of 2 Senate seats and 38 House seats. At the state level they gained 1 governorship and lost 550 state legislative seats. Goldwater's distaste for civil rights legislation had a dramatic effect on the Republican black vote. In 1960 Nixon had won some 32% of the national black vote. Goldwater, however, won only 6%,

and no Republican presidential candidate since 1964 has been
able to recover the ground lost among blacks that year.[64] Goldwater succeeded in turning the electoral geography of the Republican party upside down. His best showings were in the hitherto
solidly Democratic Deep South, whereas his worst results were in
the New England and Middle Atlantic states (many of them traditionally Republican) and in the Republican heartland of the
Midwest. In the traditionally Republican counties of New England,
which had given over 80% of their votes to Eisenhower in 1956,
Goldwater halved the Republican tally.[65] New England gave Johnson 71.1% of its total vote (an increase from Kennedy's 56% in
1960), and the Middle Atlantic states gave him 66.6% (an increase from 51.5%).[66] The only region where Goldwater im-
proved on the Republican total of 1960 was the South, where he
eked out a narrow plurality of 49% to 48.9%.[67] His southern
support, however, was not equal to that of Eisenhower or Nixon.
In 1964 the Republican ticket lost the Rim South states—Virginia,
Florida, Tennessee, and Texas—which had been leaning Republican since 1948. The growing southern black vote switched en bloc
to the Democrats as well. According to the Ripon Society's election survey *Election '64,*

> Republicans lost the southern suburban vote in which President
> Eisenhower had made such gains in 1952 and 1956. In Atlanta,
> Charlotte, Richmond, Orlando, Houston and the other metropolitan
> centers of the South Goldwater ran well behind the best Eisenhower
> and Nixon performances. The Goldwater-Miller-Burch strategy suc-
> ceeded in trading off the progressive, industrialized urban areas of
> the New South for the segregationist rural regions of the Deep
> South.[68]

Goldwater's pattern of support was more similar to that of Dixiecrat Strom Thurmond in 1948 than to that of Dewey or Eisenhower. Nevertheless, the Republican candidate was able to achieve
a net gain of 7 Republican congressmen in the region, so the advance of the conservative South as a major power within the GOP
continued.

Liberal Republicans must have hoped that 1964 would prove
to be an aberration in American electoral politics. Unfortunately
for them, the 1964 election, in retrospect, appears to have been

more a decisive stage in the realignment of factional forces within the GOP, to the disadvantage of the liberal wing. The lessons of 1964 were clear: the liberals would have to devise an attractive ideological message, organize at the electoral base of the party, and develop a communications network to propagate their message to their followers. They further needed to harness at least some of the Sunbelt elements in the Republican coalition and cease relying on the elusive eastern establishment to deliver victory for them at the national convention. The alternative to this strategy was to reach an accommodation with the conservatives around issues of party unity, as in the Eisenhower era. This option, however, carried the risk that the liberals, now clearly a minority within the coalition, would be tolerated only on sufferance by a fundamentally conservative majority on which their influence was likely to be increasingly limited.

The liberals were faced with a dilemma. They could aggressively challenge the right on its own terms and risk perpetual internal strife within the GOP, or they could seek a compromise with the right and try to maintain a united front against the Democrats, while at the same time facing the risk of gradual extinction as an effective force within the Republican party.

One final, noteworthy, aspect of the Republican debacle in 1964 is that Goldwater won his nomination in an *unreformed* party. In 1964, the process of delegate selection remained closed to the majority of Republican sympathizers in most states. Indeed, the closed process of delegate selection in many states (particularly in the South) gave the Goldwater campaign a strong advantage.[69] In some areas the party apparatus had become virtually moribund and was ripe for takeover by well-organized activists. The Goldwater movement was singular both in the purist attitudes that motivated its devotees and in the volunteer-activist nature of its organization. The success of the insurgency, however, was not achieved through transformation of a closed-party delegate-selection process but through the use of that process for its own ends.

3

From Retreat to Rout: Liberal Republicans in National Politics, 1964 to 1976

The electoral humiliation of Barry Goldwater and the conservative wing of the Republican party in November 1964 apparently left the Republican liberals ideally placed to occupy the vacuum in the national leadership of the GOP. The course of events within the party from 1964 to Gerald Ford's defeat in the 1976 presidential election did not justify the liberals' optimism, and, indeed, after 1976 liberal Republicanism appeared to be virtually extinct in American presidential politics. This chapter explains how the liberal Republicans came to be in that position and discusses the extent to which their weakness was attributable to short-term tactical errors or longer-term social and political trends.

Aftermath of Defeat

The initial weeks after the 1964 election debacle saw the replacement of Goldwater's appointee Dean Burch as RNC chairman, while the other bases of conservative power within Congress and in the ranks of the RNC itself remained unchanged. The Republican governors' meeting in December unanimously adopted a strong anti-Burch position, and liberal strategists on the national committee, George Hinman and Craig Truax, worked behind the scenes to ensure a smooth transfer of power.[1] With the liberals reluctant to antagonize the right by forcing an eastern establishment figure on the party, a staunch party regular, Ohio State Chairman Ray Bliss, was chosen as Burch's successor. The liberals were less successful, however, in the contests for the House Republican leadership in January 1965. The liberal Republican congressmen of the House Wednesday Group lacked the necessary discipline and numerical strength to be effective power brokers at the Republican conference, and in each of the leadership contests their candidate was easily defeated.[2]

The liberal Republican counterattack in the immediate aftermath of the 1964 defeat was thus limited to the substitution of the stalwart Bliss for the hapless Dean Burch as RNC chairman. Given the existence of a strong, well-organized right-wing faction within the GOP, liberal leaders, such as Rockefeller and Romney, who had an eye on the 1968 presidential nomination were unconvinced that a confrontational approach vis à vis the Republican right was in their best interests. They preferred to settle for the accommodationist strategy, relying on party professionals like Ray Bliss to keep the right in check. It was evident, however, that the GOP would face another choice between leadership from the center or the right in 1968, and the liberals were still poorly equipped for that struggle. To repair this deficiency, they needed a new locus of power within the party wherein they could coordinate strategy and assert leadership, formulate liberal ideas and policies, and build a national network of supporters as a base of electoral strength for 1968. All these initiatives were pursued to some extent by the liberals in the 1964–68 period, but for reasons to be discussed in the following pages, none of them had much chance of success.

The Moderate Revival

In ideological terms, the liberal Republicans of the mid-1960s had not advanced from Arthur Larson's prescriptions of a decade earlier. Liberal Republican candidates continued to phrase electoral appeals in terms of personality or electability, rather than of political principle, frequently acknowledging the validity of most of the right's doctrines, while arguing that they would have to be modified to win votes for the party.

Some were not so willing to concede the conservative claim to the Republican orthodoxy, however. In his book *Order of Battle* (published in 1964, and republished after the election), Senator Jacob Javits of New York took up the challenge of formulating a liberal Republican doctrine that was in harmony with the Republican political tradition and relevant for the 1960s.[3] Javits saw the Republicans as the party of the national interest in American history, weaving the disparate social and economic interests of the nation into a consensus that sought to maximize individual freedom while maintaining the unity and national security of the United States. The Republican tradition—best represented for Javits by Lincoln and Theodore Roosevelt, but also exemplified by Henry Clay's Whiggery and Alexander Hamilton's Federalism—was in accord with this pursuit of the national interest:

> This is the spirit which has represented the most dominant strain in Republican history. Hamilton—Clay—Lincoln—and Theodore Roosevelt: they represent the line of evolution embodying this tradition. Together, they became properly the progenitors of the modern Republican party, who preside in spirit over the work of that party in its finest hours. Together, also, they point to the tasks their descendants can and must undertake in the circumstances of the 1960s and the decades leading to the year 2000.[4]

Reviewing the party's history up to the New Deal era, one might agree that the GOP was the more nationally oriented of the two major parties; however, Javits did not acknowledge the fact that, since the New Deal, that tradition had been appropriated by the Democrats, with the Republicans reverting to a dogma of states' rights and economic noninterventionism. This made Javits's prescriptions less valuable as an effective modern ideology for liberal Republicans. Yet his eloquent restatement of the Republican progressive tradition did, at least, go some way toward challenging conservative claims to the party's doctrinal heritage.

Javits was not the only Republican who sought to reformulate a body of liberal Republican principle. The bulk of such work came from the Ripon Society, founded by a group of young academics, lawyers, and businessmen at Harvard in 1962, and taking its name from Ripon, Wisconsin, one of the supposed birthplaces of the Republican party. In its first public statement the society declared,

> From the outset, Ripon members have seen as their most important contribution to American politics a bridging of the gulf that has separated much of the GOP from the intellectual and professional community for the past fifty years.[5]

The Ripon Society was influenced by the British Conservative party's Bow Group, and similarly sought to establish itself as an organization of youthful Republican intellectuals oriented toward discussions of policy and the publication of position papers on a wide variety of issues. The society's founders deliberately tried to keep Ripon a select association of graduate students and policy experts.[6] By reestablishing the GOP's intellectual credentials, the Riponites hoped to attract the young, professional middle class of the ever-growing suburbs—what they called the "frontlash" constituency—to the Republican party. It was here, they argued, rather than in the pursuit of the backlash vote of the rural white South and the blue-collar North, that the Republican future lay.[7] Ripon thus urged the party leadership to endorse the civil rights revolution, decentralize political power from the federal to the state and local level, and support an end to the unpopular military draft.[8]

> This is the direction the party must take if it is to win the confidence of the "New Americans," who are not at home in the politics of another generation: the new middle classes of the suburbs of the North and West—who have left the Democratic cities but have not yet found a home in the Republican party, the young college graduates and professional men and women of our great university centers— more concerned with "opportunity" than "security"; the moderates of the New South—who represent the hope for peaceful racial adjustment and who are insulted by a racist appeal more fitting another generation. These and others like them hold the key to the future of our politics.[9]

One of the society's first acts was to issue a Declaration of Conscience on the eve of Goldwater's nomination, warning against a repudiation of the Republicans' traditional allegiance to the cause of civil rights.[10] Ripon's study of the 1964 election results, *Election '64,* was favorably received by political commentators, and the society began publishing papers on a regular basis, dealing with issues such as civil rights, the draft, welfare reform, revenue-sharing, and the opening of diplomatic relations with Red China. It also began, in 1965, to publish a monthly newsletter, *The Ripon Forum,* which featured policy proposals and political reports. The society's budget was very limited, being dependent principally on *Forum* subscriptions and donations from wealthy sympathizers such as Walter Nelson Thayer, President of the *New York Herald Tribune.* In 1968, Ripon's annual budget was $95,000, as compared to the Young Americans for Freedom's budget of $25,000 per month.[11]

Despite its limited resources, Ripon had a considerable impact on Republican party circles during the 1960s, and many of its policy proposals were to be adopted in some form by the Nixon administration. Although the membership was small (only eighty at the time of *Election '64*), the society obtained a fair amount of publicity, perhaps because it was the sole organization that could claim to provide a national voice for Republican liberals. Being based on the Harvard campus also gave Ripon some intellectual standing and access to important commentators in the news media. Finally, the society had the advantage of being led by diligent and intelligent young activists, such as Thomas Petri (Ripon's first full-time director), John S. Saloma III (the society's first president), Josiah Lee Auspitz, Bruce Chapman, and Lee Heubner.

As an Ivy League–based association of policy-oriented intellectuals, Ripon was never intended to be a crusading electoral organization. Its influence was limited to the elite; and although this was valuable, in a party where power was devolving increasingly to volunteer activists, Ripon's impact on the balance of forces between the liberal and conservative wings was more or less nil. This was noted by John Saloma in 1969:

> I think we've put too little emphasis on party affairs. If we familiarize ourselves with party matters—and it would be a full-time job—we can more effectively criticize the party and produce changes. In other words we need organization—the [Eugene] McCarthy people saw the importance of that. . . . If we can organize ourselves and

become versed in party affairs, then our criticism of the party leadership will be more than mere broadsides; instead we can promote a forward, constructive program. Maybe the leaders won't like it, but at least we are more likely to get results.[12]

The Ripon Society was never likely to acquire the funds and mass membership to become the kind of campaigning electoral group that Saloma sought. The society succeeded as an effective forum for discussion for Republican intellectuals, but the new volunteer-activist politics within the GOP remained the exclusive province of the conservative network, which possessed the necessary resources of money, manpower, and a set of polarizing issues.

The leaders of the Ripon Society did not accept Ray Bliss's prescriptions of compromise with the party's conservatives. They believed the liberals' problem to be primarily one of ideology, and they felt that unless factional differences within the GOP were aired, they could not begin to be reconciled.[13] A conciliatory approach was also likely, they felt, to maintain the defensive minority position of the liberal wing and would do nothing to challenge conservative predominance in the RNC, Congress, and the states:

> Unity is concerned with the present. It probes neither the past for understanding nor the future for direction. Unity rewards the lowest common denominator in the realm of ideas; it alone cannot generate enthusiasm or excitement for what is new and daring. Unity confirms power and discourages initiative. It is a virtue but it is not necessarily *the* virtue that will best direct the Republican party in the post-1964 political world.[14]

In 1965 the Ripon liberals acquired a champion whose ideas and political style appeared to accord with their energetic progressivism. John Vleit Lindsay's election as Mayor of New York City (overcoming a 7 to 2 Democratic advantage in registration) was the most impressive electoral triumph that Republican liberals had enjoyed for some time.[15] Lindsay had already endeared himself to the liberals through his service as a four-term New York congressman with an impressive record on civil liberties. Many Republicans nevertheless had strong reservations about him. The mayor had campaigned on a "fusion" ticket with the New York Liberal party, taking great pains to stress the fact that he was running as John V. Lindsay, not as a Republican.[16] Although the repudiation of his own party made sense in overwhelmingly Democratic New York City, it did not endear the new mayor to Republicans elsewhere. Ripon remained enthusiastic about Lindsay until his defection to the Democrats in 1971, but he seemed even less likely than Rockefeller to possess sufficient appeal to centrist party regulars and conservatives to have a chance of securing the party's presidential nomination.[17] Even within New York State, the mayor was overshadowed by Governor Rockefeller, who regarded him as something of an upstart. Rockefeller's firm control of the state party machinery further prevented Lindsay from acquiring a wider political base for his presidential aspirations.[18]

Ripon repeatedly stressed the Republicans' need to cultivate the young professional constituency, and this group was undoubtedly a key element in the electoral successes of liberal Republican candidates such as Lindsay. Yet it was a different matter to assert that these voters could be permanently wedded to the Republican party, as many of Ripon's theorists believed. The group in question was highly educated, compared to the electorate as a whole, and tended to take a more independent attitude toward electoral choice, assessing candidates on the basis of issues and ideology rather than party label. While young college-educated professionals could certainly be attracted to Republican candidates with a shrewd electoral strategy, they could be equally drawn to an attractive liberal Democrat such as Robert Kennedy or Eugene McCarthy.[19] This transitory allegiance did not seem to be a very firm foundation on which to base a liberal Republican revival.

The Ripon Society's predilection for matters of policy meant that it neglected the liberals' most serious handicap, namely, that they had a surfeit of potential leaders, but relatively few footsoldiers compared to their conservative rivals. In the 1964–68 period, further efforts were made to provide a forum for coordinating Republican liberals and to develop organizational mechanisms for presidential campaigns. One obvious approach, as mentioned above, was to revitalize the liberals' only national bastion of power: the Republican Governors' Association. Ripon issued a report entitled *The Republican Governors' Association: The*

Case for a Third Force, which urged that the RGA be reestablished as an independently staffed and financed power center within the party.[20] At the post-election governor's meeting in Denver, the Ripon program had general support, but in a repetition of the events marking William Miller's tenure at the RNC, the committee, jealous of its prerogatives, delayed the announcement of the opening of the RGA's national office for as long as it possibly could. By the time the office was finally opened in September 1965, much of the impetus for a rejuvenated RGA had ebbed away.[21]

The governors' Colorado Springs meeting in December 1966 saw a contest for the chairmanship of the RGA between Governor John Chafee of Rhode Island (who advocated strengthening the RGA as a third force in Republican party politics) and the more accommodationist Governor Love of Colorado. Only four of the twenty-five Republican governors at Colorado Springs were from the East, and this, together with George Romney's endorsement of Love, more or less disposed of Chafee's chances. The governors ended their conference by committing themselves to "a technical approach to government," and rallied rather unenthusiastically behind George Romney's presidential candidacy.[22] At the Miami convention in 1968, the RGA was unable to secure representation on the platform committee and played no significant role in the leadership selection process. Its effectiveness as a forum for liberal Republican leadership, finally, can be assessed from the unanimous election of conservative Ronald Reagan as RGA chairman at the Palm Springs conference of December 1968.[23]

While the Ripon liberals expressed bitter disappointment with the RGA, it is evident from their writings that they had extremely unrealistic expectations regarding the leadership potential of such an inherently loose and heterogeneous group as the Republican governors. Attempts to establish a national campaigning organization for liberal Republicans were equally unsuccessful. It had been hoped in some quarters that Milton Eisenhower's Republican Citizens' Committee would serve as a large-scale citizens' organization for liberal Republicans, but by 1968 the RCC had virtually petered out through lack of interest and initiative. The same fate befell the Council of Republican Organizations (CRO), a group formed in 1965, consisting of various small liberal organizations. After an initial burst of activity and attention, the council gradually faded into the background and made no real attempt to regenerate the Citizens' movement that had been so important in the nominations of Willkie and Eisenhower.[24] Finally, an effort to set up a liberal volunteer group in California, the California Republican League, was to achieve only a modest membership and minimal attention.[25]

The most serious effort at building an organizational apparatus for liberal Republicans was an entity named Republicans for Progress (RFP), established by former Cincinnati Mayor Charles P. Taft as a fund-raising committee to protect liberal Republicans from the anti-Goldwater landslide in 1964. RFP's membership never consisted fo more than one hundred people, and its board of directors was composed mainly of former Eisenhower backers. It claimed to represent the philosophy of Eisenhower, and endeavored to support candidates who espoused that philosophy. But RFP never tried to transform itself into a mass organization, seeing itself mainly as a resource for research and fund-raising. In 1965 it gave $25,000 to Lindsay for his mayoralty campaign, and gave $5,000 the following year to Senate aspirant Edward Brooke of Massachusetts. Nevertheless, Republicans for Progress ended up supporting Richard Nixon for the presidential nomination in 1968, considering him the heir to the Eisenhower legacy (some indication of Nixon's success in maintaining his credentials with the liberal wing of the party while openly courting southern ultraconservatives). After Nixon's election the group disbanded, having played only a very limited role in Republican party affairs.[26]

From these ineffectual attempts to supply liberal Republicans with a national campaigning organization, it can be seen that the liberals, in contrast to their conservative rivals, still placed their trust in personality and old-style party-elite politics rather than grass roots organization. Yet despite their lack of organizational muscle, liberal Republicans gained significantly in the 1966 congressional elections. Disenchantment with American involvement in Vietnam and Lyndon Johnson's inflationary economic policies brought the GOP a gain of 47 House seats, 3 Senate seats, 8 governorships, and 540 seats in state legislatures. Governors Rockefeller and Romney were re-elected; Ray Shafer was elected Governor of Pennsylvania; and John Chafee and John Volpe won the statehouses of Rhode Island and Massachusetts, respectively. In the Senate, the liberal ranks were augmented by the election of Edward Brooke in Massachusetts, Mark Hatfield in Oregon, and Charles Percy in Illinois. These men were all youthful, technocratic problem solvers with strong electoral appeal, but their successes were tempered by some other aspects of the midterm campaign. Conservative Republicans found a new paladin in Ronald Reagan, now Governor of California and a candidate whose potential electoral appeal far exceeded that of Barry Goldwater. The elections also saw a revival in the political fortunes of Richard Nixon, who regained a great deal of esteem within the party from his extensive campaigning on behalf of Republican candidates. The 1966 election successes could, moreover, be interpreted as a vindication of the Bliss strategy of downplaying ideology and concentrating on the electoral machinery of the party.[27]

During the interim between the 1964 and 1968 presidential elections, the liberal Republicans largely failed to take advantage of their opportunities. In the initial period after the 1964 defeat, they half-heartedly attempted to challenge conservative control in Congress and in the national party organizations, but with the notable exception of the Ripon Society, all these ventures had exhausted themselves by the beginning of 1967 and the party unity approach advocated by Ray Bliss prevailed among liberal Republican leaders (with the exception of the maverick John V. Lindsay, who was becoming increasingly isolated within the party). In addition to these disappointments, the liberals lost support in the national news media. The only liberal Republican periodical, the magazine *Advance,* went out of business, and a further mark of the decline of eastern influence over the party was the closing down in 1966 of the pre-eminent journal of the eastern Republican establishment, *The New York Herald Tribune.*[28] Looking ahead to 1968, there seemed to be a general rallying behind Romney's candidacy for the presidential nomination, although many senior liberals had reservations about the Michigan governor's competence for the job. Overall it seemed that very few of the lessons of 1964 had been learned.

The Inevitability of Richard Nixon

Richard Nixon's inexorable march toward the Republican presidential nomination in 1968 demonstrated the utter failure of the Republican liberals' efforts to recapture control of the party. As in 1964, personal rivalries and strategic ineptitude damaged their prospects. A single front-runner again became the focus of their hopes, and when he stumbled there was no one left except Nelson Rockefeller to fill the vacuum in the liberal wing of the GOP. However, Rockefeller, aside from his fundamental lack of appeal to regular Republicans, further damaged his slim chances of success by unnecessarily delaying his entry into the race. Nixon repeated his 1960 strategy of cultivating the centrist party professionals, who still revered him, and outmaneuvered the ultraconservatives by gaining the allegiance of the southern Republican leadership. Once he had established his center-right coalition, Nixon was virtually assured of the nomination, and his success can be seen as the final triumph of a strategy of conciliation vis à vis the Republican right over the ideological-adversarial approach favored by the liberal intellectuals of the Ripon Society. Liberal Republican leaders were prepared to tolerate the centrist organization candidate Nixon rather than risk the nomination of another right-winger, when victory at the polls seemed to be a much more likely prospect than it had four years earlier.

Almost as soon as the 1966 midterm election returns were in, a liberal Republican consensus (partly fueled by press speculation) considered George Romney the strongest contender for the presidential nomination in 1968. The Michigan governor seemed to possess the requisite qualities for a successful liberal Republican candidate. He came from a small-town, western background; he was noted for his nonpartisan, "citizen politics" style; he cultivated a public image of sincerity and high personal integrity; and in Michigan he had demonstrated formidable electoral appeal to normally Democratic-voting groups, sucs as union members and blacks. Romney, however, had several serious shortcomings as a presidential contender: his Mormon religion; his lack of experience in national politics and international affairs; and his refusal to endorse Goldwater in 1964, which made him unpalatable to the right wing of the party.[29] On the other hand, Romney had carried Michigan by 383,000 votes in 1964, while Goldwater had lost the state by over 1 million, and after his re-election in 1966 (by a record margin), the Michigan governor's front-runner status appeared to have been consolidated.[30] By the spring of 1967 Romney was leading Johnson by 54% to 46% in the polls.[31]

Romney benefited from the support of Nelson Rockefeller, who still dominated the liberal forces within the party in spite of his failure in 1964. Having apparently concluded that he could never be nominated by the Republican party after the events of 1962–64, the New York governor placed his considerable organizational resources—research, speech-writers, funds, personnel—at the disposal of the Romney campaign, and publicly endorsed Romney's candidacy as early as May 1966.[32] Scranton's successor in the Pennsylvania statehouse, Ray Shafer, also endorsed Romney, and he seemed assured of solid support from the traditional liberal bastions of Pennsylvania and New York at the 1968 convention. This eastern establishment support restricted Romney's appeal to other sections of the party, however. From the moment that Rockefeller gave his endorsement, Romney found it impossible to evade his shadow. Many still suspected that the New Yorker would jump into the race at the first suitable opportunity and that the lackluster Romney was merely serving as a Rockefeller stalking horse. Yet for Romney to distance himself from Rockefeller would have estranged him from the most influential figure in the liberal wing of the party and endangered his ready access to funds and personnel. Romney was never able to get out of this impasse.

Rockefeller's desire to be kingmaker prevented other liberal candidates from entering the race. His so-called "non-proliferation treaty" was intended to force Republican liberals to unite behind Romney, but once Romney's shortcomings as a presidential candidate had been exposed by the rapacious press, there was no alternative candidate in the field. Lindsay was effectively confined to New York City by Rockefeller, and Charles Percy and Mark Hatfield lacked the national visibility and organizational resources to mount a presidential campaign. So if Romney fell, Rockefeller was the only other liberal Republican who could mount a serious challenge to Nixon.

After his notorious "brainwashing" remarks on a Detroit television show, Romney's stock in the polls began to fall precipitously, and some liberals, such as Massachusetts Governor Volpe, drifted toward the Nixon camp.[33] Rockefeller stepped in to try and sustain Romney's candidacy, but the more Rockefeller campaigned for Romney, the more speculation about his own intentions increased, and Romney's independence was further compromised in the process. It was not Rockefeller's embrace that ultimately destroyed Romney's chances, however, but his bad press and poor television image. The Michigan governor came across as shallow, unctuous, and out of his depth in national politics.[34] On February 28, 1968, after his pollsters presented him with figures showing Nixon ahead by 70% to 11% in New Hampshire, Romney withdrew from the race and his humiliation was at an end.[35]

It seems odd that Richard Nixon's comeback in 1968 was regarded as so surprising at the time since, with Eisenhower incapacitated by illness, Nixon (although only in his mid-fifties) had become the elder statesman of the Republican party. After his experiences in California in 1962, he was well aware of the dangers of publicly repudiating the right-wing activists. In 1964 he had refused to ally himself explicitly with the "stop Goldwater" forces and was a loyal supporter of the Goldwater-Miller ticket in the fall campaign, thereby rebuilding his bridges to the conservative wing of the party. Nixon's campaigning for Republican candidates in 1966 endeared him even more to the local party stalwarts, who had always appreciated his talents. The former vice president now found that his interests dovetailed nicely with those of the party as a whole:

> I felt that two things would be necessary to keep the party together: we would have to be on constant guard against attempts by leaders of the left or right to take over the party; and we would have to convince the party rank and file that there were better times ahead. I knew from experience that this would be hard, long and sometimes thankless work. But this was the job that I increasingly saw as my own. It was pragmatism more than altruism that led me to take it on, because I believed that whoever did would gain a significant advantage in the race for the 1968 presidential nomination. This enabled me to reconcile the paradox of having to help my Republican competitors—Rockefeller, Romney and Reagan. I felt that if the base of the party were not expanded, the 1968 nomination would be

worthless. If the party were expanded by the victories of others, I thought I had a good chance of benefiting from its greater strength.[36]

Nixon also benefited from the 1964 defeat, insofar as it had weakened the right's chances of nominating one of their own in 1968. With the liberal wing of the party gaining most of the media attention in 1965–66 because of the victories of Lindsay, Brooke, Percy, and Romney, Nixon appeared to be the only presidential candidate who could prevail against them. As a result, many former Goldwater supporters decided to cut their losses and rally behind the centrist Nixon in order to prevent the detested eastern establishment from regaining control of the party.[37] Garry Wills perceived the right's rationale for supporting Nixon:

> In 1965 and 1966, when it looked as if Rockefeller or Romney had the nomination, Nixon was the only palatable candidate surviving on the Right. . . . He played this role carefully, giving and getting support from all the leaderless Goldwater types still running or maneuvering to run. He earned their gratitude and prior commitment.[38]

The southern Republican leaders were particularly anxious to prevent the nomination from falling to an eastern liberal. Peter O'Donnell and Senator John Tower of Texas were early (if tacit) Nixon backers, as were Mississippi Chairman Fred LaRue, Georgia's Howard "Bo" Callaway, and South Carolina Senator Strom Thurmond.[39] Goldwater supporters, such as Richard Kleindienst and Senator Everett Dirksen, and Goldwater himself all fell in behind Nixon. According to Fred LaRue,

> Nixon's dilemma was that he had to win the nomination basically with the same forces Goldwater had in 1964, but without associating with them or being associated.[40]

By the beginning of 1968, Nixon had constructed a broad and formidable coalition behind his candidacy. He had the support of the regular Republicans and of most of the important figures on the party's right, while still maintaining his ties to the liberals in the eastern states. As the organization candidate, Nixon was acceptable to the pragmatists in both liberal and conservative camps, who valued his ability to prevent the leaders of their ideological opponents from securing the nomination.[41] When his experience in national and international affairs was compared to that of Romney or Reagan, Nixon's standing gained all the more. The problems facing the Nixon forces were the candidate's image as a "loser" and his equivocal positions on major issues, particularly the Vietnam War. The later difficulty actually became an asset to Nixon in the pre-convention campaign, in which he was running as the unity candidate, repudiating rigid ideological stances that might offend an important section of the party. The "loser" image was largely disposed of when Nixon completed a series of primary victories over desultory opposition, commencing with a 77% triumph in New Hampshire. The liberals, having stayed loyal to the hopeless Romney for so long, now found themselves stranded in the face of the Nixon advance.

Those conservatives who found it impossible to accept Nixon had not given up all hope. Ronald Reagan's landslide victory in the 1966 California gubernatorial election immediately made him the new hero of the conservative volunteer network. Handsome and affable, Reagan was a far more electable candidate than Goldwater, and it soon became apparent that, despite his frequent disavowals, the California governor entertained presidential ambitions.[42] Goldwater's organizational maestro, F. Clifton White, became the director of a conservative effort to keep Reagan's name before the voters as a possible Republican nominee in 1968. It was evident that, despite the conservative leadership's dalliance with Nixon, there was considerable sentiment for Reagan in the lower echelons of the movement, particularly in the South. Reagan's presence in the race as a conservative alternative ironically gave the liberals their only opportunity of stopping Nixon. If Reagan could secure a sizable number of southern conservative delegates, Nixon's nomination on the early ballots might be prevented. Some of his supporters might then be inclined to deviate toward a liberal candidate who appeared to have a better chance of winning in November. Despite all that had passed in the previous eight years, the only liberal who seemed to meet the requirements was Nelson Aldrich Rockefeller.

Rockefeller was a reluctant candidate. Personal abuse from his opponents and what he interpreted as the ungrateful attitude of Republican liberals gave the New York governor strong reasons for not embarking on another grueling and probably hopeless quest for the Republican presidential nomination.[43] By early March 1968, however, the pressures on Rockefeller to stand were becoming irresistible and, together with his most trusted advisers, Emmett Hughes and George Hinman, he began to explore the possibilities of a third try at the nomination. By entering the Oregon primary, Rockefeller could challenge Nixon on favorable terrain, where he had triumphed four years previously. A group of governors—Chafee, of Rhode Island; Agnew, of Maryland; Shafer, of Pennsylvania; Winthrop Rockefeller, of Arkansas; Love, of Colorado; McCall, of Oregon—with the additional support of Senator Scott of Pennsylvania and Senator Morton of Kentucky, and even Mayor Lindsay—all put pressure on Rockefeller to run. Agnew, moreover, became chairman of a National Draft Rockefeller Committee, established on March 6, 1968.[44] Nevertheless, the political soundings from Oregon were not impressive, and Rockefeller announced on March 21 that he would not be a candidate.

The public relations blunders surrounding this announcement more or less doomed Rockefeller's chances when he later decided to enter the race. Governor Agnew, infuriated by Rockefeller's procrastinating, defected to the Nixon camp.[45] Senator Javits was of the opinion that Rockefeller's elaborate staff system let him down; that "he wasn't getting good advice from his aides."[46] Former RNC Chairman Meade Alcorn, who was heavily involved in the Rockefeller campaign, believed that the governor suffered from family pressure and a failure to follow his own instincts and announce his candidacy at an early date. According to Alcorn: "Had Nelson—the figure around whom we were building—been willing to take an aggressive lead, he would have succeeded in 1968."[47] The view that Rockefeller was impeded by his staff system is endorsed by Connery and Benjamin in their study, *Rockefeller of New York*. The governor's excellent staff, accustomed to rational decision making and pragmatic problem solving, were ill-suited to advise him on such an unpredictable and irrational process as a presidential race:

> Rockefeller's vast staff resources made him cautious. The essential element of throwing caution to the winds, of standing early and going all out, was lacking in all but the 1964 presidential effort.[48]

No sooner had Rockefeller resolved his dilemma by renouncing his candidacy than the pressures to run manifested themselves once more, this time from a quarter that had not been overly-friendly toward him in the past, despite his image as the quintessential eastern plutocrat. Two old Eisenhower allies and pillars of the eastern business establishment, John Hay Whitney and Walter Nelson Thayer, now began an effort to rally the support of big business for Rockefeller as the only viable alternative to Nixon:

> Irwin Miller, John Whitney and myself all called Rockefeller the next day [after the withdrawal statement], and said: "You can't do this." We set up an organization called "Rockefeller for President" without Rockefeller's permission. Nelson was a very able man and a good Governor. He did a marvellous job in New York. Nixon just did not have the same stature.[49]

H. J. Heinz II, Henry Ford II, and J. Irwin Miller of the Cummings Diesel Company all joined in the effort to persuade Rockefeller to change his mind. Many non-Republican Jewish businessmen in New York, eager to block Nixon's chances of becoming President, also contributed support.[50]

All this pressure did not fail to impress Rockefeller, and at the end of April he at last announced his candidacy, claiming that he had been influenced primarily by the urban discontent following Martin Luther King's assassination. On the same day as his announcement, Rockefeller won a surprise write-in primary victory in Massachusetts, winning all the state's 34 convention delegates and defeating Nixon's stand-in, Governor Volpe. However, the New York governor's late start and his image of indecision were serious disadvantages. After the Oregon primary in late May, Nixon had won 112 delegates from the primary states plus another 108 in the Rocky Mountain area. A successful meeting with senior southern Republicans in Atlanta helped to forestall Reagan's advance in the South, and Nixon's managers felt sure that they could count on another 394 delegates from the southern and Border states.[51] Thus Nixon appeared to have the nomination more or less sewn up before Rockefeller even began to campaign.

Rockefeller knew that he could not win the nomination through his personal appeal to regular Republicans. In those quarters he was still regarded as the spoiler of 1960 and 1964, and his belief in dynamic, problem-solving government—which led to a fourfold increase in the New York State budget, from $1.79 billion in 1958 to $8.3 billion in 1973, when Rockefeller left office—hardly accorded with the Republican tradition of fiscal rectitude.[52] The costly public projects that were necessary to appease the liberal interest groups of New York State offended the parsimonious, limited-government, small-business sensibilities of the Republican mainstream. That mainstream was the basis of Richard Nixon's strength, and Rockefeller's only hope of defeating Nixon was to convince the stalwart Nixon delegates that their man would drag the party down to another defeat, while Rockefeller was a certain winner in November. Since he had failed to enter any primaries, the only means that Rockefeller could use to demonstrate his superior electoral appeal were the opinion polls. Rockefeller's aspirations depended wholly on his being able to demonstrate from poll data that he could clearly outrun Nixon against Vice President Humphrey, the likely Democratic nominee. A total of $8 million, $5.5 million of which came directly or indirectly from the Rockefeller family, was raised for the campaign, and $4.4 million of that was spent on a massive media campaign to increase the governor's poll ratings.[53] The efforts of the eastern establishment and Madison Avenue on Rockefeller's behalf did begin to have some effect, and his standing in the polls began to improve steadily as many former Kennedy and McCarthy supporters began to look favorably on the dynamic New York governor. The decisive blow to Rockefeller's hopes was an eve-of-convention poll conducted by Gallup that showed Nixon leading Humphrey 40% to 38%, while Rockefeller ran level with the vice president at 36%. There was nothing in these figures to convince the Nixon devotees among the delegates that they ought to desert their favorite, and a later Harris poll that put Rockefeller ahead came too late to repair the damage.[54]

Liberal Republican hopes at Miami were only kept alive by the hope that a sudden boom in support for Reagan would detach enough of Nixon's southern support to prevent him winning on the first ballot. For a time it did seem that the California governor might be capable of halting the Nixon bandwagon as he began to charm the conservative southern Republicans over the heads of their state party leaders.[55] If southern defections could stop Nixon's nomination on the first ballot, there was an outside chance that

Nixon delegates in northeastern and midwestern states such as New Jersey, Illinois, Ohio, and Pennsylvania could be won over to a more liberal candidate on succeeding ballots. For this reason, Ohio's Governor James Rhodes and New Jersey's Senator Clifford Case remained "favorite son" candidates in order to dilute Nixon's first-ballot strength. The major southern leaders, Strom Thurmond and John Tower, together with Barry Goldwater, succeeded in extracting a pledge from Nixon that no vice-presidential nominee unacceptable to them (namely, a northeastern liberal) would be chosen for the second place on the ticket. Thurmond's influence over the wavering southern Republicans was such that they were more or less held in line for Nixon.[56] On the first ballot Nixon won by 692 votes to 277 for Rockefeller and 182 for Reagan, with the remainder going to various moderate favorite sons—Rhodes, Romney, Case, Carlson, Winthrop Rockefeller, and Hiram Fong—totalling 162 votes in all.

The liberals came quite close to blocking Nixon in the end, and had they been better organized, would probably have succeeded in doing so. However, their failure to contest a single primary election against Nixon and their continuing weakness in the South were the decisive factors that rendered Nixon's eventual victory certain (see Tables 3-1, 3-2, and 3-3). The pattern of Nixon's support was similar to that of Goldwater in 1964: solid in the Rocky Mountain and Plains states, strong in the industrial Midwest and the rural Northeast, with the margin of victory being provided by firm support in the southern and Border states. Reagan had California and scattered support in the southern and western states. Rockefeller and the liberals were confined, as in 1964, to their northeastern ghetto, with the addition of the favorite sons' totals in Michigan, Ohio, Arkansas, Hawaii, Utah, and Kansas.

Nixon owed his nomination largely to the southern conservative Republicans, and this factor was a major consideration in the future president's strategic thinking. The selection of Spiro T. Agnew of Maryland as Nixon's running mate might have appeared on the surface to be a concession to the eastern liberal wing of the party. But Agnew had shed his connections to Rockefeller after the public relations debacle of March 20, 1968, and several "law-and-order" pronouncements against civil rights activists in Maryland had endeared him to the southern Republican leadership. The lib-

TABLE 3-1.   Republican Convention, 1968, First Ballot[a]

Region	Nixon	Rockefeller and Others	Reagan
South	Alabama Florida Georgia Kentucky Louisiana Mississippi Oklahoma South Carolina Tennessee Texas Virginia	Arkansas (W. Rockefeller)	North Carolina
West	Alaska Arizona Colorado Idaho Montana Nevada New Mexico Oregon Washington Wyoming	Hawaii (Fong) Utah (Romney)	California
Midwest	Illinois Indiana Iowa Missouri Nebraska North Dakota South Dakota Wisconsin	Kansas (Carlson) Minnesota Ohio (Rhodes)	
Northeast[b]	Delaware Maryland New Hampshire Vermont West Virginia	Connecticut Massachusetts New Jersey (Case) New York Pennsylvania Rhode Island	

a List of states in which the respective candidates secured a majority of the delegation. The Rockefeller states and states in which liberal Republican favorite sons
(either alone or in combination with the Rockefeller vote) secured a majority
have been counted together.

b The Maine delegation was divided equally between Nixon and Rockefeller.

Source: Bain and Parris, *Convention Decisions and Voting Records.*

TABLE 3-2.   Republican Convention, 1968: Regional Support for Candidates

Region	Number of Delegates	% Of total vote[a]	% For Nixon	% For NAR and others	% For Reagan
South	356	26.7	74.2	7.6	18.2
West	262	19.6	47.7	11.8	40.4
Midwest	352	26.4	52.6	44.6	2.8
Northeast	346	26.0	31.8	67.9	0.3
Total convention vote = 1333.					

Source: Bain and Parris, Convention Decisions and Voting Records.

erals had been outmaneuvered once again, and the selection of Agnew illustrated their diminishing influence within the national party. The auguries for a liberal Nixon presidency were not very hopeful. Because he had not been reliant on the liberals for victory, Nixon could afford to ignore their claims during the fall campaign. They might grumble about the Border state strategy, but they were unlikely to bolt for Hubert Humphrey, the incarnation of the New Deal, or for George Wallace.[57]

The story of the 1968 general election campaign has been well documented by Theodore H. White, Chester et al., and Joe McGinnis in *The Selling of the President 1968*.[58] Nixon's campaign manager, John Mitchell, relied on an Upper South and Border state strategy rather than concentrating on the urban Northeast (the Deep South was written off to George Wallace), but there

TABLE 3-3.   Republican Convention, 1968: Candidate Support by Region

Candidate	Vote	% From South	% From West	% From Midwest	% From Northeast
Nixon	692	38.1	18.1	26.7	15.9
Rockefeller and others	459	5.9	6.8	34.2	51.2
Reagan	182	35.5	58.2	5.5	0.5

Source: Bain and Parris, Convention Decisions and Voting Records.

were still enough liberals in Nixon's entourage (principally California's Lieutenant Governor Robert Finch) to prevent the candidate from being totally won over to the backlash camp.[59] The result of this tension was a rather lackluster campaign, with the ghosts of 1960—vacillation and ambiguity—returning to haunt Nixon. The election outcome also mirrored that of 1960: a desperately close margin in the popular vote, with Nixon winning this time by 1%. His comfortable electoral college victory indeed came from carrying the Rim South and Border states (with the exception of Texas), as well as pluralities in the crucial midwestern states of Ohio, Illinois, and Wisconsin. Nixon's ambiguous mandate in 1968 illustrated the continuing change in the pattern of Republican support since 1952. The Republican presidential vote was becoming more southern and western, and less northeastern, with each succeeding election; Nixon's neglect of the metropolitan Northeast meant that he carried virtually no big cities, and his percentage of black votes was little better than Goldwater's had been: 12% to 6% in 1964.[60]

The new president remained difficult to define ideologically, and as his administration commenced it was not certain that he would move in a rightward direction. Yet the conservative South had assured Nixon of the nomination and had been crucial to his election. This factor, plus the presence of the southern strategist John Mitchell in the Nixon cabinet as Attorney General, rightly gave Republican liberals cause for foreboding as the Nixon administration took office.

The Nixon Administration

Richard Nixon owed his elevation to the vice presidency in 1952 to the influence of Thomas E. Dewey and Herbert Brownell, and he had taken care to keep open his lines of communication to the Republican liberals.[61] It was not surprising, therefore, that there was a strong liberal presence in the first Nixon administration, particularly at the cabinet level. In the foreign policy area, William Rogers, an old associate of Dewey's, was made Secretary of State, and Rockefeller's protégé, Henry Kissinger, became National Security Adviser. On the domestic front, Alaska Governor Walter

Hickel became Secretary of the Interior, George Romney became Secretary of Housing and Urban Development, Massachusetts Governor Volpe became Secretary of Transportation, and Nixon's long-time confidant, Robert Finch, became Secretary of Health, Education and Welfare (HEW). According to Nixon's own assessment of his first cabinet:

> As a group its members were less conservative than Eisenhower's Cabinet, and in fact somewhat to the left of my own centrist positions. But each man knew his subject and each brought both competence and imagination to his job.[62]

Even the Ripon Society had a foothold in the new administration. Lee Heubner, a former Ripon president, joined the White House staff, and two other Ripon activists. John Price and Christopher DeMuth, became assistants to White House Domestic Counsellor Daniel Patrick Moynihan.

In a modern American presidency, however, the cabinet and a few lower-level assistants do not make major policy decisions, and the Nixon administration was certainly no exception in this regard. Essential decisions were made by the president and a small circle of trusted advisers, and the liberal presence here was negligible. Nixon's closest aides, H. R. Haldeman and John Ehrlichman, were fiercely loyal to the president, rather than to any specific ideology. Arthur Burns and Bryce Harlow were cast in the stalwart mold, and Kissinger had his own idiosyncratic views on foreign policy. Strom Thurmond's aide, Harry Dent, also served as a special counsel to the president. Nixon's three major speech-writers reflected the major ideological currents within the Republican party: Robert Price was a liberal, Patrick Buchanan represented the views of the radical right, and William Safire was a less strident conservative. The nearest thing to a liberal Republican among the senior aides was Pat Moynihan, but he was a registered Democrat![63]

The adviser on whom Nixon relied most heavily on matters of political strategy was his former law partner and 1968 campaign manager John Mitchell, who had been persuaded to take the post of Attorney General. According to Evans and Novak,

> His [Mitchell's] conviction was that a certain definable constituency elected Richard Nixon, and the correct political course of the Presi-

dent now was to satisfy its needs, not those of his enemies, who would never vote for him anyway. To Mitchell, a second Nixon term depended on keeping his own vote of 1968, and being able to win over the vote of segregationist third-party candidate George Wallace, should Wallace not run again.[64]

Mitchell's approach entailed cultivating the backlash blue-collar and southern Democratic vote, and statistical justification for the southern strategy was provided by his assistant, Kevin P. Phillips. In his 1969 book, *The Emerging Republican Majority,* Phillips used charts and maps to demonstrate that electoral trends in the United States were moving in the direction of a national conservative (and he hoped, Republican) majority based on the states of the South and West—the Sunbelt. This majority was formed by adding the Nixon and Wallace totals of 1968:

> The emerging Republican majority spoke clearly in 1968 for a shift away from the sociological jurisprudence, moral permissiveness, experimental residential, welfare and educational programming and massive federal spending by which the liberal (mostly Democratic) Establishment sought to propagate liberal institutions and ideology and all the while reap economic benefits. The dominion of this impetus is inherent in the list of Republican-trending groups and potentially Republican Wallace electorates of 1968; Southerners, Borderers, Germans, Scotch-Irish, Pennsylvania Dutch, Irish, Italians, eastern Europeans and other urban Catholics, middle-class suburbanites, Sun Belt residents, Rocky Mountains and Pacific Interior populists.[65]

Phillips's thesis appeared to confirm the old claim of the Goldwater movement that the Republicans could succeed electorally only by appealing to the barely concealed conservative majority in the hinterland. The liberal states—New York, Michigan, Massachusetts, and Pennsylvania—were no longer essential to Republican success.

The Ripon Society naturally had a strong adverse reaction to Phillips's book. The *Ripon Forum,* in a lengthy editorial devoted to a discussion of the Phillips thesis, retorted:

> The party that abdicates its considered judgement of the nation's needs and priorities to the fears and prejudices of a narrow class of

voters may profit temporarily though even that is doubtful; but in
the end it is bound to fail. And the government that keys its programs to the excesses and injustice of the White South will find to
its shame that it has sown the seeds of tragedy across the nation.[66]

The Ripon activists and their liberal allies in Congress adhered to
their standard argument, that the Republicans' future prospects
depended on the growing young, middle-class constituency in the
Northeast and the Sunbelt.[67] Yet the electoral logic of 1968 seemed
to be on Phillips's side, Nixon had not, after all, been nominated
by liberal suburban professionals in the Northeast, but by businessmen, farmers, and lower-income conservatives in the Midwest,
South, and West. In the general election, his margin of victory had
come from his solid support in the West, the Great Plains, the rural and suburban Upper Midwest, and his scattered gains in the
South and Border. The president owed his strongest campaign
debts to Barry Goldwater, Strom Thurmond, and John Tower.
With the leading proponent of the southern strategy as his closest
political adviser, it appeared likely that Nixon would incline more
toward the views of Mitchell than toward those of the Ripon
Society.

The policy output that actually resulted was largely in accordance with the proposals of the Ripon Society, with a rhetorical
style that reached out toward the "forgotten Americans" and the
putative "new majority" of which Phillips and Mitchell spoke.

The Nixon administration implemented a fair proportion of the
Ripon policy agenda. The military draft was abolished, revenue-
sharing between federal, state, and local governments was introduced, détente with the Soviet Union and an opening to Communist China were zealously pursued by Nixon and Kissinger,
and Moynihan put together his Family Assistance Plan (FAP)
to reform the nation's welfare system through the concept of a
guaranteed income (although this was later defeated in Congress).[68]
Most important, perhaps, Nixon withdrew increasing numbers of
American combat troops from Vietnam during his first term. In
terms of substance, then, much of the public policy output that
emanated from the first Nixon administration could, with some
justice, be called liberal (certainly more so than the legislative
output of Eisenhower's first term).

But there was another side to the story. With an eye to sustaining Nixon's southern support, Mitchell's Justice Department gave the impression of seeking to slow down the pace of school integration and enforcement of the 1965 Voting Rights Act.[69] Leon Panetta, the head of the Office of Civil Rights at HEW, resigned in 1970 over the reluctance of the administration to pursue school integration.[70] Nixon also went out of his way to court the favor of southern conservative Democrats, such as Senators Eastland, of Mississippi and Byrd, of Virginia. The nominations of southerners Clement F. Haynsworth and G. Harrold Carswell to the Supreme Court (both were ultimately rejected by the Senate) were further designed to consolidate the administration's southern support.[71]

Nixon's leading agent in wooing conservative Democrats was his vice president. In a series of speeches (written mainly by Pat Buchanan), Agnew railed against the new left, anti-war students, militant black leaders, and the liberal eastern news media, which he accused of condoning their activities.[72] This strategy of reaching out to the new majority was continued into the 1970 midterm elections, with Agnew again playing the leading role. At this time of considerable campus unrest and rising urban crime, "law and order" and the "social issue" became the prevailing themes of the Republican campaign.[73] *The Real Majority,* a book written by electoral analysts Richard Scammon and Ben Wattenberg, which argued that the Democrats could not succeed electorally as long as they were perceived by the electorate as soft on the social issue, apparently had a profound effect on speech-writer Buchanan, and through him on the president:

> If this analysis [Scammon and Wattenberg's] was right, and I agreed with Buchanan that it was, then the Republican counterstrategy was clear: we should preempt the social issue in order to get the Democrats on the defensive. We should aim our strategy primarily at disaffected Democrats, and blue-collar workers, and at working-class white ethnics. We should set out to capture the vote of the forty-seven year old Dayton housewife.[74]

This tactic was highly uncongenial to the liberal Republicans in Congress, many of whom had supported the Democratic liberals on the civil rights and foreign policy questions that troubled the administration; but the White House was mainly content to leave the

Republican liberals undisturbed, since they needed their votes on other issues, such as the Family Assistance Plan, and also because most of them were well entrenched in their states and districts.[75]

There was one important exception to this rule, however. Senator Charles Goodell (appointed by Nelson Rockefeller to fill Robert Kennedy's unexpired Senate term) was a fairly stalwart upstate New York congressman while in the House of Representatives. On his elevation to the Senate, however, Goodell was the first Republican to support an immediate American military disengagement from Southeast Asia. He began to speak out frequently against the war and introduced an amendment in the Senate providing "for the complete withdrawal of U.S. forces from Vietnam one year after its enactment."[76] As an appointed Republican senator in a generally Democratic state, Goodell was highly vulnerable in the 1970 midterm elections. Moreover, the White House had a ready alternative: James Buckley (a brother of William F. Buckley), who was running on the Conservative party line as a supporter of Nixon on the war and the social issue.[77] In William Safire's account, Nixon briefed his staff as follows:

> Another thing—we are not out for a Republican Senate. We are out to get rid of the radicals. The point is that the only Republican coming up who is a radical is Goodell. Now about him I'll give you the line: Both major party candidates in New York oppose the President. The only candidate who doesn't is Buckley. The President's rule of endorsing all Republican candidates is being revoked in this case. We are dropping Goodell over the side. Everyone knows it.[78]

Nixon was true to his word, and both he and Agnew lost no opportunity to make clear which candidate they favored in the New York Senate race:

> It was made very clear to me that my opposition to the war would cause trouble from the Nixon White House. Colson and others sent out letters to Republican state party leaders in New York, and to Wall Street which basically dried up all the normal campaign contributions that a Republican candidate in New York could have expected. . . .
> They never openly endorsed Buckley but they came close to it.

Agnew openly campaigned against me, and at the time I thought that it was Agnew on his own. Subsequently, having seen the papers and transcripts of the Nixon tapes, it was clear that Nixon had authorized it.[79]

Ultimately Goddell finished in third place behind the winner, Buckley, and Democrat Richard Ottinger.

Despite the efforts of Nixon and Agnew, there were few other dividends at the polls for the administration. The GOP lost 9 House seats and 11 governorships, while gaining 2 Senate seats. Under the influence of Democrat John Connally, brought into the administration as Treasury Secretary in 1971, Nixon moved to the left on economic policy, introducing wage and price controls, ending the system of fixed currency-exchange rates, and publicly declaring "I am now a Keynesian".[80] The strident attacks on the liberals and the media were also temporarily suspended. Nevertheless Nixon was not turning for advice to liberal Republicans; rather, with the departure of Moynihan in 1970 and his replacement by John Ehrlichman, liberal influence within the administration was further diminished.[81]

Even after the Goddell affair, Nixon maintained some contact with the liberal Republicans in Congress. Together, the moderates and progressives accounted for some 16 of the 43 Senate Republicans, and 69 of the 189 House Republicans in the Ninety-first Congress elected in 1969, and the administration needed their support on key votes.[82] Nixon and has aide for congressional liaison, Bryce Harlow, initially pursued a legislative strategy of trying to keep the Republican minority together on most issues, and then adding liberal or conservative Democrats as the situation demanded.[83] In the House, the greater ideological homogeneity of the Republicans enabled the strategy to prevail in most cases, but in the more intractable and individualistic Senate, the "floating coalition" strategy encountered greater difficulties. According to Reichley:

> The Republican minority was less cohesive in the Senate than in the House. Many of the Republican progressives and moderates—a larger share of the total representation in the Senate than in the House—felt that they had little to gain politically by supporting the administration.[84]

Most of the liberals had run ahead of Nixon in their states in 1968, and were electorally beholden to constituencies that were not in ideological or cultural accord with those the administration was trying to reach. Some Senate liberals, such as Charles Percy, Edward Brooke, and Mark Hatfield, had been elected primarily because of opposition to President Johnson's Vietnam War policies, and they sought to disengage the United States from Southeast Asia as quickly as possible. Others were committed to supporting many federal programs that the administration wanted to dismantle. Relations were tense between the Nixon White House and Republican Senate Minority Leader Hugh Scott, who the administration had hoped would loyally serve their interests in the upper chamber. The Pennsylvania Republican took a serious view of his responsibilities toward his fellow Republican senators, however, and did not regard himself purely as a servant of the White House. Scott was further distrusted for having been a Rockefeller supporter in 1968:

> The palace guard people didn't like me. Haldeman felt that talking to me was beneath him, and Ehrlichman was always looking for ways to get rid of me. He was responsible for a story in *Newsweek* that Nixon didn't want me re-elected in 1970.[85]

The Republican liberals in the Senate voted solidly against Nixon's proposed Anti-Ballistic Missile system in 1969, and they also played a significant role in defeating the Haynsworth and Carswell nominations.[86] The Senate liberals were further instrumental in passing the Cooper-Church Amendment of 1970, which prohibited the use of funds for American military operations in Cambodia, and in defeating an anti-busing amendment that the administration supported.[87] While they supported Nixon on FAP and revenue-sharing, the administration was already beginning to omit the liberal Republicans from its strategic considerations.[88] According to Congressman Gilbert Gude.

> Under Nixon I was over at the White House very few times. I'm not sure that many other Republicans were going there a good deal either. I became convinced that the Vietnam war was not for us, and I was among the first to attempt to repeal the Gulf of Tonkin resolution, together with Paul McCloskey. This was my big area of difference with the administration.[89]

Dissatisfaction with Nixon's continuing support of the war in Vietnam was the catalyst for a minor revolt against him, orchestrated by two young liberal Republican congressmen, Donald Riegle, of Michigan and Paul (Pete) McCloskey, of California. Together they organized a quixotic campaign by McCloskey for the Republican nomination in 1972. According to Riegle,

> In the midst of the 1970 campaign McCloskey and I concluded that the emerging profile of the Nixon administration was a distressing one. The war continued in Vietnam. There were incursions into Laos and Cambodia and the administration's election tactics hinged around the unfortunate southern strategy. Reluctantly, we decided that Nixon was not the man we'd hoped he'd be. . . . Even more worrisome was the fact that citizen faith in the whole self-government process was continuing to deteriorate. At that time our heads were not yet into the notion of challenging him in the primaries. Then, last February, Pete made his impeachment comments at Stanford University. We began to consider the challenge seriously.[90]

Riegle and McCloskey hoped to do to Nixon in the New Hampshire Republican primary what Eugene McCarthy had done to Lyndon Johnson in 1968. But although McCloskey got 20% of the New Hampshire vote, his challenge to Nixon from the left faded as rapidly as that of Congressman John Ashbrook from the right.[91] No senior Republican liberal, such as Rockefeller, Percy, Javits, or Hatfield, wanted to be associated with the insurgency, and McCloskey's campaign was a shoestring operation with little money or organization. Anti-war activists applauded the California congressman, but they were more interested in securing the Democratic nomination for George McGovern than in pursuing their aims within the fundamentally hostile GOP.

John Lindsay, once the bright hope of the Ripon Society and the Republican liberals, campaigned for the presidency in 1972 as a Democrat, and he was soon joined in changing parties by Riegle and former *New York Herald Tribune* publisher, Congressman Ogden Reid. These switches by ambitious young liberal Republicans give some indication of the lack of influence that Republican liberals possessed over the Nixon administration. Those who continued to give general support to the administration while voting against most of its legislative proposals were not rewarded with a hearing from the increasingly intransigent and insular Nixon White House. The major liberal leader in the nation was still Nelson Rockefeller, although his fourth and final administration in New York was taking an ever more conservative stance on the social issue, as demonstrated by his anti-drug bill and his response to the Attica prison riot. Unlike many other liberals, Rockefeller also gave full support to Nixon's Vietnam policy.[92]

In 1972, Nixon was able to win re-election by a landslide, with barely a whimper of opposition from within his own party. Even the usually critical *Ripon Forum* found some nice things to say about the president when they compared him to the Democratic alternative, George McGovern. With Wallace eliminated from contention after the attempt on his life, Nixon at last found his new majority, as southerners and urban blue-collar Democrats in the North defected in droves and the incumbent carried every state save Massachusetts. The Republicans gained 12 House seats, lost 2 Senate seats and 1 governorship: not a very impressive showing, given the dimensions of the Nixon landslide; it was apparent that Nixon's new majority was largely a negative vote against McGovern, rather than a positive endorsement of the president or his party.[93]

Negative or not, Nixon, reinvigorated by his renewed mandate, was determined to launch a full-fledged assault on the "liberal bureaucracy" and to use American force to the limit to enforce Kissinger's Vietnam peace agreement.[94] His move to the right was impeded by the Watergate scandal, however, and as he sank deeper into the morass, survival became the sole object of his administration. Nixon's increasingly conservative tone in his second term, and the flood of disclosures concerning wrongdoing in the 1972 campaign, finally alienated his remaining supporters among liberal Republicans.[95] The latter were fortunate, however, in that most of those disgraced, from Nixon and Agnew on down, were not closely associated with their section of the party. In fact, given the administration's rhetorical tone, Nixon's downfall appeared to be a disastrous reversal for the conservative wing and another possible opportunity for the liberals to revive. Nixon's successor, Gerald Ford, had a stalwart, midwestern background, had been a popular House minority leader, and was sufficiently malleable on most issues for liberals to feel that they might be able to influence his administration and fill the ideological vacuum left by the temporary eclipse of the right.

Richard Nixon remains an elusive and enigmatic figure as far as his relationship with the Republican party is concerned. His belief in using strong—almost authoritarian—presidential powers to achieve the conservative goal of reducing the size of the federal government, and the realpolitik characteristic of the Nixon-Kissinger foreign policy, was reminiscent of the concept of the presidency held by the Progressive Theodore Roosevelt and his latter-day descendant, Nelson Rockefeller. In the areas of welfare policy, economic policy, and foreign and defense policy, it is difficult to conceive of Rockefeller's pursuing a course drastically different from Nixon's, were he the president. To that extent, Nixon falls into the liberal-activist Republican tradition of Theodore Roosevelt and his original mentor, Dewey.

Yet Nixon's willingness to countenance populist attacks on institutions dear to liberal Republicans—the Ivy League universities and the news media, for example—and his lack of enthusiasm for civil rights enforcement made it difficult for many modern liberal Republicans to support him. Before Nixon's fall, more Hamiltonian and Rooseveltian liberals, such as Rockefeller, felt ideologically comfortable with much of what he did, while the younger generation of more rights-conscious Jeffersonians—Weicker, Brooke, and Riegle—grew ever more uncomfortable. At the root of the tension between Nixon and the liberals lay differing conceptions of the kind of electoral strategy the Republicans ought to adopt. Nixon sought to make a populist conservative appeal to disenchanted middle- and low-status Democrats—his forgotten Americans—although, as we have seen, this did not necessarily entail a conservative policy output. To the liberals, this involved an appeal to groups with which they had never felt socially and intellectually comfortable: southerners, blue-collar ethnics, Roman Catholics, and so forth. They would have preferred to orient the GOP toward the middle- and upper-income suburbanites, whose political culture was more in accord with their own—individualistic, culturally and socially liberal, and distrustful of government intervention in all its forms.

At the turn of the century and up to the 1950s, it had been Republican liberals who had advocated strong government and "big stick" diplomacy. Rockefeller may well have been the last of this breed. The more contemporary Republican liberal has been preoccupied with human rights questions and distrusts government activism and American military intervention overseas. By the 1970s, ironically, it was the conservatives who were the advocates of overseas intervention and strong presidential leadership. It was this fundamental divergence of political outlook that brought about the conflict between the *etatiste* Nixon and the more liberal elements in his party.

The Ford Administration and the Election of 1976

In the aftermath of Watergate, with many leading conservatives "tainted" by being associated with Nixon, circumstances temporarily favored the liberal Republicans. Ford's appointment of Nelson Rockefeller to the vice presidency seemed to be an indication of the direction in which he was heading.[96] However, the political climate of the mid-1970s was not particularly well suited to a revival of Republican liberalism. Bold government initiatives in the style of Johnson, Nixon, and Rockefeller seemed out of place at a time of record inflation and demands for financial retrenchment on the part of the federal government. Because of Watergate and Vietnam, there was also a widespread lack of confidence in the institutions of the federal government, in contrast with the traditional progressive faith in strong executive leadership. This crisis of confidence engendered demands from both liberals and conservatives for a reduction in the scope of federal government activity and a return to more participatory politics at the state and local level. In many respects the stalwart Republicanism of Gerald Ford fit the prevailing climate of opinion more closely than did the interventionist activism that had characterized the political career of his vice president.[97]

Rockefeller sought an activist role for himself as the administration's authority on domestic policy, and Ford duly promised to make him head of the Domestic Council:

> Ford, Rockefeller understood, wished to move in a somewhat more liberal direction. And Rockefeller could provide him with the planners, the researchers, the conceptualizers who would design pro-

gressive new programs, always staying within the bounds of fiscal soundness and Republican concern for local self-determination and economic freedom. . . . But for that to happen, Rockefeller quite naturally believed it would be necessary for Ford to govern along the lines that would be recommended by the new Vice-President.[98]

Unfortunately for Rockefeller, the overriding preoccupation of the Ford administration was reducing the rate of inflation by restraining the growth of government expenditure. By the time Rockefeller had completed his lengthy confirmation hearings before Congress, the administration's policy had already been firmly set on this path by Ford's conservative economic advisers, Chairman of the Council of Economic Advisers Alan Greenspan and Treasury Secretary William Simon.[99] The combination of Watergate and economic recesssion inflicted severe losses on the Republicans in the 1974 midterm elections: the party lost 49 House seats, 5 Senate seats, and 4 governorships. With large Democratic majorities in both houses, Ford's only hope of preventing Congress from passing appropriations measures of which he disapproved was to veto them and hope that his managers in at least one house could summon up enough votes to sustain the vetoes.[100] This situation left Rockefeller, the foremost liberal in the administration, in a hopeless position. His bold new domestic programs never saw the light of day, and he encountered hostility from Ford's White House staff, led by Chief of Staff Donald Rumsfeld, who feared that Rockefeller was trying to encroach on the president's prerogatives.[101] According to one Rockefeller biographer,

Nelson found himself negotiating for power with Ford's Chief of Staff Donald Rumsfeld, a tough forty-two year old former Congressman. At first, Rockefeller emerged from those bargaining sessions elated. "He acted as if he were President," Mrs. Whiteman remembered. "He'd come back from a meeting announcing that he was going to run the White House." But in the end, Rumsfeld outboxed him. Nelson moved like an aging heavyweight dazzled by a fast, young puncher. As his capture of the machinery of domestic policymaking became less certain, Nelson muttered darkly about "people only out to serve themselves and who don't give a damn about the country." With Rumsfeld, it was the Rockefeller-Lindsay rivalry all over again, youth and age in collision.[102]

Ford had sound political reasons for wishing to distance himself from his vice president, since after the initial shock of Watergate, the Republican right had rapidly regained its former organizational strength. The conservatives' champion was still former California Governor Ronald Reagan, whose telegenic campaigning skills and ready access to the right's network of fund-raisers and pressure groups made him a formidable obstacle to Ford's prospects of renomination. The right had been generally quiescent during the Nixon years, and many conservatives in Congress had been among the president's diehard supporters during Watergate. In the wider conservative political network, however, there was a continuing distrust of Nixon, and veterans of the movement, such as William F. Buckley and William Rusher, had distanced themselves from the administration after Nixon's pursuit of détente with the Russians and the opening to China.[103] Appalled by Watergate, the right was originally prepared to give Ford the benefit of the doubt, but after his selection of their arch enemy Rockefeller as vice president, right-wing interest groups, think tanks, and journals began to give encouragement to the Reagan candidacy. Some of the Californian's supporters even urged Reagan to reject the Republicans entirely and form a new party, since the experience of the Nixon and Ford administrations had demonstrated that the GOP, with its seemingly permanent liberal wing, could never be an effective vehicle for their version of conservatism. Rusher, the foremost advocate of the "new party strategy," described the Republican liberals as follows:

> There is nothing inauthentic about the Republicanism of these people. They are "Republican" all right; they are merely not conservative. Like the drone bee, they have (whether they like it or not) only one function: to work for liberal principles and defend liberal interests *within the Republican party,* and thereby prevent it from ever uniting the conservative majority in America and leading that majority to victory.[104]

Of course, Rusher exaggerated the influence of the liberals within the GOP. During the Nixon and Ford administrations their direct influence on the White House increasingly diminished, and whatever bargaining power they might once have possessed at Republican National Conventions was being vitiated by the proliferation of presidential primaries (discussed at greater length in the next chapter). Reagan appears to have been apprised of these developments, since he never gave serious consideration to the notion of an Independent or Third Party campaign. The Reaganites realized that they had a reasonable chance of securing the Republican nomination, since Ford was a particularly vulnerable incumbent because of (a) the peculiar circumstances of his accession to the presidency and (b) the transformation of the presidential nominating system (also discussed in the next chapter).[105] According to Reagan's campaign manager John Sears:

> I had real doubts about Gerald Ford. I was asked to participate in Ford's campaign, but I never thought he could win a national election, because of all the Watergate and recession baggage he had to carry around. In 1974–5 I didn't think that the race would be close with Ford as the nominee. The Republicans were in a real downslide. I felt it was important to have a race within the party, to get people reinvolved. The party needed a diversion from Watergate.
>
> Ford was a unique incumbent, and I hoped somebody else would come in so as to drain away votes from him on the moderate side of the party. Howard Baker and "Mac" Mathias both came close to coming in. But the Ford people pressured them into not running. As for Rockefeller—there was no way that he could get out there once he agreed to be Ford's vice-president.[106]

More accurately than those of Rusher, Sears's comments depict the parlous situation of the Republican liberals. Had Nixon served out his second term, there can be little doubt that at least one leading liberal—probably Senator Percy—would have been an active contender for the 1976 nomination. But Nixon's resignation and the likelihood of Ford's running for a full term changed the whole picture. The liberals never regarded the stalwart president was one of their own, and his apparent ineptitude in office discomforted them even further. There seemed to be the added danger, after Ford's pardon of Nixon, that many of those suburban professionals who constituted what strength the liberals had among Republican supporters in the electorate would drift away from the party, refusing to get involved in a struggle between the mainstream Republican Ford and the conservative Reagan. At least one liberal senator, Charles Mathias of Maryland, did give serious consideration to entering the race, if only to try and create some counterweight to Ford's shift to the right to meet the Reagan challenge:

> President Ford was still thinking about running in 1975. Obviously either as a candidate or potential candidate he was going to be heavily pressured by Reagan and the right. Some of us felt that it was necessary to create a counterforce so as to keep equal pressure on each side. If Ford were to be a candidate it would obviously be an extremely difficult thing to do. The question hinged on what his plans were, and how the party would coalesce around him. If the party were to coalesce around an incumbent, it would not have been prudent to run.[107]

Yet the liberals were as well aware as John Sears was that if one of them ran against Ford, it would make Reagan's task much easier. Ultimately the liberal challenge came to naught, like so many in the past, and Ford continued to move rightwards to deal with the threat from Reagan.

One aspect of that shift was the decision to arrange Vice President Rockefeller's withdrawal from consideration for renomination in November 1975. According to Rockefeller's counsel, Peter Wallison, the reasoning behind this decision was as follows:

> Because of the challenge from Reagan on the right, Ford had to throw off some ballast, and Rockefeller was the biggest piece of ballast that he could throw aside. The Republican perception was that Rockefeller was interested in the Presidency, and interested in the Republican party only as the vehicle to get him the Presidency. Rockfeller could have changed that perception. He could have gone to fundraisers around the country. But he chose not to do that. He preferred the more ceremonial functions, in the hope that he would be able to participate in the great issues of foreign and domestic policy. As a result Rockefeller hadn't ingratiated himself with the party when Ford came under pressure from the Reagan people. Ford had good reasons to dump him, but Rockefeller always said that he wanted to be dumped. He couldn't stand another four years of humiliation.[108]

The "dumping" of Rockefeller led to further murmurs of discontent from the liberals, but by now it was too late for them— given the new dynamics of the presidential nominating process—

to do very much about it. The Ripon Society bitterly regretted its unequivocal endorsement of Nixon in 1972, and it moved to Washington the following year in an attempt to build a better relationship with party regulars (a move vehemently opposed by many leading Riponites). But Ripon still lacked the basic organizational and financial infrastructure to mount anything like a serious presidential campaign.[109] The House Wednesday Group and Senate Wednesday Club continued to exist, but they could not overcome the indiscipline that characterized the leading liberal Republicans in Congress.[110] In the absence of Nelson Rockefeller's personal organization and financial resources, there was an organizational vacuum in the liberal wing of the party. In a thoughtful article entitled "The Plight of Progressive Republicans," former Ripon Executive Director Robert D. Behn gave a candid analysis of the liberal predicament:

> As the presidential campaign season opened, the progressive Republicans were the only major section of the nation's political ensemble that was unable to compose a serious presidential overture. Consequently, during the spring and summer of 1976, as Ford and Reagan played to a strictly conservative audience, the only parts open to the GOP's progressives were in a small uninfluential section of the chorus singing hosannas to Ford.[111]

Behn also pinpointed one main reason for the liberals' organizational weakness:

> For individual candidates, regardless of party, the liberal maverick is a valuable resource and a reputation for independence a major asset. Yet for a party—or any political group with a common set of policy objectives—independence and accomplishment are incompatible. If the liberal Republicans wish to achieve some specific public policy goals, they will have to sacrifice some of their sacred independence for the cooperation that is a prerequisite for performance.[112]

These problems of selfishness and lack of cooperation were made even more conspicuous by developments in the technology and environment of American electoral campaigns at all levels. Thomas Dewey had triumphed in state and national politics because he had built alliances with state and local leaders who could deliver support to him when he required it. By the mid-1970s most Republican state and local parties had to contend for influence over party nominations with single-issue groups, ideological activists, and campaign-management specialists. In these circumstances, liberal Republicans were successful when they succeeded as individual personalities, owing little to party activists, who frequently remained fundamentally hostile toward them.[113] Direct appeals to the voters, using the rhetoric of independence mentioned by Behn, were the best means of overcoming that liability. These matters will be discussed further in the next chapter; it will suffice to say here that the absence of a single obvious national leader, and the loss of party control over nominations, had succeeded in moving the Republican liberals of the 1970s toward a public demeanor reminiscent of the western mavericks' of the 1920s, an attitude characterized by professions of independence from nefarious special interests, by volatility, and by irresponsibility. Like their forebears, these latter-day mavericks exerted some influence in the U.S. Senate (as will be shown in Chapter 5), but also, like Borah and company, they were a beleaguered minority within the national party.

With the grudging support of the liberals and the strong support of most party regulars, Ford was able to prevail over Reagan by a narrow margin at the 1976 Republican Convention in Kansas City.[114] The president's crucial early primary victory in New Hampshire (he won by a margin of approximately 1%) saved him by giving him sufficient momentum to win other early primary states, such as Florida and Illinois. Reagan launched a strong counterattack after his victory in North Carolina in April, sweeping most of the South and West (see Table 3-4). Ford, however, succeeded in uniting the traditionally liberal states— Massachusetts, Connecticut, New York (still under Rockefeller control), and Michigan—with most of the stalwart states of the Midwest, and this, together with his early successes, was sufficient to win a narrow triumph at the August convention. Reagan's forces tried a last gamble when the Californian announced that he would select the liberal Republican senator from Pennsylvania, Richard Schweiker (the first and only Republican senator endorsed by the AFL-CIO), as his running mate. This did not break the solidarity of the Ford ranks, however, and the move probably lost Reagan support among conservative southern Republicans.[115] With the

TABLE 3-4.   Republican Convention, 1976: Regional Support for Candidates

Region	% Of total vote	% For Ford	% For Reagan	% Ford's total vote	% Reagan's total vote
Northeast	26	88	12	43	6
Midwest	27	68	32	35	18
West	20	18	82	7	34
South	27	27	73	14	41

Total convention vote = 2,259.
Total Ford vote = 1,187.
Total Reagan vote = 1,070.

Source: Congressional Quarterly, National Party Conventions 1831–1980 (Washington, DC: Congressional Quarterly, 1983).

polls indicating a likely electoral disaster in November, the president chose to consolidate his basic Republican constituency by selecting a stalwart midwestern conservative of an ideological stamp similar to his own—Senator Robert Dole of Kansas—as his vice-presidential running mate

If the Dole selection was an exercise intended to limit the electoral damage, the result in November seemed to justify it. Ford held all of the western states (save Hawaii) and most of the Midwest. He lost the election because of narrow defeats in the crucial states of Ohio, Pennsylvania, Texas, and Florida. Running against southern Democrat Jimmy Carter, Ford lost the entire Confederacy except for Virginia, and all of the Border states but Oklahoma. Eight years after Kevin Phillips had published his *Emerging Republican Majority,* the party had lost the presidency (albeit narrowly), held only a handful of statehouses, and still represented only a pitiful minority in both houses of Congress. Republican identification in the electorate had dropped to 22–23%, and the very survival of the party seemed to be in doubt.[116]

Watergate was undoubtedly a major factor in retarding the Republicans' electoral progress so severely, but this had not enhanced the viability of the party's now virtually moribund liberal wing. On the contrary, control of the party now fell into the conservatives' hands, and perhaps the major success of Reagan's effort in

1976 was that he was able to distance conservative Republicanism from the discredited administration of Gerald Ford and from the specter of Richard Nixon. In 1980, the right-wingers could thus more easily achieve the complete domination of the Republican party they had sought since 1952.

Liberal Republicans in Retreat, 1964 to 1976

The underlying demographic and ideological trends that had contributed to the liberal Republican failure in 1964 accelerated during the 1960s and 1970s. Population, and economic and political power, continued to drift away from the northeastern United States toward the conservative South and West.[117] The Democratic party remained a staunch defender of the public philosophy of the New Deal, but the political upheaval generated by the Vietnam War and the civil rights movement forced the party to the left, particularly on foreign policy and the so-called social issue. As a consequence the conservative Wallaceite element of the Democratic coalition—predominantly southern, but with an important element of support among urban, northern, lower middle-class, and blue-collar voters—became more susceptible to Republican appeals, at least in presidential elections.[118] The drift away from the Democrats among southerners and northern ethnics augmented the ranks of the conservative Republicans and reinforced the minority status of the liberal wing, which had consistently argued that the path to Republican electoral success lay in courting the so-called frontlash voters, those socially liberal suburban professionals who were becoming ever more ideologically and culturally alienated from the majority of Republican activists.

These underlying trends were reinforced by the liberals' organizational shortcomings in the 1968–80 period. Through persistent ineptitude and irresolution, they succeeded in transforming their perilous position in presidential politics into an unseemly rout. The initiatives undertaken by the liberals in the wake of the 1964 debacle amounted to very little with regard to subsequent presidential campaigns. As a small policy and discussion group, Ripon succeeded in forcing Republicans to think originally about concrete policies, but it was unable to alter the overall ideological direction of the party and lacked the resources to establish the national grass-roots organization that the liberal cause required.

Many talented young liberal Republicans were elected as senators and state officials in the mid-1960s reaction against the Johnson administration. But they were elected in large part as individual personalities, not on their political principles. Liberal Republican leaders continued to lack a coherent ideology (save for technocratic pragmatism), were envious of each others' successes, and remained reluctant to challenge entrenched conservatives in their respective state parties. Many of the new liberal Republican stars, particularly Mayor Lindsay of New York, won office primarily by playing down their party affiliation.

In the crucial 1968 nomination battle, the fact that Nelson Rockefeller—probably the liberal leader who was farthest from the mainstream of the GOP in terms of background, style, and policy—was again the liberal Republican candidate was fatal to their chances. The New York governor's vast resources and national stature prevented any other liberal with a potentially broader electoral appeal from entering the presidential stakes once Rockefeller's chosen candidate, Romney, had fallen at the first hurdle. Easy as it is to criticize Rockefeller's "nonproliferation treaty" and his jealous grip on the leadership of the liberal faction, it is by no means clear that any of the other liberals had any stomach for the fight whatsoever.

Much of the criticism directed at the liberal wing of the Republican party in this work and elsewhere views its major problem as being the lack of a viable network of local volunteer organizations to transform liberal Republicanism from a vague abstraction into a national political movement. As politics in the United States began to move in a more ideological direction during the 1960s, and as power within political parties became more diffuse, the Republican liberals were left stranded with an outdated, elite-oriented approach to political campaigning. Liberal Republican initiatives were invariably "top-down" rather than "bottom-up," originating from a small group of established senior Republican figures rather than as a response to a clearly delineated body of opinion within the American electorate.

Yet in attributing the liberals' electoral mishaps to a lack of grass-roots organization, it is valid to ask whether there was an identifiable constituency for liberal Republicanism. The Riponites could point to the fact that Eugene McCarthy had won an estimated 25% of the registered Republican vote in Wisconsin's open primary in 1968 (Nixon's was the only name on the Republican ballot), but this does not necessarily imply that liberal Republicans had an equal claim to the McCarthy constituency, as many Ripon supporters seemed to believe.[119] Lee Heubner asserted in May 1968,

> If the Republican party is to avoid even further isolation from a changing electorate and a rising generation, it must learn to speak to the new forces that are moving in American life.[120]

However, it would be equally true to say that the Republican conservatives were also speaking to "new forces in American life"—perhaps unpalatable forces such as the white backlash or the Sunbelt as far as the easterners were concerned, but forces that were as potent as the college-educated suburbanites' revolt against the New Deal party system. In the final analysis, it is also somewhat dubious that Eugene McCarthy's and Robert Kennedy's broad anti-war support constituted a constituency susceptible to Republican appeals in the long term. These voters had not, after all, flocked to the candidacy of George Romney, who had accused American generals of brainwashing him about the war. This group might vote for a liberal Republican occasionally to punish a Democratic candidate whom they found distasteful, but it was too fluid and amorphous a constituency to constitute a solid electoral base for the liberal element in the Republican party.

If this is correct, then the much-maligned accommodationist approach favored by the liberal Republican leaders, although primarily defensive, appears much more realistic than the confrontational stances advocated by Ripon. The liberals' problems were not only technical and logistical in 1968, but also stemmed from the fact that their old base of support—urban eastern Republicans and affluent northern white Protestants—was becoming a less important element in the party's electoral base.[121] The Republicanism of Goldwater and Nixon was better suited to the changing composition of the Republican electoral constituency: Sunbelt nouveaux riches, low-status social conservatives, and small-town and rural Americans. The liberals' fundamental problem was that their old base was rapidly eroding, while they had little to offer the new forces within their party coalition but the platitudes of another era.

4

Liberal Republicans and the Changing American Party System, 1968 to 1980

In this chapter we consider the impact of the transformation of the U.S. party system on the liberal wing of the Republican party. As we have seen, the liberal Republicans were already losing ground in the national Republican party by the early 1960s through the effects of long-term electoral trends accelerated by short-term strategic ineptitude. The impact of the reforms in the presidential nominating process confirmed the elimination of the liberal Republicans from presidential politics. Some other aspects of the reform process, on the other hand, have probably helped liberal Republicans survive at the state and local level.

The first section of this chapter surveys the changes in the U.S. party system over the last two decades. The second section analyzes the effects of reform on the Republican party, and particularly on liberal Republicans since the mid-1970s. Finally, there is a brief sketch of the contrasting effects of the new politics on the Republican parties of Massachusetts and Connecticut.

The Transformation of the U.S. Party System

The changing role of political parties in the United States can be understood in terms of three interrelated factors: the decline of party strength within the electorate; organizational transformation; and changes in the political environment within which party competition takes place.

The decline in the strength of political parties among voters has been analyzed most thoroughly by Nie et al., with additional contributions from Kirkpatrick, Ladd, and Burnham.[1] These authors have demonstrated that the role of the party in structuring the vote in American elections has diminished considerably since the 1950s.[2] Self-described partisan identities—which earlier studies had found to be the crucial determinants of electoral choice for most voters—declined precipitously from 1956 to 1976. Intensity of partisanship declined and increasing numbers of voters described themselves as Independents, attached to neither party (see Table 4-1). In addition to the decline in party identification, other significant indicators of popular disaffection with the major parties were discovered by scholars of American electoral behavior in the 1956–76 period. Voter turnout declined at all levels of electoral competition; there was a much greater incidence of partisan defection and split-ticket voting; and there was also evidence of an increasing hostility toward political parties in general, accompanied by a declining belief in their efficacy as political institutions.[3] At the same time that American voters were becoming detached from the major parties, however, it was discovered that they were politically motivated by issues and ideology to a greater extent than they had been in the 1950s.[4]

American political scientists had previously stressed the importance of "critical elections" and "realignments" in bringing about necessary changes both in the party system and within the political system as a whole.[5] They now summarized the developments noted above as evidence of "dealignment": instead of moving between the parties as in a realignment phase, the electorate appeared to be increasingly estranged from the party system in general.[6] This conclusion appeared to be corroborated by the fact that new age-cohorts of voters were entering the electorate without having inherited their parents' partisan preferences, and continued to remain less partisan despite the passage of succeeding elections.[7]

The erosion of partisan attachments in the electorate has been regarded as both cause and effect of the disintegration of traditional party organization. The welfare functions that were once performed by urban party machines have been taken over by state and federal authorities. Patronage—the adhesive that held together many state and local party organizations—has largely disappeared through the development of a nonpartisan, merit-based civil service at all levels, the reduction in the number of patronage jobs, and the declining attractiveness of such jobs. The reforms of the Progressive era introduced nonpartisan elections at the local level in many areas and the widespread use of the direct primary for party nominations at all levels. The effects of the political upheaval of the 1960s and the demands for openness and participation in the selection of delegates to the national party conventions have led to the more widespread use of binding presidential primaries in both parties. Presidential nominations are no longer determined by bargaining between state party chiefs congregated at the quadrennial national party convention. The convention has ceased to be the decisive element in the presidential candidate selection process and now, in most instances, merely ratifies decisions already made in the primary elections. Table 4-1

TABLE 4-1. The Republican Shift to a Candidate-Based Delegate Selection Process

	Republican National Convention Delegates	
Year	Party-based delegates[a]	Candidate-based delegates[b]
1936	66%	34%
1952	56	44
1968	52	48
1972	39	61
1976	15	85
1980	14	86
1984	13	87

[a] Delegates selected by party committees, party caucuses, or delegate primaries.
[b] Delegates "bound" to candidates by participatory conventions or candidate primaries.

Source: Tables kindly provided by Byron Shafer from his *Bifurcated Politics: Evolution and Reform in the National Party Convention* (Cambridge, Mass.: Harvard University Press, 1988).

illustrates the increase in the number of convention delegates who arrive committed to candidates by essentially nonpartisan methods of candidate selection. The advent of the direct primary and the campaign finance reforms of the early 1970s have decreased the role of the party in financing presidential and congressional election campaigns and enhanced the influence of interest groups (in the form of Political Action Committees), candidates' personal organizations, and professional political consultants.[8]

Some authors, such as Polsby, Ranney, and Kirkpatrick, have tended to emphasize the importance of the reforms of the 1970s as the decisive factors in the decline of party organizations.[9] Others such as Burnham, have seen the disintegration of the parties as the culmination of a long-term process of party decomposition dating from the turn of the century.[10] All of these authors, however, see the transformation of the party system as one aspect of a more general change in the political environment in which party competition takes place. The growth in the power of the federal government and the "nationalization" of American politics reduced the importance of state and local government, which traditionally provided the base of party activity. Bureaucratization and the technocratic public philosophy of progressivism and the New Deal have all but eliminated the traditional incentives for partisan involvement. Electronic communications media—particularly television news—have supplanted the parties as mediating institutions through which most American citizens relate to politics and receive political information. The more widespread availability of higher education, suburbanization, and the disintegration of traditional urban ethnic communities, added to the development of independent media for dispensing political information, have created an electorate that is better educated and more politically active, but that is also more antipathetic toward traditional party politics. The increasing political sophistication of the electorate discovered by Nie et al. has engendered a greater concern with specific issues and ideology, as opposed to a perception of politics through family or community ties.[11] These changes in the context of American electoral competition brought the traditional norms of American party behavior—bargaining, building coalitions, patronage, concentration on victory at the polls rather than doctrine—into disrepute, and the public became more receptive to demands for party reform as the parties were perceived to be inimical to the health of the body politic.

One important aspect of the debate about the decline of parties has been the attention given to the conflict between amateurs (or purists) and professionals within American parties since the 1950s. This distinction was first introduced by James Q. Wilson in *The Amateur Democrat,* a study of Democratic party reform clubs published in 1962. Wilson defined the professional as follows:

> The professional, for whom politics has extrinsic rewards, is pre-occupied with maintaining his position in party and elective offices. Winning is essential, although sometimes electoral victory must be subordinated to maintaining the party organization.[12]

The amateur, on the other hand,

> would in the ideal situation prefer to recruit candidates on the basis of their commitment to a set of policies. Voters would be mobilized by appeals to some set of principles or goals. The party would be held together and linked to the voters by a shared conception of the public interest.[13]

Aaron Wildavsky (as we have seen) applied Wilson's distinction between types of party activists to the conflict over the Republican party nomination in 1964, although he focused on style rather than attitude as the key factor in distinguishing between the two types, substituting the term "purist" for Wilson's "amateur":

> Purists are interested in being interested in politics. They care about people caring about politics. They are far more concerned about the need for substantial differences between the parties than they are about the differences themselves. If only one has principles and stands up for them, their position seems to suggest, the uneasy world of politics—compromise, bargaining, exceptions, modifications, inconsistencies—will disappear. Political style thus becomes a substitute for politics itself.[14]

The upheaval in American politics in the 1960s consisted largely of purist attacks on the political establishment from both right and left. The ideologies were distinctive but the basic approach was the same. The shortcomings of American democracy were attributed to professionalism in politics and to the failure of the existing compromise-oriented system to accommodate radical demands for change. One consequence of this was the reform of the political parties in order to bring them more in line with the purist conception of politics. According to Kirkpatrick, Polsby, Ranney, and Shafer, the opening up of the parties and the assault on the power of the party bosses has had the desired effect, as new political elites have taken over the presidential selection process.[15] Indeed, it is asserted that these new elites have not so much taken over the parties as reformed them out of existence, making them extraneous to a political process that is based on plebiscitary appeals in terms of single issues, personality, or ideology. The transformation of the party system is a manifestation of the triumph of the purist conception of politics, which has rendered obsolete the traditional accommodationist politics of American parties. Presidential candidates put forward by the reformed parties are more likely to be ideologues with a "principled" political style, while the more centrist elements in both parties are virtually excluded from the nominating process.

About the future development of the party system there is no general agreement among scholars. One school, perhaps best represented by Walter Dean Burnham, sees American parties as having been in an irreversible secular decline since the turn of the century, a process that will ultimately lead to a fragmented, irresponsible, and ungovernable polity.[16] As correctives to the theory of party decline are the more sanguine analyses of Cotter et al., Reichley, and Kayden and Mahe, which stress that national party committees in the United States now exercise much more authority over state and local parties than ever before in American history, and that party organizations in the 1970s and 1980s have been playing a greater role in election campaigns at all levels than they did twenty-five to thirty years ago.[17] Regardless of which assessment is more accurate, it is undeniable that a considerable transformation of American party politics has taken place.[18]

Party Reform and the Republican Party

All the trends discussed above were discerned through a rigorous analysis of the raucous and highly visible debate over party reform that took place in the Democratic party after 1968. In comparison, consideration of the impact of reform on the Republican coalition has received scant attention. In an effort to rectify this imbalance, the effects of reform on the GOP and the ambivalent relationship between its liberal wing and party reform will now be discussed.

In one major respect, change in the Republican party followed the Democrats, namely in the proliferation of presidential primaries. The 1968 struggle between Nixon, Rockefeller, and Reagan for the Republican presidential nomination saw primary elections in just seventeen states, with only 36% of the national convention delegates being committed to candidates by primary elections. By 1980, over 70% of the Republican delegates were bound by primaries or open caucuses (see Table 4–1). The most obvious explanation for the proliferation of Democratic primaries was the complexity of the McGovern-Fraser rules on delegate selection and affirmative action. These frequently conflicted with established state laws, and made primary elections easier to operate than the caucus system in many states. Another consideration was that pragmatic state party leaders often sought to distance the presidential candidate selection process as much as possible from the procedures of the state party so as to protect their own fiefdoms against incursions by radical activists and avoid credentials challenges at the convention.[19] The urge for reform in delegate selection and for affirmative action procedures was present to some extent among the Republicans, particularly from the liberal wing of the party.[20] But, as will become evident, the Republicans' delegate-selection reforms were far too limited to serve as the sole explanation for the increase in the number of Republican presidential primaries.

The main reason that primaries increased within the GOP is related to the Democratic dominance of most state legislatures during the 1970s. In order to bring the state parties into line with the McGovern-Fraser guidelines, Democratic state party leaders were frequently required to write provisions for presidential primary elections into state law. This, in most cases, bound the Republicans to hold a presidential primary as well. Even had the Republican state leaders not been compelled by state electoral law to conduct a presidential primary, they would not have wanted to permit the Democrats to gain the registration advantages and media attention that would have been exclusively theirs had the GOP refused to hold a primary on the same day. Electoral and legal realities thus forced the Republicans at the state level to follow behind their Democratic rivals.[21]

Both ideological wings of the Republican party could see advantages to their cause in moving toward an open system of convention delegate selection through primaries. Conservatives saw primaries as a means by which liberal or stalwart control of many local party organizations might be weakened, particularly in states where the right did not have a strong foothold, such as New York, Pennsylvania, and Ohio.[22] Liberal Republicans hoped that an open system of delegate selection might avert another Goldwater coup, in which conservative party activists had overridden the wishes of Republicans in the electorate as a whole through winning control of unrepresentative state and local party organizations.[23] Thus there was little resistance to the opening up of the presidential nomination process in the Republican party, as contrasted with the widespread intraparty antagonism engendered by the Democrats' reforms.

Procedural reform had less impact on the Republican party than among the Democrats because, unlike their opponents, the Republicans already had a codified set of party rules (codified in response to the disastrous schism of 1912) which explicitly laid down the precise powers of the Republican National Convention, the Republican National Committee, and the Republican state parties.[24] Yet the bitter struggle over representation in the Democratic party did infect the Republicans to the extent that, in 1969, RNC Chairman Rogers Morton appointed a sixteen-member Delegate and Organization (DO) Committee to consider proposals for reform in delegate-selection procedures. This committee reported in January 1971, recommending a ban on proxy voting, a ban on ex officio delegates, open caucuses to select delegates, and action on the party's Rule 32, which dealt with the representation of women and minorities. According to John F. Bibby,

> The key difference between the McGovern-Fraser guidelines and the recommendations of the DO Committee was that the McGovern-Fraser guidelines called for a mandatory quota system and affirma-

tive action program, whereas the DO Committee only recommended the election of greater numbers of minority delegates. Thus whereas the Democrats moved in the early 1970s toward a nationalized set of procedures for delegate selection, the GOP retained the confederate legal structure of its party, with a states' rights approach to delegate selection procedures.[25]

In 1973, a second reform commission, known as the Rule 29 Committee, was set up by RNC Chairman George Bush. This committee proposed a series of reforms dealing with the national committee itself. Its proposals included direct election of the membership; the enlargement of the committee (ending the principle of three members from each state regardless of population); open RNC meetings; and the establishment of a select committee on presidential affairs under the national chairman. In March 1975, the RNC rejected the Rule 29 Committee's "positive action plan," and most of its proposals were negated by the 1976 convention as infringements on states' rights. In the final analysis, the procedural reforms advocated by the Republican National Committee were largely cosmetic, with the main emphasis of the delegate-selection regulations remaining on the confederal and decentralized nature of the party structure.[26]

One procedural matter did arouse some debate within the GOP, however. Since the 1920s the Republicans had used an apportionment formula that gave bonus delegates to states that had elected Republican governors, senators, and congressmen, and had also voted for the Republican presidential candidate at the previous election. This plan obviously favored the small, conservative western states against the liberal states of the Northeast, and the Ripon Society twice challenged its constitutionality in the courts.[27] The first suit was declared moot when delays postponed a decision until after the 1972 Republican convention. The second case, in 1975, challenged the reapportionment formula on the basis of the Supreme Court's "one man, one vote" rule, but was rejected by the District of Columbia Court of Appeals; the Supreme Court also refused to hear the case.[28]

The minimal procedural reforms undertaken by the RNC were to have negligible impact on the balance of ideological forces within the party. The one major change in the Republican presidential nominating process was the proliferation of primaries, which was of little advantage to the Republican liberals. The shift from an elite-oriented to a plebiscitary selection procedure ultimately benefited the conservatives even further. According to Reagan's 1976 campaign manager, John Sears,

> The nominating process had also changed drastically. With all these primaries, internal party officers played a less significant role. Republicans could afford to disregard the obligations which the party leaders felt to the man in office. It was now possible to run against an incumbent and win. In the Democratic party, the reforms further alienated those voters who felt that the party was moving too much to cater to the needs of a minority. The party leaders lost the ability to maintain order in that party, and the blue-collar people stopped participating. Watergate had a similar impact on the Republican party. Lots of moderates just stopped participating. In this country the system functions best with broad-based parties. Now we have a system of Left and Right.[29]

It was symptomatic of the decline in the influence of party leaders in the new nomination system that Sears's candidate could only get the support of three major Republican officeholders—New Hampshire's Governor Meldrim Thomson and Senators Jesse Helms and Paul Laxalt—yet was almost able to win the 1976 nomination:

> We were very shy on officeholders. . . . but the new nominating system helped us, even though few high-ranking officials in the regular apparatus in the states could afford to support us.[30]

There can be little doubt that the new dynamics of presidential nominations were a godsend to the militant right. Their ever-expanding network of pressure groups, campaigning organizations, and single-issue activists could be effectively mobilized for primary elections or open caucuses, where the total turnout of registered Republicans was likely to be low. Republicans less committed to the conservative cause and to conservative candidates were simply less likely to feel sufficiently motivated to vote. Many of these people had also rejected the GOP entirely out of disgust with Nixon and Watergate. In addition, the advent of candidate-centered organizations and political-consultancy firms meant that candidates could win election independent of the support of most state party organizations. Traditionally, Republican liberals had relied on controlling the large delegations to the Republican convention from the northeastern industrial states in order to check the power of the more conservative Republican organizations in the Midwest and West. Dewey and Rockefeller were able to control the votes of the large New York delegation at Republican conventions through the closed selection process and their command of the state party machinery. The opening up of the nominating procedures meant that the liberal Republicans were now open to attack on their own turf, and were no longer able to exert full control over the Republican convention delegations from their own states. In 1976 Reagan had made little effort in these states because his financial resources had dried up after early primary defeats.[31] In 1980, however, he was able to win a significant number of delegates in the liberal Republican bastions of Massachusetts, New York, Connecticut, and Pennsylvania (although he scored an outright victory only in New York).

One further aspect of party reform also assisted the right. It has already been mentioned that the changing electoral geography of the Republican party was shifting power away from the eastern, liberal, big-business establishment toward Sunbelt conservatives and the business interests that supported them. This trend was consolidated by the reforms in the Federal Elections Campaign Amendment Act of 1974 (FECA). FECA further reduced the influence of eastern "big money" within the Republican party by placing severe restrictions on the amounts that the national party could contribute to a presidential campaign; it also introduced provisions for public financing of both primary and general elections. It has already been noted that the Goldwater campaign had been extremely successful in soliciting large amounts of funds from small donors through direct mail. Now that Republican presidential candidates had to raise $5,000 in contributions, not exceeding $250 in at least twenty states, to qualify for matching federal funds, the conservative Political Action Committees (PACs) and interest groups, with their lengthy mailing lists, found themselves ideally equipped for this task. Moreover, the 1976 Supreme

Court decision in *Buckley v. Valeo* permitted unlimited "independent" expenditures by a PAC on behalf of a candidate, provided
these were not made in coordination with the candidate's official
campaign. This, of course, benefited the right even further, since
it possessed a growing infrastructure of PACs and lists of thousands of donors to solicit for funds.[32] Eastern financial influence
was rapidly declining within the Republican party, and the Republican liberals, who had relied heavily on Wall Street as a financial base and as a source of power over the national party, suffered accordingly.

This analysis of the impact of party reform and the reformed
nominating process on the Republican party indicates that those
who attribute the ascendancy of ideological activists in modern
American party politics to the opening up of the presidential nominating process are only partially correct with regard to the Republicans. The unreformed Republican party had already come
under the temporary control of conservative ideologues in 1964,
and the drift of power away from the party's liberal wing was a
long-term process that antedated the advent of demands for party
reform and the growth in the number of primaries. Nevertheless,
the increase in the number of presidential primaries and the campaign finance reforms undoubtedly expedited the efforts of the
militant right to become the predominant force within the national
party and completed the utter destruction of whatever organizational and financial power the party's liberal wing still possessed in
the late 1960s. Had the liberals erected anything like the grass
roots fund-raising organizational and propaganda structure that
had been developed by the radical right over the previous two decades, they could have adapted more easily to the new system.
Unfortunately the liberals, who led the demands that the party be
opened up and its electoral base broadened, failed to develop the
necessary political infrastructure. They had little money, no national organizations (except Ripon), no PACs, and, it seemed in
the increasingly issue-oriented political environment of the mid-
1970s, no issues. Hence the substitution of the participatory model
of candidate selection for the pluralist model served merely to ac-
celerate the decomposition of the liberal wing of the Republican
party.

Republican Party Renewal and the
Election of Ronald Reagan

Although the Republicans did not directly revise their procedures for delegate selection in the 1968–80 period, the national Republican party was transformed during the 1970s from a skeletal organization that existed only during presidential election years into a national fund-raising and campaign-management operation unprecedented in American party history.[33] This organizational strength enabled the Republicans to run the nationally directed partisan campaign that got Ronald Reagan and a Republican Senate elected in 1980. Organizational regeneration also held out some (limited) promise of a "reprofessionalization" of Republican party politics, which might assist the survival of the residue of liberal Republicans in the 1980s.

The Republicans' party-renewal projects were made possible for the RNC only because of the strong financial base they had been building at the national level since Ray Bliss's time as national chairman in the 1960s. In response to the shattering defeat of 1964, Bliss inaugurated an RNC national fund-raising program by direct mail, which was maintained and expanded by his successors.[34] For the 1983–84 election cycle, Republican party committees (the RNC plus the House and Senate campaign committees) raised $298 million to the Democrats' $98 million.[35] With this fund-raising base, the RNC was able to undertake a program of strengthening its organizational resources, particularly during the chairmanship of William Brock from 1977 to 1981. State and local parties were given access to national party funds and services (e.g., candidate and manager training, computer facilities, polling) in an effort to build up the party at the grass roots level.[36] This helped create a new interdependence between the RNC and the state and local parties and made possible the Republicans' coordinated national campaigns in 1980 and 1984.

The nationalization and organizational regeneration of the Republican party structure since the mid-1960s is an interesting adaptation to the new disaggregated electoral environment in which American parties have to compete. Whether this will have any significant effect on the ideological balance of power within the Republican party is another matter. The national party's increasingly important role in the financing and direction of state and local campaigns might, nevertheless, act as a barrier to the influence of conservative candidate organizations, PACs, and single-issue activists at the lower levels of electoral competition. As the national organization is interested in electing Republicans regardless of ideological affiliation, the type of approach pioneered by Bliss and Brock may yet help Republican liberals survive in the party, since they are the only type of Republicans who could conceivably be elected in several areas. Such an approach represents at least a partial return to professional thinking in party politics, as opposed to the purist attitudes prevalent in the 1960s and early 1970s.[37]

With the onset of the economic recession and foreign policy frustrations of the Carter administration, Republican prospects for the 1980 elections looked increasingly bright. The conservative movement was now enjoying an intellectual respectability that had not been theirs ten years previously. Liberalism and government activism were out of fashion, as were dovish attitudes on foreign policy. The crisis in American liberalism was made further apparent by the increasing number of neoconservative critiques that emanated from a group of disillusioned liberal intellectuals—Irving Kristol, Norman Podhoretz, Nathan Glazer, Daniel Patrick Moynihan, and Daniel Bell among others—in magazines and journals such as *Commentary* and *The Public Interest*.[38]

Another development that assisted the electoral advance of the conservatives was the opposition to Carter's Panama Canal treaty led by Ronald Reagan and North Carolina Senator Jesse Helms.[39] In addition to opposing the Canal, the new right's PACs were also soliciting the support of anti-abortionists, anti–gun control activists, and, most important, evangelical Christians. This enabled them to make further inroads into Democratic support among northern blue-collar and lower middle-class Catholics, as well as southern and western fundamentalists. The latter group had given considerable support to Southern Baptist Jimmy Carter in 1976, but after the disappointments of his administration, they found themselves more in accord with the moralistic, pro-family crusades of the new right.[40]

The right-wingers were now better organized than ever before. Their PACs (led by Senator Helms and his Congressional Club) built up formidable lists of financial contributors around the country.[41] During the Carter administration they also coordinated their forces more effectively, bringing in groups such as antifeminist Phyllis Schlafly's Eagle Forum and the Christian fundamentalist leaders Jerry Falwell (the Moral Majority) and Ed McAteer (the Religious Roundatable).[42] In addition, the right derived intellectual sustenance and substantive policy proposals from the new conservative think tanks such as the Heritage Institution in Washington, DC and the Hoover Institution at Stanford.[43]

The new right's relationship with the Republican party remained tense, however. In contrast to the conservatives of the 1950s, who had operated almost exclusively within the GOP, many new right leaders claimed the label "populist" and regularly repudiated the Republican party as being dominated by elitist businessmen and effete Yankee liberals.[44] According to new rightist Paul Weyrich in a 1981 interview,

> The Republican party is not built on principles, it's a tradition maintained by effete gentlemen of the northeastern Establishment who play games with other effete gentlemen who call themselves Democrats.[45]

Although Weyrich was being more than a little disingenuous in making these remarks, his comments do illustrate the mutual suspicion that existed between the social conservatives of the new right and the more laisser faire, business-oriented conservatism characteristic of the Republican tradition.

The liberal Republicans remained disorganized and seemingly divorced from developments within the Republican ranks. They had nothing with which to compete against the formidable organizational resources of the conservatives, and thus they continued to rely on their independence and their personal organizations to survive in uncongenial times. When Connecticut Senator Lowell Weicker was asked for the best political description of himself, his response was typical of latter-day Republican liberals: "Maverick is fine . . . I like 'Independent' too. Independence is the key to political success in the future."[46] The 1978 midterm election was not a happy experience for the liberals. Senator Edward Brooke had to fight a tough Republican primary against conservative Avi Nelson, and subsequently lost his Massachusetts Senate seat to liberal Democrat Paul Tsongas. In New Jersey, veteran liberal Republican Clifford Case was defeated in the Republican primary by Jeffrey Bell, a former director of the American Conservative Union and aide to Ronald Reagan. Bell attracted enthusiastic support from conservatives and raised considerable amounts of money from conservative sources through direct mail.[47] According to the *Congressional Quarterly,* Case's apparent disdain for the exigencies of soliciting electoral support—a not uncommon attitude among liberal Republicans in the 1970s—led to his defeat:

> Case did not set up his campaign committee until January of this year, and by late May had spent only one third the money Bell had. Case also irritated rank-and-file Republicans during the campaign when he did not personally attend Republican gatherings and instead sent stand-ins.[48]

Case and Brooke were both caught in the dilemma of the contemporary liberal Republican. In order to win the Republican primary, a liberal candidate has to prove his right to the Republican label in an increasingly conservative party. Yet should he succeed, the liberal can win the general election in a predominantly Democratic state only by stressing his independence from partisan considerations, which antagonizes regular Republicans and initiates the cycle all over again. These prerequisites of electoral survival often led liberals to adopt militantly antipartisan positions (which would have appalled a Dewey or Brownell), culminating in a state of near-warfare with their respective state parties. This was true of Governor Francis Sargent in Massachusetts, Charles Mathias in Maryland, and particularly of Lowell Weicker in Connecticut. In an era of conservative dominance among Republican activists, this appeared to be the only means by which a Republican liberal could remain liberal and survive electorally. At the national level, of course, these tactics engendered further disaffection and the alienation of stalwart party regulars who disliked the antipartisan tone of much liberal Republican rhetoric. (They were not overly pleased with some of the new right's activities either, but the latter seemed to have the tide of events on their side in the late 1970s, and Republican loyalists—like all party loyalists—like winners.)

All of this did not lead one to expect liberal Republicans to fare well in the battle for the Republican nomination in 1980. After

Messrs. Weicker and Pressler had made their brief entries and exits from the race, there remained only one liberal Republican contender, Illinois Congressman John Anderson. The effort of Senate Minority Leader Howard Baker was hopelessly disorganized and, shackled by his vote for the Panama Canal treaty, he never really got off the ground as a presidential contender. Also on the stalwart side of the field stood Senator Robert Dole, but his less than impressive performance as Ford's running mate in 1976 was a serious handicap and he, too, rapidly disappeared from contention. This left former U.N. Ambassador and former RNC chairman George Bush, a patrician Yankee by birth, a Texan by adoption, and a stalwart Republican in his ideological orientation. Bush's base of support within the party lay with party regulars and those liberals who preferred him to any of the right-wing alternatives. On the right, Reagan remained the most charismatic and significant contender. His only serious rival was former Texas Democratic Governor and Treasury Secretary John Connally, who had moved rightward to try and capture Reagan's support in the South and West (and succeeded in getting the support of direct-mailer Viguerie). But Connally was handicapped by his identification with Lyndon Johnson and Richard Nixon—hardly an impressive pedigree in the political atmosphere of 1980.

Bush was the early front-runner after a surprising victory in the Iowa caucuses, but Reagan's convincing victory in New Hampshire stopped his momentum. Reagan then went on to dispose of Connally in South Carolina, and of the gadfly Anderson in Illinois. Bush proceeded to win victories in the old liberal strongholds—Michigan, Massachusetts, Connecticut, and Pennsylvania—and he made an impressive showing in his adopted state of Texas; but the South, West, and Midwest were solid for Reagan, and, after seeing off his early challengers, he could not be deprived of the nomination. According to Charles O. Jones, Reagan profited by winning the media-expectations game that had so badly damaged him in New Hampshire in 1976:

> Iowa created Bush for Reagan to defeat in New England, Connally offered himself in South Carolina, and New England produced Anderson as an Illinois sacrifice. The media (including the polls) played the important role in each case of advertising the potential

strength of Reagan's opponents. There were two important consequences of these developments: (1) The margin of victory for
Reagan was always "surprising" and (2) the cumulative effect of
the surprises was to convince the pundits that Reagan was in-
vincible.[49]

It is necessary to discuss the Anderson campaign further, for it
betrayed many of the characteristic features of the decayed Republican liberalism of the post-Rockefeller era. Anderson had be-
gun his political career as a stalwart midwestern Republican congressman from Rockford, Illinois, but during his time in the
House his issue positions had moved increasingly toward the center. Respected by Washington's political community as a forthright
and capable politician, Anderson was elected Chairman of the
House Republican Conference, the third-ranking post in the House
Republican hierarchy. His outspoken liberalism, however, antagonized many of the members of the conservative-dominated House
Republican delegation (see Chapter 5), and having to fight extremely hard to cling to his largely ceremonial leadership post became increasingly wearisome:

> I was increasingly harassed and isolated. I was the first Republican
> in the House to call for Nixon's resignation. The Republican Whip
> at the time waved an AP press dispatch in front of my face and
> upbraided me for not being a loyal Republican. This kind of thing
> led to increasing feelings of isolation and frustration. I realized that
> I could never be elected Minority Leader. I gave thought to run-
> ning for the leadership after Ford became Vice-President, but some
> friends came and told me that there was not a snowball's chance in
> Hell that I could win. So I had no chance of advancement in the
> House. I had the feeling that the party was going down the wrong
> road. A feeling that it was hopelessly wedded to policies that were
> appropriate to the past but not the future.[50]

The final indignity for Anderson came in the Republican congressional primary in 1978, when a conservative television evan-
gelist made an issue of Anderson's opposition to constitutional
amendments on abortion and school prayer, and of his support
for the Panama Canal treaty. Anderson was held to 58% of the
primary vote and, deciding that he was fighting a losing battle,
abandoned the House and entered the national arena.[51] The Illi-

nois congressman's bid for the presidency initially looked like a quixotic venture, since he had no national recognition and no natural base of electoral support. On the other hand, Anderson felt that his bid was justified because none of the other contenders adequately represented the liberal viewpoint.

Anderson attracted support from the remaining Ripon activists, and Ripon's National President John C. Topping, Jr. was campaign director for the Anderson prenomination effort.[52] According to Howard Gillette (who worked as an issues director for the campaign), the original Anderson strategy was based heavily on the early New England primary states:

> There was a short period in the Anderson primary campaign when we had high expectations. Initially we had a five state strategy—Massachusetts (which we thought we could win), Vermont, New Hampshire (we didn't really expect much there), Illinois, and Wisconsin. There were four potentially liberal states where we hoped to stop Reagan. The whole game was Massachusetts and Vermont.[53]

Anderson won only 9.8% of the vote in New Hampshire, but he came tantalizingly close to winning Massachusetts and Vermont, losing by a hairs-breadth to Bush and Reagan, respectively. A sizable proportion of the Anderson vote, however, was coming from Independents and Democratic crossovers and was concentrated in New England's academic communities.[54] In his home state of Illinois, Anderson was convincingly beaten by Reagan (37% to 48%), and on April 1 he came in third in the Wisconsin primary, which he had at one stage expected to win. The relatively low level of support for Anderson among registered Republicans (he never exceeded 37% in any primary) illustrated just how meager the liberal base of support had now become at the Republican grass root level. Without the support of the Independents and crossover Democrats, his early primary showings would have looked far less impressive. Yet the Anderson following was large enough to damage the Bush candidacy in those crucial early contests. By dividing the liberal-to-stalwart vote, Bush, Baker, and Anderson ensured Reagan's success. According to Jones,

> Bush must have felt totally boxed in during the New England primary campaign period. Anderson and Baker got support he might

otherwise have claimed. One can appreciate his fascination in watching moderates split the vote. If Bush had received the Anderson and Baker vote in New Hampshire, Reagan would still have won, but by just 4%. With the Anderson and Baker votes, Bush would have won by margins of approximately 38% in Massachusetts and 33% in Vermont. These results surely would have changed the competitive standing of both Bush and Reagan.[55]

This did not greatly trouble Anderson, who, despite his less than spectacular performances in the primaries, was enjoying the considerable media attention that his campaign had engendered. According to Howard Gillette, the possibility of an Independent candidacy by Anderson in November had been present from the start:

> Some people were thinking about it very early. Lee Auspitz urged Anderson to run as an Independent from the start. He felt that the Republican party was no longer capable of a progressive campaign. . . . There were people counselling him very early to go Independent—[Wall Street financier] Felix Rohatyn, [leading political consultant] David Garth, Mrs. Anderson. . . . Once Anderson started breathing in the air of national attention, he was lulled into the belief that he could do it.[56]

Campaign Director John Topping was further aware that Anderson was taking far too liberal positions on various social issues to have a serious chance of winning the nomination:

> Anderson had a tendency to flaunt his liberal positions on social issues. He gained to some extent politically but his liberalism skewed his position on every other issue. This was helpful in Cambridge, Massachusetts, and among Democrats and Independents in crossover primaries in the first four New England primary states. . . . Anderson's advertising agency was basically liberal Democratic in outlook and they never took seriously the chance that the Republicans would ever nominate him. There was a split in the campaign between those interested in the nomination and those interested in building up a direct-mailing list for Common Cause type liberalism or something like that.[57]

Anderson began to give an Independent candidacy serious consideration after April 1, 1980. While it is possible to argue that Anderson, having demonstrated his broad popular appeal, should have stayed and fought for his ideas within the GOP, the candidate had become disenchanted with the failure of prominent liberals like Mark Hatfield and Charles Percy to rally to his banner. Moreover, his private polls and the publicity that he had received gave him the impression that he might be able to win as an Independent.[58] Anderson eventually decided that it was worthwhile to take the risk, and by the end of the month his Independent effort had been launched:

> On April 1st I said that I would begin the Independent effort. I have no regrets about that decision. People have asked me, "Wouldn't you like to run for your House seats again or perhaps for the Senate?" I turned them down because I wanted to set up a new party, and I thought I would find being in the Senate a rather lonely experience. My friends are deluding themselves that there is any future in the Republican party. The GOP has metamorphosed into an ultra-conservative party. They should make the clean break that David Owen and Shirley Williams have done in Britain, and found a new party.[59]

Initially Anderson's prospects looked encouraging. As the campaign progressed, however, he began to fade, and Reagan's selection of George Bush as his vice-presidential running mate helped forestall a substantial Republican defection to Anderson (although many Ripon activists stayed with him to the end). In the November election Anderson won 7% of the national vote and carried no states. He ran relatively strongly in the old Yankee progressive areas of New England, the Upper Midwest, and the Pacific Northwest. Whether the Anderson constituency of moderate Yankees, affluent suburbanites, university towns, and high-tech areas is stable enough to sustain a national political movement is another matter.[60]

The Anderson campaign illustrates the problems of the modern Republican liberal in presidential politics. Lacking a stable base of support within Republican ranks, candidates like Anderson are compelled to put their major emphasis on winning the support of Democrats and Independents. This immediately raises doubts as to the genuineness of the candidate's commitment to the Republican party and estranges him even further from the party's mainstream. Anderson might have attempted to convert his primary support into a liberal constituency within the GOP. By withdrawing as he did, he left the Republican field clear for the militant right and the stalwarts. There was no liberal bloc of delegates for the Reaganites to bargain with in Detroit, and thus the right was able to dictate the party platform virtually unopposed. Individual liberals could still be elected in their states or districts, but they lacked any real national power or leadership, or even an effective national voice. Anderson, who might have provided that leadership, disdained the opportunity by opting to run as an Independent. Had he stayed within the Republican fold and gone to Detroit, his might have been a more significant voice in national politics than it was in the 1980s.

Anderson's aspirations were also thwarted because Ronald Reagan proved to be a much more astute party leader in the 1980 campaign than his antagonists and detractors had anticipated. From the start of his campaign, it was apparent that Reagan, although perceived as the candidate of the right, was eager to win the nomination with as little intraparty strife as possible, and thereby benefit from a united party in the fall election. The experience of 1964 had taught experienced conservative Republicans an important lesson. Reagan avoided personal attacks on his opponents, retained William Brock as national chairman for the general election, expanded his organization to include personnel from other campaigns, such as Bush's campaign manager James Baker III, and met with Republican leaders throughout the nation. The selection of George Bush as his running mate was another part of this party unity strategy.[61] At the Detroit convention there were some grumblings from right-wingers who were appalled at the selection of the patrician New Englander Bush as vice president. But having secured the major prize, they more or less accepted the decision, and even William Rusher conceded that Bush was the logical choice for the second spot on the ticket.[62] A flurry of speculation as to the possibility that former President Ford would accept the vice-presidential nomination ultimately served only to excite television viewers.

There was one aspect of the convention that did arouse controversy, however. Other sections of the party grudgingly accepted the conservative platform's planks on foreign policy, defense policy, and the new conservative panacea of supply-side economics, but this was not the case with women's rights and abortion. The 1980 platform omitted the longtime Republican commitment to support the Equal Rights Amendment (ERA) to the Constitution, and also included a plank that stated that Republicans would "work for the appointment of judges at all levels . . . who respect traditional family values and the sanctity of human life." These sections were the result of the assiduous lobbying of the Platform Committee by Senator Helms and the pro-family forces of the new right.[63] Mary Dent Crisp, the Republican National Co-chair, and many other Republican feminists were outraged by these commitments, but they were unable even to get their own amendments to the convention floor. According to Mrs. Crisp,

> In 1980 we held regional hearings on the platform. The panel was John Tower, Trent Lott, Bill Brock and myself. Hearings are controlled by virtue of who you select to give testimony. At that point I saw a deliberate refusal to have women testify in favour of the ERA. Reagan wanted to have a platform that he could control. The whole theme of the 1980 convention was "Together a New Beginning" and no dissent was allowed.[64]

Mrs. Crisp subsequently resigned in disgust and later joined the Anderson campaign. The enmity between Reagan and American feminists would prove to be a persistent grievance of liberal Republicans against his administration.

In November, Reagan won the presidency by 489 electoral votes to Carter's 49, and the popular vote with 51% to 41% for Carter and 7% for John Anderson. In addition, the Republicans gained 12 Senate seats, giving them control of that body for the first time since 1954, with 33 House seats, and 4 governorships. In the Senate elections the new right PACs claimed to have had a decisive influence in defeating Democratic liberals such as Birch Bayh, Frank Church, John Culver, Gaylord Nelson, and George McGovern, but more credit should possibly go to the party's national committees, which targeted vulnerable Democratic Senate and House seats, recruited strong candidates, and spent the maximum amount permissible on House and Senate campaigns.[65] The new Republican senators were not uniformly militant conservatives either. Along with new rightists Steven Symms, Jeremiah

Denton, and Don Nickles, there were liberals such as Slade Gorton and Arlen Specter and old-fashioned stalwarts such as Charles Grassley, Mark Andrews, and Warren Rudman.

One of the 1980 results in the Senate was, however, symptomatic of the erosion of liberal Republican support in the state that had been the foremost bastion and source of national liberal leadership. In New York, veteran liberal Republican Senator Jacob Javits, running for a record fifth term, faced a strong challenge from Conservative party candidate Alfonse M. D'Amato in the Republican primary. In previous years Javits had been well protected by Nelson Rockefeller's tight control of the state committee, and indeed this was the first statewide primary that he had ever faced in New York. D'Amato eventually prevailed after an aggressive campaign that focused on the incumbent's advancing age and declining health. The basis of D'Amato's success was his overwhelming vote in the New York suburban centers—Nassau, Suffolk, Westchester, and Rockland Counties. Javits stayed in the race on the Liberal line, but finally could win only 11% of the vote, while D'Amato won a narrow 45% to 44% victory over Democrat Elizabeth Holtzmann. D'Amato's success seemed to confirm the impact of the Conservative party in moving New York Republicans sharply to the right, particularly in the absence of strong leadership of the state Republican party. The fact that New York—the quintessential liberal Republican state—had elected a conservative Republican senator for the second time within a decade spoke ill for the state of Republican liberalism at the dawn of the 1980s.[66]

Liberal Republicans at the State Level in the 1980s: Massachusetts and Connecticut

While liberal Republicanism was disintegrating as a national political force, its position in several state parties was also weakened by the effects of realignment-dealignment and the transformation of the party system. This was true even in former liberal Republican strongholds such as the lower New England states. In this section we contrast the disintegration of the GOP in Massachusetts with its healthier position in Connecticut, and seek to explain why the liberal Republicans (and Republicans per se) have been better able to survive in the latter state.

Massachusetts

Massachusetts was a bastion of patrician Republican liberalism in the 1940s and 1950s. The state's two liberal Republican senators during this period, Leverett Saltonstall and Henry Cabot Lodge, were internationalists, interventionists in economics, and represented the tradition of enlightened progressivism prevalent among the Brahmin families who dominated Massachusetts' Republican politics.[67] As late as the mid-1960s, distinguished liberal Republicans such as John Volpe, Edward Brooke, Elliot Richardson, and Frank Sargent were being elected statewide. But at the mass level, Massachusetts politics were changing rapidly. As late as the 1950s, the Republicans held a majority in the Massachusetts legislature. Yet by 1982, as the effects of reapportionment, demography, and the national party's shift to the right took hold, the Republicans held only 30 of 160 House seats, 7 of 40 Senate seats, and elected only 1 of 11 U.S. congressmen. All the state's leading Republican liberals had either retired from active politics or had been defeated at the polls by this time, and the party's highest elected officeholder in Massachusetts was Middlesex County Sheriff John Buckley. In terms of registration, the Democrats enjoyed a 4 to 1 advantage by 1984.

There were three main factors involved in the Republican collapse in the Bay State. First, owing to the bitter ethnic conflict that had characterized the state's politics for almost a century, Massachusetts Republicans gained a reputation for social exclusivity. According to former Republican National Committee member Eunice Howe,

> The Republicans had a traditional appeal to the middle-income WASP, and they had an image of excluding ethnic types who were arriving on the scene. As the ethnics became active the Democrats were more responsive to them. Herter, Morse, Richardson and Sargent were Yankees, dedicated to public service, but the party failed to purvey a public image which could match their successes.[68]

The Republican legislature of the 1950s further antagonized the state's Roman Catholic voters by advocating liberalization of the birth control laws. With the changing demographic and denominational balance in Massachusetts, the Republicans' failure to attract the growing Roman Catholic vote was a severe blow when their own Yankee electoral base was diminishing. Moreover, the Kennedy brothers were able to reach beyond the Democrats' Catholic, working-class base and attract formerly Republican professional and middle-class voters.[69]

The second factor involved in the Republican decline was the political style of the GOP's liberal officeholders. Many of the latter including Governor Sargent and Senator Brooke, deliberately neglected the infrastructure of the party in their anxiety to appear "above party" and independent. According to 1984 State Chairman Andrew Natsios,

> Governor Frank Sargent was a Republican in name only. He was suspicious of the party organization and he proceeded to take it apart. When Sargent became governor we had 14,000 ward and town committee members. When he left there were 7,000.[70]

Finally, the Republican decline was exacerbated by bitter factional divisions within the state party. The tempestuous period of Sargent's governorship (1969–74) saw a takeover by Republican conservatives of the party organization, culminating in the election of right-winger Gordon Nelson as state chairman in 1976. In other northeastern states (particularly New York), conservative Republican candidates had been able to win by appealing to traditionally non-Republican ethnic groups on moral-social issues, Ronald Reagan, through a similar appeal, carried the Bay State narrowly in 1980 and 1984, but at the state level the popularity and influence of Senator Edward Kennedy and the Republicans' supposed exclusivity prevented this from occurring on a significant scale. In fact, the Republican decline continued under conservative rule because it alienated the nonsectarian younger professional vote, which had supported Sargent and Brooke. Eunice Howe accurately summarized the dilemma that brought the Massachusetts GOP to its weakened state:

The conservative image brought in some ethnics, but the Yankee exclusivist image lingered. The conservatives seemed to have blinders on, and they excluded other people. So we still have the same problem but in a different context. Now the party is seen as ideologically rather than socially exclusive. It still has that same exclusivity.[71]

If ever there was a need for a revival of liberal Republicanism in the early 1980s, it was in its former Massachusetts bastion, and the unexpected retirement of incumbent Democratic Senator Paul Tsongas in 1984 provided an apparently heaven-sent opportunity for a Republican victory after years of electoral misery. Republican liberals had a ready-made candidate. Former Lieutenant Governor Elliot Richardson came from the long tradition of patrician liberal Republican Yankees characteristic of Massachusetts. He had served with some distinction in Washington as Secretary of Health, Education and Welfare (1970–73); Secretary of Defense (1973); Secretary of Commerce (1976–77), and as U.S. Ambassador to the Court of St. James (1975–76) and to the Law of the Sea conference (1977–80). As Attorney General under Nixon, he achieved almost heroic stature because of his dismissal by the president for refusing to fire Watergate Special Prosecutor Archibald Cox. The National Republican Senatorial Committee (NRSC) tacitly encouraged Richardson to enter the race in the belief that he was likely to be a formidable general election candidate in a year in which the GOP was struggling to hold onto the Senate. Many state party officials, although distrustful of Richardson's liberalism, were so desperate for a long-awaited electoral success that they viewed his candidacy with relish. Nevertheless, there remained the obstacle of the Republican senatorial primary, where Richardson was opposed by Raymond Shamie, a local businessman who had run an energetic but hopeless race against Senator Edward Kennedy in 1982. Shamie ran with the endorsement of the national right-wing PACs and as a Reagan loyalist. The race developed as a classic confrontation between liberal and conservative Republicanism.

Richardson's strategy was to run as a supporter of Reagan, but on a distinctly liberal platform, stressing the possible need for tax increases to meet the deficit crisis, the nuclear freeze, and his pro-choice position on abortion (a potentially important issue in a state with a large Catholic population). These positions, plus Richardson's personal reputation, would, it was hoped, attract enough Independent voters to the Republican primary to guarantee a margin of victory. Shamie's strategy, by contrast, was to play to the small, conservatively inclined Republican electorate, and he thus emphasized his ideological harmony with Reagan. At the same time he also sought to appeal to socially conservative middle-class and lower-status Catholic Democrats. One of Shamie's campaign staffers summarized the essential differences between the two candidates as follows:

> Ray's close alignment with the President and his views is well known. Even Richardson has stated that Shamie is more closely aligned with the President than himself. In 1976 Ray Shamie was supporting Reagan. Ray goes along with supporting the reduction of taxes. Mr. Richardson does not. We appeal to the blue-collar, two wage-earner family. We appeal to those who earn their money.[72]

The campaign waged between the two candidates followed the course that might have been predicted, given their respective strategies. Richardson stressed his experience and his independence from the Reagan administration, going so far as to repudiate the 1984 Republican platform:

> That platform, as it finally emerged, does not reflect my position on a number of fundamental issues. It does not adequately reflect the needs and desires of the people of Massachusetts. It is deficient both in terms of what it says and what it fails to say.[73]

Shamie, on the other hand, emphasized his adherence to the platform and attacked Richardson on the tax issue. He also reminded the voters of his close ties to Massachusetts, in contrast to Richardson's 16-year absence from the state, and he ran an exuberant and lively campaign on television and on the stump, performing well in debates with his more experienced opponent.

Shamie's 62% to 38% victory in the September primary was nevertheless a considerable surprise. It appeared that the tax issue had been decisive. The Republican turnout in recent Massachusetts primaries had been around 200,000, but the Richardson camp had been hoping for a higher-than-average turnout through attracting non-Republican Independents to the polls. In this respect their wishes were fulfilled, since the Republican turnout rose by 80,000 in 1984; however, the Independents who participated assisted Shamie rather than Richardson, since liberals were more attracted to the tightly contested Democratic primary. According to the *National Journal,* the new Republican voters came preponderantly from heavily Democratic blue-collar areas, and they swung the race decisively to Shamie.[74]

Richardson's defeat was a bitter blow to liberal Republicans nationwide, who had hoped for a Richardson victory as a mark of their resurgence. In retrospect, however, the result was not so surprising. Shamie ran as a Reagan loyalist in a year in which identification with the popular president did no harm to a candidate's electoral prospects. Richardson's patrician background and his dull campaigning style also proved to be severe liabilities in a state that had undergone many changes since his last campaign there in the mid-1960s. The liberal *New Republic* provided a harsh but accurate appraisal of Richardson's defeat:

> When he [Richardson] came back to Massachusetts to run this year, more than a little diffidently, he also seemed more than ordinately ill at ease. What one has to do to win in Massachusetts Republican politics now, in Massachusetts Republican politics no less than among the traditionally cruder Democrats, is something Brahmins find distasteful. Power, they seem still to be thinking to themselves, ought to flow to them naturally. It doesn't. Mr. Richardson would have had an easier time running for the Board of Supervisors of Harvard College. But he might not have won there either. The whole world has changed. And really over a very short time.[75]

Despite his ethnic "breakthrough," Shamie lost the general election to Democrat John Kerry, thus indicating that realignment in the Bay State had some way to go.

Connecticut

At the state level, one of the Republicans' best performances in 1984 was in Connecticut, where they gained 11 seats in the Senate and 24 in the House to take control of the legislature. With no statewide races intervening, much of this advance could be attributed to the Reagan landslide in Connecticut (the president won

61% of the vote); however, the vitality and competitiveness of the predominantly liberal Connecticut Republicans, in contrast to their Massachusetts brethren, may also have contributed to electoral success.

Massachusetts and Connecticut shared broadly similar political characteristics. Both had long-entrenched patrician Republican political establishments with a liberal tradition, and in each state that establishment was electorally overwhelmed by the mobilization of Roman Catholic ethnic voters into the Democratic party (and also, in Connecticut, by the ending of severe malapportionment in the state legislature).[76] The comments of former Republican gubernatorial candidate and national committeeman John Alsop give some impression of the type of Republicanism that prevailed in the Constitution State as late as the early 1960s:

> We had a group of very good leaders—liberal, but worthy Yankees. I was one of them. However, it was hard for the melting pot population to identify with us. . . . The last legislature which I served in was in 1947, and we passed a fair employment practices bill, and state aid to education. The interesting thing about that period is that the state was very well run. We had terrific people putting on hairshirts, doing things that we knew had to be done. We passed the state's first anti-discrimination bill and desegregated the National Guard. That was the sort of party it was then. We looked to the old eastern establishment for leadership. They had a sense of *noblesse oblige* similar to the British system. And like the collapse of the British system, our establishment fell too. . . . The basic thing about Connecticut in those days was that although it was very undemocratic and represensible, the state got good, clean government in terms of personal freedom, administration and opportunity.[77]

Although the Republican establishment of which Alsop spoke did lose its firm grip on Connecticut politics, a comparison between the recent Republican electoral results in that state and Massachusetts is interesting. In Massachusetts the Republicans have only a handful of legislators, one congressman, and a county sheriff. In Connecticut the GOP now controls the state Senate, holds 3 of the state's 6 U.S. House seats, and has held 1 U.S. Senate seat since 1970.

One factor that has contributed to the greater success of the Connecticut party has been their effectiveness in shedding the exclusivist WASP image that has bedeviled the Massachusetts Republicans. In Connecticut the GOP has been quite successful in tapping the Irish and Italian vote by putting forward candidates with similar ethnic backgrounds, such as former Governor Thomas Meskill, former Congressman Lawrence J. DeNardis, and former gubernatorial candidate Lewis Rome.[78] It has also benefited from divisions within the Democratic party, where a split developed between partisans of the old state machine built by John Bailey and "reform" Democrats such as former Congressman Toby Moffett. The Connecticut GOP has, moreover, profited electorally from a reputation for pragmatic moderation, currently represented by the state's Republican congressmen, all of whom were prominent Gypsy Moths (see Chapter 5, p. 186), and principally by the Connecticut GOP's liberal enfant terrible, Senator Lowell P. Weicker.

Weicker's wealthy background is that of the typical New England liberal Republican, but in his first U.S. Senate race in 1970, he won election as a "law-and-order" Republican endorsed by Vice President Agnew. The senator's experience on the Senate Watergate committee, where his voluble indignation at the misdemeanors of the Nixon administration gained him national attention, acted as the catalyst for his transformation into a liberal Republican. Indeed, Weicker was to be the Reagan administration's most persistent liberal critic within the Republican ranks in 1981–4 (see Chapter 5).

At home, Weicker's brand of independent Republican politics has been electorally popular, although among Connecticut's Republican party activists his standing has rarely been so high. Like many other liberal Republicans, Weicker has had an antipathy toward partisanship and has appeared to revel in his strife with the regular party apparatus. Even those Connecticut Republicans in ideological sympathy with the Senator have found his behavior exasperating. According to John Alsop,

Weicker's problem is that he doesn't understand party politics and he doesn't believe in it. That is where he and I have our big difference of opinion. In my view party politics is the only means by which we can protect freedom and have effective government. In the old days practically everybody went uncommitted to the convention, and these were people whose livelihoods depended on the candidates the convention selected. Weicker believes in winning but in the process he has found it to his advantage to disregard or kick around the Republican party.[79]

Weicker's anti-Reagan rhetoric in the Senate earned him opposition from the right in the 1982 Senate primary. New right forces already had Weicker on their target list for 1982, and some elements within the White House appeared to have given at least tacit encouragement to Prescott Bush, the brother of the vice president, to challenge the incumbent in the primary. In the spring of 1982 Bush's prospects of unseating Weicker looked favorable. He had raised a lot of money from new right sources and gained the support of most state party leaders. The then state chairman Ralph E. Capecelatro adopted a neutral attitude which was interpreted as being favorable to Bush. The latter, however, showed little political ability on the stump, and as Weicker counterattacked with polls showing that he was the only Republican who could defeat Toby Moffett, the likely Democratic nominee, Bush's support evaporated. Although Bush won sufficient support to force a primary challenge, his momentum had been broken and he abandoned the race shortly afterwards.[80] In November Weicker ran with full White House and NRSC backing and won a third term with 51% of the vote.

The events of 1982 appeared to portend the development of divisive factionalism within the Connecticut GOP, which could potentially weaken the party as similar conflict had done in Massachusetts. Weicker, however, in contrast to the liberal Republican officeholders in the Bay State, decided to end his deliberate neglect of home-state party politics and reinforce his political base among Connecticut Republicans. While he persisted in emphasizing his differences with the national Republican mainstream on the Senate floor, he used his 1982 victory to secure the state party chair for his campaign manager, Thomas J. D'Amore, and proceeded to enforce his authority over a body that he had regarded with near-contempt for almost a decade. According to Weicker's Special Counsel Steve Moore, "The Senator wants the party to focus less on ideological purity and more on electability."[81] In line with this rediscovery of party "professionalism," Weicker used D'Amore to mend fences with several embittered Republican opponents and to reunify the state party.

Weicker and D'Amore further succeeded in getting the state party's 1984 convention to adopt a rules change enabling Independents to participate in Connecticut's Republican primaries. Aside from enhancing Weicker's own electoral prospects, it was argued that this would expand the party's base of support by including new voters in the selection process. D'Amore refused to support Weicker on a further change that would have abolished the 20% convention-support requirement for a primary challenge, and this proposal was defeated.[82] The original reform package was opposed by national committeeman Alsop, but it was adopted nevertheless by the convention by a vote of 531 to 344.[83] Alsop was supported by a panel of eleven Connecticut political scientists, led by former Ripon activist Professor Howard L. Reiter, who challenged Weicker's arguments in favor of the open primary by pointing out its potential defects:

> The party's registration figures would probably stabilize or drop, because an incentive to join would be lost. Nominees would be less loyal to Republican values because they would have to appeal to non-Republicans in order to get nominated. After all, on most issues unaffiliated are somewhere in between Republicans and Democrats. And maverick candidates would win more often.[84]

Whatever the merits of the criticism of Weicker's open primary from those who believe in strong party politics, there is little doubt that the Weicker-D'Amore brand of Republicanism enjoys considerable popular support in Connecticut. With the increasing professionalization of the southern New England primary electorate engendered by the new high-technology industries and prestigious institutions of higher education in that region, the local Republican party needs support from independent, white-collar suburbanites to carry Connecticut and Massachusetts. According to a recent study of southern New England politics,

> Having largely ignored the Catholic ethnic groups earlier, the GOP has now also forfeited the support of the professionals by articulating a *laissez faire* philosophy that most of them view as antiquated. The Republicans' failure to align their policies with the

interests of this burgeoning new class is readily apparent in the election results.[85]

Weicker's political style is attuned to the social and political attitudes of this sector of the electorate, which recoils from strong partisanship and applauds individualism and independence in political life. Thus the Weicker-D'Amore strategy may well make short-term electoral sense in Connecticut, although the long-term implications for political party structures may be more serious. (After all, opening up partisan primaries to Independents in the name of greater participation could also enhance the influence of the nonpartisan new right and other single-issue groups, as has occurred in other states. Independents were decisive, as we have already seen, in the defeat of Elliot Richardson in Massachusetts in September 1984.)

The success of the Republican party in Connecticut at all levels of government in 1984 appears to have served as a resounding endorsement of the activities of the senator and the state chairman, and was a rare instance of a liberal Republican officeholder's being prepared to use the regular party organization for his own ends. The organizational renewal of the Connecticut GOP, with strong assistance from the national party, also demonstrates how this aspect of the new American party system can actually help liberal Republicans. The contrast with the bitterness and factionalism that pervades the Massachusetts GOP is stark, and if there is to be any revival of liberal Republicanism in American national politics, then party-building efforts in states predisposed toward Republican liberalism, such as Connecticut, are a prerequisite for success.

Conclusion

The period from the re-election of Richard Nixon in 1972 to the re-election of Ronald Reagan in 1984 witnessed the destruction of Republican liberalism as a force within the national Republican party. When Nelson Rockefeller departed from the political scene, there was nothing left to replace his electoral, financial, or organizational base for liberal Republicanism at the national level. As a consequence, Republican liberalism virtually disappeared as an important factor in the presidential equation.

The liberals also fell victim to the vicissitudes of the American electorate. Its increasing conservatism during the 1970s, particularly on questions of economic and social policy, was exploited effectively by Republican conservatives, whose demands for an end to "big government" and "social engineering" now found receptive ears. Reform of the presidential nominating process and the long-term transformation of the party system in general confirmed the extirpation of the liberal Republicans from presidential politics. The proliferation of presidential primary elections ended the influence of state and local party leaders over national politics, and gave a more influential role to the media, candidates' organizations, and the ideological activists of the right. By organizing an effective network of think tanks, journals, PACs, direct-mail specialists, and campaigning organizations, the right wing was far better equipped than were the liberals to deliver the vote in low-turnout primary elections.

Some liberal influence remained. Anderson's early showings in the 1980 primaries indicated at least some electoral support for liberal Republican ideas, and liberal Republicans continued to survive at the congressional level (as we shall see in the next chapter) as a result of the different dynamics of congressional elections and the more successful adaptation to the requirements of the new politics on the part of Republican candidates. There were still important politicians who called themselves moderate or progressive Republicans in the early 1980s, and they still accounted for some 15 U.S. senators, 30 congressmen, and almost all of the party's incumbent governors. Electoral necessities in states such as Connecticut still demanded a liberal on the ticket for any prospect of Republican success. Yet, unless these electorally attractive individuals could somehow be welded into a cohesive force with a national constituency, their role in presidential politics was likely to remain limited.

5

Liberal Republicans in Congress, 1932 to 1984

The congressional Republican party has traditionally been regarded as a conservative bastion. Republicans in Congress during the 1940–52 period generally supported Senator Taft, while the strength of the liberal wing of the party was felt at the quadrennial national convention and among the governors of the major states. It has already been shown how the presidential Republican party ceased to be a base of support for liberals. In the contemporary Republican party, the more liberal element—perhaps rather surprisingly—relies on the Congress, and particularly the Senate, as its main area of support in the national government. The roles of the presidential and congressional parties have been reversed, and Republican presidents in recent times have been more susceptible to conservative influence, while Republicans in Congress have tended to act as a moderating influence on policy.

In this chapter I attempt to account for this development by examining changes within the Republican party in both houses of Congress from the New Deal to the present. The part played by organizations such as the Wednesday Group, and the extent to which they succeeded in coordinating Republican liberals into an important force within Congress, will also be considered. Finally, in order to assess the extent of liberal Republican influence in Congress in recent times, I will examine the status and behavior of Republican liberals in the House and Senate during the first Reagan administration.

The Republican Party in Congress, 1920 to 1960

The Republican congressional majority of the 1920s was divided between the progressive senators of the Great Plains and the West and the more conservative eastern business wing. The diffuse and fragmented nature of power in Congress after the downfall of the "strong Speaker" system in 1910, together with the East-West division within the GOP, precluded the adoption by congressional Republicans of positive policy initiatives, and a complacent attitude prevailed.[1] A look at the regional distribution of Republican House and Senate seats in 1924 (see Table 5-1) reveals a congressional party based predominantly in the northeastern and midwestern states. In the Senate the Mountain and Pacific regions were somewhat better represented, but the Republican majority was firmly grounded in the American heartland, as opposed to the peripheral areas of the West and South.

TABLE 5-1.   Regional Distribution of Republican Seats in Congress, 1924–1980

Region	1924	1936	1948	1960	1972	1982
Senate:						
South and Border	9%	0%	5%	11%	28%	26%
New England/ Mid-Atlantic	30	50	33	37	26	18
Midwest/Plains	37	25	43	34	21	24
Mountain/Pacific	24	25	19	17	26	32
House:						
South and Border	9%	4%	4%	7%	22%	26%
New England/ Mid-Atlantic	38	50	37	34	24	22
Midwest/Plains	42	37	44	24	36	29
Mountain/Pacific	11	8	15	15	18	23

Source: Norman J. Ornstein, Thomas E. Mann, Michael J. Malbin, Allen Schick, and John F. Bibby, *Vital Statistics on Congress 1984–1985* (Washington, DC: AEI, 1984).

The impact of the New Deal was disastrous for the Republican party in Congress. Initially the Republican leadership in the House and Senate—Representative Snell of New York and Senator Mc-Nary of Oregon—supported Roosevelt's relief measures in the financial crisis of 1933.[2] Yet bipartisan harmony was ephemeral, and by the mid-1930s congressional Republicans (urged on by ex–President Hoover and RNC Chairman Fletcher) were attacking FDR as a "traitor to his class."[3] As their numbers sank to 16 senators and 89 representatives by 1937, however, congressional Republicans became a negligible force in opposing the Democratic administration until Roosevelt's court-packing plan of 1937 at last provided them with an opportunity to oppose FDR effectively.[4] The court-packing fracas also acted as the catalyst for the birth of the famed conservative coalition of Republicans and southern conservative Democrats, which predominated in Congress after 1938.[5] Republicans could usually be relied upon to join with the southerners in impeding liberal interventionist policies at home and abroad, and until the Democratic landslide of 1958, the coalition had a firm hold on Capitol Hill.

Apart from this *de facto* influence, the Republicans enjoyed two brief periods of *de jure* ascendancy from 1938 to 1958. The GOP controlled the Congresses elected in 1946 and 1952, although in both cases they lost control at the succeeding congressional election. Leadership of the Republicans in Congress during this period came principally from three figures: Taft, the Republican leader on domestic policy in the Senate; Arthur Vandenberg, Chairman of the Senate Foreign Relations Committee; and House Speaker Joseph Martin of Massachusetts.[6] While there were obvious tensions within the leadership—Vandenberg became a convinced internationalist on foreign policy, while Taft remained fundamentally isolationist—the general tone of Republican rhetoric remained overwhelmingly conservative, notwithstanding Taft's initiatives in the fields of housing policy and education. American labor was particularly incensed by the Taft-Hartley Act of 1947, which restricted union privileges, and President Truman made great political capital from the fact that measures endorsed by the 1948 Republican platform, such as broadened civil rights, inflation control, and the minimum wage, had all been blocked in the Republican-controlled Eightieth Congress.

In the second Republican-controlled Congress of 1953–4, conservative predominance was maintained, although by this time the GOP was burdened by the increasingly embarrassing activities of Senator McCarthy, whom the Senate leadership and the White House appeared either unwilling or unable to control. Republicans in the Eighty-third Congress loyally supported the first Republican president since 1933, illustrating that Eisenhower was by no means a particularly liberal president in the domestic sphere. According to Gary Reichard,

> The strong backing which congressional Republicans gave to the President deflates the argument that Eisenhower presented a program more appealing to Democrats than to his own party. Indeed the striking contrast between the degrees of support from the two parties indicates that the administration program of 1953–4 was solidly Republican. Only in foreign policy (where Eisenhower was admittedly tugging the Republicans in a new direction) and welfare policy (where he attempted some "middle-way" measures) did Democrats support the President nearly to the extent that Republicans did.[7]

Strong support for the Eisenhower administration did not benefit the Republicans, however, and they lost control of both houses in 1954. Two years later, despite Eisenhower's landslide re-election as president, with 57% of the popular vote, they were unable to regain control. In 1958 they suffered an electoral disaster in the midterm elections, losing 47 House seats and 13 in the Senate. Eisenhower's popularity did not extend to his party, which—in Congress at least—still appeared both antiquated and irrelevant.

The ouster of Joseph Martin from the House leadership in 1959 demonstrated some restiveness within the Republican ranks, although it was based on Martin's leadership style rather than on policy grounds. The Republican insurgents of 1959 were disenchanted by the poor election results of 1958, and, moreover, distrusted Martin's close relationship with Democratic Speaker Sam Rayburn. But the heart of the discontent with the minority leader lay in his relegation of the House Republican Policy Committee to a state of inactivity.[8] According to one disgruntled House member, the committee was ". . . more a debating society—a more or less academic procedure to endorse Joe's decisions."[9] Martin's successor, Republican Whip Charles Halleck, was a colorless member of the Republican Old Guard, but he did pledge to separate the posts of Minority Leader and Policy Committee Chairman. This hardly seemed to constitute a long-term solution to the Republican problem in the House, and Halleck's Senate counterpart, Everett Dirksen of Illinois, although a superb parliamentarian, was equally bereft of imagination or new ideas with which to regenerate the Republican party in Congress.

Prior to concluding this brief sketch of the congressional Republican party from 1933 to 1960, its geographical and ideological composition in the late 1950s should be examined more closely (see Tables 5-1 and 5-2). The regional distribution of the GOP had not altered a great deal since 1924, and in 1960 most Republican senators and congressmen still came from the northeastern and midwestern regions. In terms of voting patterns within Congress, Barbara Sinclair found that the Republicans adopted the

TABLE 5-2.   Republican Party Strength in Congress by Region

Region	1948	1960	1972	1982
Senate:				
South	0%	0%	32%	50%
Border	20	40	50	30
New England	75	58	42	50
Mid-Atlantic	62	75	62	50
Midwest	80	30	40	40
Plains	83	75	42	75
Mountain	25	25	56	69
Pacific	67	20	40	60
House:				
South	2%	6%	32%	29%
Border	12	16	23	24
New England	61	50	36	33
Mid-Atlantic	51	51	46	42
Midwest	56	59	61	45
Plains	84	84	67	50
Mountain	25	27	58	65
Pacific	62	49	42	38

Source: Ornstein et al., *Vital Statistics on Congress 1984–1985.*

TABLE 5-3.　Mean Republican Support in Congress on Selected
Issue Areas[a]

Congresses	All Democrats	All Republicans	Northeastern Republicans
Government management of the economy:			
83–86 (1953–60)	85%	13%	14%
87–90 (1961–68)	85	17	25
91–94 (1969–76)	70	25	39
Social welfare:			
80–82 (1947–52)	64%	16%	20%
83–86 (1953–60)	72	33	43
87–90 (1961–68)	76	33	43
Civil liberties:			
84–86 (1955–60)	55%	62%	76%
87–90 (1961–68)	53	42	54
91–94 (1969–76)	59	40	56

International involvement:

Congresses	All Democrats	All Republicans	Northeastern Republicans	Pacific Republicans	Interior[b] Republicans
76–82 (1939–52)	88%	43%	62%	58%	25%
83–86 (1953–60)	69	61	87	74	41
87–90 (1961–69)	77	40	64	39	29
91–94 (1969–76)	64	52	73	52	36

[a] Issue areas are based on issue clusters discovered by Clausen and Sinclair. Party influence is assessed by the correlation between the party and the scores of individual members of Congress. The influence of region is determined by multiple-regression analysis within each party.
[b] Excludes the South.

Source: Adapted from tables in Barbara Sinclair, *Congressional Realignment 1925–78* (Austin, TX: University of Texas Press, 1978).

more conservative position on three of her four issue areas during the Eisenhower years.[10] Her results (shown in Table 5-3) indicated, however, that northeastern Republicans were more likely than the party as a whole to support liberal positions on civil rights, social welfare, and international involvement. In the area of government management of the economy, the northeasterners did not deviate substantially from the Republicans as a whole in their low level of support. One of Sinclair's more interesting findings is that Republicans in the late 1950s were still predominantly supporters of civil rights legislation. This reflected the party's Lincolnian heritage, but northeastern Republicans were again significantly more favorable to civil liberties than were congressional Republicans as a whole. The northeastern Republicans were thus becoming the deviant group within the GOP, as opposed to during the 1920s and 1930s, when they had been in the stalwart mainstream.[11]

With lackluster leadership that failed to make any significant national impact and a crisis in policy direction, congressional Republicans were not particularly impressive or effective in the late 1950s. Conflict with the Democrats and partisanship gained them little but contempt from the wider public. On the other hand, cooperation with the Democrats, as practiced by Joe Martin, did not gain them anything of substance either. The public image of reaction that they conveyed was still damaging electorally, although the congressional Republicans were almost certainly more conservative in style than in substance. Republican liberals were generally ineffective and noninfluential, tending to act as isolated individuals rather than as party leaders. In the decade of the 1960s considerable efforts would be made by congressional Republicans to address some of these problems. The following section will assess how successful these efforts were to be.

Years of Unrest: Congressional Republicans, 1960 to 1980

The 1960s were years of ferment in the ranks of Republicans in Congress. The deposition of Joseph Martin was a harbinger of that unrest, and there was wide agreement between both liberal and conservative Republicans that the party as a whole was failing to provide constructive or effective opposition to Kennedy's New Frontier. To meet this problem, Republican liberals in the House formed the Wednesday Group as a forum for discussion and coordination among like-minded Republicans in that chamber. In the Senate, the 1960s saw an influx of younger liberals, whose influence will also be considered in this section. Overall however, these were years of lost opportunities for Republican liberals in Congress as elsewhere.

One key vote that indicated the divisions within the Republican ranks in the early 1960s concerned President Kennedy's proposal to reform the House Rules Committee. The conservative coalition had a firm grip on this important committee, which determined whether legislation reached the floor of the House for debate. Kennedy's proposal to expand the membership of the committee as a means of overcoming the conservative majority was opposed by the House Republican leadership, but 21 Republicans voted for the proposal and proved decisive in its passage. According to the veteran Massachusetts Republican Congressman Silvio O. Conte,

> Twenty one of us liberal Republicans voted in favor of expanding the committee, and that was the key thing that started the Wednesday Group. . . . At the time we felt that we were like skunks at a lawn party, so we might as well stink together.[12]

John V. Lindsay (a New York congressman at the time) also emphasized the importance of the Rules Committee vote in the founding of the Wednesday Group:

> Two years later, under the Kennedy administration, we had a showdown vote on expansion of the Rules Committee. A handful of Republicans broke ranks and voted to expand the committee—about 12. The Republican leadership were incensed and they took steps to retaliate. Bradford Morse of Massachusetts was blackballed by the Acorns and other established clubs. So a small group of us founded the Wednesday Group.[13]

The group formally came into existence in 1963, the principal instigators being six very junior House Republicans—Lindsay (New York), Morse (Massachusetts) Sibal (Connecticut), Tupper (Maine), Ellsworth (Kansas), and Mathias (Maryland)—who lacked the seniority and ideological soundness necessary for advancement in the House Republican hierarchy.[14] Even at the beginning, there were some doubts as to whether the Wednesday Group should be an exclusively liberal Republican group. An analysis of its membership in the early years (1963–7) reveals that some members could hardly be described as liberal Republicans, although there was a clear bias toward the more liberal northeastern states.[15] There was no clear view of what exactly the group's role was intended to be, and over the years the group became less liberal in its orientation and more concerned with providing various services to its members. However, in the early days some members believed that it might be able to provide a crucial bloc vote in the House Republican Conference.

The discontent of the Wednesday Group members with the leadership was shared by a broader group of younger House Republicans, the Young Turks. Like the members of the Wednesday Group, these were junior House Republicans frustrated by the GOP's continuing minority position in the chamber, but ideologically the Young Turks inclined more to the conservative side, although some liberals were also associated with the group.[16] What united this disparate band was general discontent with the inadequate levels of staffing and support services for the House Republican minority (a discontent shared equally with the Wednesday Group members) and the desire for more positive leadership than that being provided by Minority Leader Halleck and his deputy Les Arends.[17] According to Charles Goodell, their aim was to offer "constructive alternatives to Democratic proposals, rather than merely saying 'no' like Dirksen and Halleck."[18]

> We were unhappy that the House Republican Policy Committee was not really representative of the House Republican membership. 50% of House Republicans had been elected in the previous six years but they had virtually no representation on the Policy Committee. We felt that the Republicans should come up with alternative programs to those of the Kennedy Administration. We put up a number of "Quie-dell" bills on Education for instance.[19]

The Young Turks concluded that the leadership would have to be challenged directly. The first major rebellion came in January 1963, when they ran Michigan Republican Gerald Ford against the Chairman of the House Republican Conference, Charles Hoeven of Kansas, a rigid Old Guard Republican. Ford's victory—organized by Griffin and Goodell—was an ominous sign for Halleck.[20] The direct challenge to his leadership eventually came after the 1964 Republican election debacle:

In November 1964, after the election, Griffin and I met with Ford. We urged him to announce early that he was running against Halleck. In early December 1964 the campaign was announced at a press conference. After a month's campaign we won by 73 votes to 67. We made a big point of the fact that there was no way we could win if we made the Ford-Halleck contest a liberal versus conservative matter. Some of the fifteen or so liberals openly supported Halleck.[21]

The Wednesday Group mounted its challenge in the balloting for the positions of Conference Chairman and Party Whip. In the former contest the group ran Peter Frelinghuysen of New Jersey, an old fashioned patrician liberal, against conservative Melvin Laird, who proceeded to defeat Frelinghuysen by 77 votes to 62. The vote for Party Whip saw the indefatigable Frelinghuysen (with the support of Gerald Ford) challenging the veteran incumbent Leslie Arends of Illinois, but the liberal candidate was once more defeated by 70 votes to 59. These contests served only to illustrate the Republican liberals' weakness and indiscipline. According to Peabody,

> Little attempt seems to be made by conservatives, who outnumber liberals by six or seven to one, to tolerate dissent or elect liberals to the party leadership. If the activities of the Wednesday Club [sic] in a series of contests taking place at the opening of the 89th Congress were at all characteristic, liberals have seldom been cohesive enough to form a balance of power between personal or sectional interests within the predominantly conservative Republican ranks.[22]

These results suggested that the Wednesday Group was too ill-defined and structurally loose to exert much influence over the House Republican leadership. Although the group included some of the more capable House Republicans, the leadership and the conference as a whole tended to regard the group as a cabal or a liberal conspiracy. In order to allay these fears, the group deemphasized ideology and became more oriented toward pragmatic activities, such as research on legislation and reports on the business of various House committees. After being badly burned in the 1964–65 leadership contests, it did not again engage in open challenges to the party hierarchy.

Liberal Republicans in the House were still in a very weak position in the mid-1960s. The overall thrust of the Young Turk revolt had been supported by most liberals, but that insurgency had been primarily conservative and more concerned with vigorous opposition to the Democrats, while the liberals sought to be more conciliatory. This again illustrates the dilemma of the self-proclaimed "moderate" in two-party politics, who often finds himself more in agreement with moderate members of the opposite party than with many of his partisan allies. The assault of consensus politics and the status quo from all directions during the 1960s only made the Republican liberals feel this dilemma more keenly.

The smaller numbers and less hierarchical nature of the Senate gave liberal Republican senators more opportunity for influence in that chamber. In the elections of 1966 and 1968 Republican liberals gained considerable ground in the Senate with the election of Charles Percy, Richard Schweiker, Mark Hatfield, Robert Packwood, Edward Brooke, William Saxbe, and Charles Mathias. The influence of this group was crucial in the election of Hugh Scott of Pennsylvania to succeed Everett Dirksen as Minority Leader in 1969. Scott had already defeated Roman Hruska of Nebraska in the contest for party Whip in 1968 (although Dirksen preferred Hruska), and his success came in spite of the fact that only a handful of Republican senators, led by Jacob Javits, had more liberal voting records.[23] Seniority counted for more than ideology in the contest to succeed Dirksen for the leadership, in which Scott was opposed by the more conservative, but more junior, Howard Baker of Tennessee. The fact that Scott had been a loyal Nixon supporter in early 1969 helped him shed some of his eastern establishment image, and he also used the advantages of incumbency to good effect. According to a conservative Scott supporter,

He did not conduct himself as an eastern establishment liberal. First and foremost he was a Republican Senator and a loyal supporter of the President's program.[24]

This helped Scott win the votes of 6 conservative senators. Of the moderate-liberal bloc he lost only Cook (Kentucky) and Packwood (Oregon) in his 23 to 20 victory, and won the votes of all 13 eastern Republican senators. Scott confirmed his victory in 1971

TABLE 5-4.   Republican Ideological Divisions in Congress, 1970–1984[a]

Ideology	91st Congress, 1969–70	94th Congress, 1975–76	97th Congress, 1982 session	98th Congress, 1984 session
Senate:				
Fundamentalist	17 (40%)	16 (42%)	31 (57%)	35 (64%)
Stalwart	10 (23)	10 (26)	11 (20)	12 (22)
Moderate	7 (16)	3 (7)	6 (11)	7 (13)
Progressive	9 (21)	9 (24)	6 (11)	1 (2)
Total	43	38	54	55
House:				
Fundamentalist	72 (38%)	71 (49%)	95 (49%)	112 (67%)
Stalwart	48 (25)	48 (33)	59 (31)	35 (21)
Moderate	44 (23)	15 (10)	23 (12)	13 (8)
Progressive	25 (13)	11 (7)	14 (7)	8 (5)
Total	189	145	191	168

[a] The ideological classifications are those used by Reichley, and are based on the *Congressional Quarterly*'s annual Conservative Coalition scores, as follows: Fundamentalist = 81% or greater support for the coalition; Stalwart = 61–80% support; Moderate = 41–60% support; Progressive = under 40% support.

Sources: Reichley, *Conservatives in an Age of Change,* Chapter 2; *Congressional Quarterly Almanac, 1982* (Washington, D.C.: Congressional Quarterly, Inc., 1983), and *Congressional Quarterly Almanac, 1984* (Washington, D.C.: Congressional Quarterly Inc., 1985).

by defeating Baker again, this time by 24 votes to 20. The fact that the stalwart grip on the Senate Republican leadership had been broken gives some indication of the liberal influence within the Senate Republican Conference during Nixon's first administration.[25]

The difference between the numbers of liberal Republicans in the House and Senate, which was minimal in 1970, became more pronounced during the following decade (see Table 5-4), yet the reasons for this development were not immediately obvious.[26] John Lindsay suggests one explanation:

To make a career in the House, it is best if you are compatible with the mainstream of your party. It's very exhausting to be seen as a maverick all the time, and it's not very effective for your district. It is very difficult for a Congressman when he's constantly isolated from the power structure. In the Senate it's a little easier because you have a statewide base, but even there it is getting more dangerous.[27]

The size of their constituencies and the different natures of Senate and House electorates might also have contributed to the liberal decline in the latter chamber. House districts and primary electorates are generally more socially and politically homogeneous and can be held by appealing to hard-core party identifiers in many instances. By contrast, winning and holding a Senate seat more often involves appealing to more ideologically and socially heterogeneous electorates, and statewide primary elections are more visible. Thus liberal candidates can most easily survive Senate primaries because of broader electoral participation, and in general elections their moderation, pragmatism, and independence have tended to be strong assets.

One final consideration regarding this point is the effect of the geographical realignment of electoral forces in the United States. It has already been stressed that since the 1930s the liberal Republicans have been strongest in the northeastern quadrant of the country. Population changes have entailed an overall shift of House seats from this region to the South and West, as the Republicans have been winning fewer and fewer races in the Northeast. In the Senate the variations in constituency size and the fixed geographical limits of the states have helped to conceal this shift, which meant that many fewer liberal Republicans could be elected to the House as formerly Republican districts became Democratic in the 1960–80 period, and particularly in the landslide years of 1964 and 1974 (see Table 5-2).

President Nixon's uneasy relationship with Republican liberals on the ABM, busing, the Haynsworth and Carswell nominations, Cambodia, and the War Powers Act has already been discussed. These issues gained the liberals little electorally, however, and their gradual decline in numbers was not arrested. Gerald Ford's use of the presidential veto as his main legislative strategy was generally supported by congressional Republicans. Ford vetoed sixty-six bills in his two-and-a-half years in the White House, and all but twelve of these were sustained in Congress. He did have

some failures: In July 1975 his veto of the Education Appropriations Bill for 1976 was overridden in the House, with only 27 Republican fundamentalists and 9 stalwarts voting to sustain it, and
Congress also cut off American aid to South Vietnam and to the
Angolan guerillas.[28]

During the Carter years the Republicans were able to present a
reasonably united front against the Democratic administration. But
there were tensions and long-term ideological and geographical
shifts underlying this prima facie unity. Geographically the party in
Congress mirrored the national party in becoming ever more southern and western, while losing its former strength in the Northeast
and Midwest (see Tables 5-1 and 5-2). On the whole gamut of issue
areas, ranging from social welfare to international affairs, northeastern Republicans were becoming more and more divergent from
the Republican Conference as a whole (see Table 5-3). The most
interesting change from the 1950s was in the area of civil liberties.
The decline in Republican support for such legislation became no-
ticeable in the mid-1960s, when the focus of civil rights legislation
began to move from political rights to questions of economic rights,
which placed demands on the GOP's suburban, middle-class, and
business constituency.[29] The increasing willingness of Republicans
at the national level to court southern conservative white Democratic voters and exploit the white backlash in the North also probably had an effect on congressional attitudes on this matter. The
trends in Republican voting on the various issue dimensions during
the 1960–78 period are summarized by Barbara Sinclair (see Table 5–3):

> During the 1920s and throughout most of the 1930s, northeastern-
> ers were the conservative mainstay of the Republican party; mem-
> bers from the West–North Central states were the most likely to
> defect. By the mid-1940s, the latter group no longer deviated from
> the Republican opposition stance on government management or
> social welfare issues, but continued to defect on agricultural assis-
> tance legislation. Northeasterners, by the early 1950s, had become
> the most deviant section of the Republican party on social welfare,
> and in the 1960s and 1970s, this deviance was extended to govern-
> ment management issues. As Republican support on civil liberties
> began to decline in the late 1950s, a regional split developed, with
> northeasterners providing significantly more support than their

party colleagues from other areas. This split intensifies in the 1960s and continues in a somewhat milder form in the 1970s. The decline in mean Republican support also continues. By the mid-1970s, southern Democrats are more supportive on the civil liberties dimension than the Republicans.[30]

William Shaffer's findings from an analysis of Americans for Democratic Action (ADA) scores in Congress (see Table 5-5) further indicated that the two major parties had become more ideologically homogeneous and distinct since the mid-1960s, this distinctiveness extending to all regions of the country:

Certainly there are still a few liberal and moderate Republicans but their presence cannot be taken seriously, at least not when describing the prevailing philosophical orientation of the GOP.[31]

TABLE 5-5.   Average ADA Ratings by Party and by Region in Congress, 1965–1976[a]

Region	Democrat (mean, 1965–76)	Republican (mean, 1965–76)	Difference (mean, 1965–76)
House:			
All	56	17	39
Northeast	77	31	46
South	21	4	17
Border	49	19	30
Midwest	75	15	60
Mountain	57	9	48
Far West	78	13	65
Senate:			
All	58	27	31
Northeast	84	55	29
South	21	5	16
Border	64	32	32
Midwest	81	17	64
Mountain	59	7	52
Far West	73	42	31

[a] ADA scores measure votes of members of Congress on key issues and range from 0 (conservative) to 100 (liberal).

Source: William R. Shaffer, *Party and Ideology in the United States Congress* (Washington, DC: University Press of America, 1980).

The shift to the right was reflected in the House of Representatives as the conservative Republicans began to organize in response to what they termed "Nixon's move to the left" in 1971, particularly his Family Assistance Plan (FAP), the Child Development Act, the introduction of wage and price controls, and détente with the USSR. The House Republican leadership—Ford, Arends, and Conference Chairman John Anderson—all supported FAP, which passed the House in April 1970 (the plan was subsequently defeated in the Senate Finance Committee). However, the main opponents of the FAP on the Republican side—Phil Crane (Illinois), Edward Derwinski (Illinois), and John Ashbrook (Ohio)–used this occasion to found the Republican Study Committee (RSC).[32] Modeled on the Democratic Study Group of liberal Democrats, the RSC sought to coordinate the legislative activities of conservative Republicans, reach out to the academic community, and get involved in electoral activity.[33] According to Edwin Feulner, the former RSC staff director,

> The primary reason for the foundation of the Republican Study Committee was to give conservatives a more immediate and coordinated impact on the legislative activities of the House of Representatives.[34]

By 1981, 80% of House Republicans were members—a mark of the extent of conservative influence within the House GOP.

In the Senate, Senator Carl Curtis of Nebraska founded the Steering Committee for similar reasons. Its aim was to try to increase the influence of conservatives in that chamber. In its early days this committee had only four or five senators attending its weekly meetings. It was revitalized, however, when North Carolina Republican Jesse Helms became chairman in 1981, with attendance rising to some twenty-five to thirty senators. The committee had a staff of four, answerable to the chairman.[35]

The growth of conservative ideological groupings in both houses of Congress was symptomatic of the decline of the authority of the party leadership in both chambers and in many states and districts. Members of Congress became less dependent on the party organization and resources in getting elected, and instead relied more on personal organization, campaign consultants, and donations from Political Action Committees. Since senators and representatives relied less on the party leadership in Congress for their electoral survival, maintaining links to ideological or single-issue groups, paying attention to constituent services, maintaining name visibility, and securing access to funds became far more important. As was mentioned in Chapter 4, the new right was far more adept at playing this new congressional election game than were the party regulars or the liberals. The defeats of Clifford Case and Jacob Javits in Senate primaries, and the harassment of House Conference Chairman Anderson, were examples of conservative influence over Republican primary electorates, although in the case of Javits and Case there were mitigating factors, such as age and infirmity, that contributed to their defeats. The considerable electoral resources of the new right further discouraged Republican liberals even from entering primary elections, since they had not developed an equivalent network of PACs to serve their interests. Single-issue and ideological politics thrives on polarizing issues that have the power to mobilize large numbers of voters and dollars. Pragmatic, centrist politics rarely arouses such intensity of political commitment.

The 1970s, then, witnessed an apparent transition in congressional Republican politics away from the stalwart-liberal axis toward the fundamentalist rights. The new right constructed an impressive electoral network for use in congressional elections, and found the fragmentation of power within Congress conducive to their aggressive, negativistic style of politics. Nevertheless, liberal Republicans were still being elected to Congress even in the banner conservative year 1980 (see Table 5-5). In the Senate there were still enough liberals to exert some influence over the leadership and to play an active part in formulating policy. In the House, by contrast, the prospects for liberals were grim as their numbers continued to dwindle, and with the departure of John Anderson they became more remote than ever from the House leadership.

Liberal Republicans in the Ninety-Seventh and Ninety-Eighth Congresses

The 1980 election results in the United States were perceived by many as a triumph for conservative Republicanism. The Republicans gained 12 Senate seats and 33 House seats, and most of the publicity given to these gains was concerned with the apparent success of the new right PACs in defeating incumbent liberal Democrats and replacing them with right-wing Republicans. In 1970–84 the strength of the fundamentalist element within the Republican party in the Senate increased from 40% to 64% (see Table 5-1) and in the House from 38% to 67% (Table 5-4). The regional distribution of Republican seats in both chambers also continued to change. Tables 5-1 and 5-2 show that, in Congress, the GOP became ever more southern- and western-based, reinforcing the movement to the right among Republicans in Congress, and leaving the liberals in the vulnerable position of representing areas where the GOP was in electoral decline. This last factor would be important in the development of the Gypsy Moth movement, to be discussed later (see pp. 186–188).

This section, however, should impress upon the reader that reports of the death of the Republican liberals in the early 1980s were somewhat exaggerated. While it is true that there were fewer out-and-out liberals or progressives among congressional Republicans, a moderate element survived within the Republican Conference in both chambers. The Gypsy Moth insurgency influenced policy in the House of Representatives and the Wednesday Group still thrived there. In the Senate, liberal Republicans obstructed the new right's "social agenda" and came to play an increasing role in determining the direction of economic policy. Examining each chamber in turn, I shall now discuss how the Republican liberals were able to defend their position, and why they have remained a force among congressional Republicans.

The Senate

The conservatism of Reagan has had a dampening effect on moderate tendencies. Moderates tend to be more quietly persuasive of their point of view. The big contradiction to this is when you find people like Lowell Weicker standing up and shouting that this won't do. They also tend to get very upset about attempts to tamper with the Constitution. In the intensity of their opposition on these matters, they've been very effective, and they've stopped each one of these

> social issues from passing the Senate even though the Pres-
> ident has wholeheartedly supported their passage.
> Senator Richard Lugar[36]

In 1981 the Republicans in the Senate—controlling the chamber for the first time since 1955—achieved an extremely high level of party unity (Table 5-6). Republican senators voted unanimously on 30% of the votes taken between January and August of that year. On 67% of those votes only 5 or fewer Republican senators defected, and on the 101 recorded Senate votes on which a majority of Republicans lined up against a majority of Democrats, the average Republican lined up with a majority of his party 84% of the time.[37]

Much of the credit for this high degree of Republican cohesion was given to Senate Majority Leader Howard Baker. The majority leader's genial manner and accessibility to Republican colleagues

TABLE 5-6.   Support for Party on Votes in Congress[a]

Year	Senate		House	
	Democrat	*Republican*	*Democrat*	*Republican*
1970	71	71	71	72
1971	74	75	72	76
1972	72	73	70	76
1973	79	74	75	74
1974	72	68	72	71
1975	76	71	75	78
1976	74	72	75	75
1977	72	75	74	77
1978	75	66	71	77
1979	76	73	75	79
1980	76	74	78	79
1981	77	85	75	80
1982	76	80	77	76
1983	76	79	82	80
1984	68	78	74	71

[a] The percentage of members voting with a majority of their party on party unity votes, i.e., roll calls on which a majority of one party votes on one side of the issue and a majority of the other party votes on the other side.

Sources: Ornstein et al., *Vital Statistics on Congress, 1982; Congressional Quarterly Almanac 1984.*

regardless of ideology appear to have been significant factors in Republican legislative successes. The following statements by liberal Republican senators, who were among the most persistent defectors, give some impression of Baker's general popularity:

> *Senator Mark Andrews:* "Who could disagree with an individual as genial as Howard Baker?"[38]

> *Senator William S. Cohen:* "I think that the high cohesiveness of the Senate Republicans is due to Howard Baker and Paul Laxalt. They have been the key to holding the GOP together. I feel that you've got to give the credit to Baker."[39]

> *Senator Charles Mathias:* "The Republicans have done well in running the Senate, and much of the credit for that must go to Howard Baker."[40]

Baker's task was facilitated by the close ties to the legislative branch the Reagan administration had cultivated in its early days.[41] The Reagan White House decided early in 1981 to give priority to the administration's budget and tax proposals; and fundamentalist Republican senators eager for debate on controversial legislation such as constitutional amendments on abortion, busing, and school prayer were assuaged by promises of action on these matters at a later date.[42] In keeping the Republican coalition in Congress together, the Reagan administration relied to a large extent on Reagan's personal friend, Senator Laxalt of Nevada, who served as liaison between the Senate and House leadership, the White House, and the Republican National Committee, of which he became General Chairman in 1983. The creation of this office was a clear attempt to coordinate the separate elements of the Republican national party.

Tables 5-6 and 5-7 show a diminishing level of Republican unity and a rise in Republican opposition to the Reagan administration in the Senate from 1981 to 1983. After spectacular success in passing the 1981 package of tax and expenditure reductions—on which the Senate Republicans were generally united—divisions emerged on a range of issues.[43] On some Senate committees Republican dissenters allied with the Democrats to obstruct administration proposals. This happened most frequently on Labor and Human Resources, where Senators Weicker and Stafford frequently joined

TABLE 5-7.   Presidential Opposition Scores in Congress, 1981–1983
(by Region)[a]

Year	All Republicans	East	Midwest	South	West
Senate:					
1981	15%	21%	16%	11%	11%
1982	21	31	19	17	18
1983	22	27	20	23	20
1984	18	30	19	10	14
House:					
1981	26%	31%	29%	22%	21%
1982	27	35	30	23	18
1983	25	35	25	22	19
1984	33	40	33	30	28

a The scores show the percentage of times Republican congressmen from each of the four regions voted against the Reagan position. Northeast: New England/Mid-Atlantic and West Virginia. Midwest: Midwest/Plains. South: The Old Confederacy, Oklahoma, and Kentucky. West: Mountain/Pacific.

Source: Congressional Quarterly Almanacs 1981–1984.

the Democrats in opposing the fundamentalist Republican chairman Orrin Hatch. In the area of national security Senators Andrews, Durenberger, Hatfield, Stafford, and Weicker opposed the administration's position on MX missile development; on an amendment prohibiting the production of nerve gas, seventeen Republicans defected; and during the confirmation hearings on Kenneth Adelman to head the Arms Control and Disarmament Agency, the nominee was opposed by Senators Andrews, Gorton, Mathias, and Pressler.[44]

New right Republicans found the four-year period of Republican rule in the Senate particularly frustrating. In 1981 Senator Helms secured passage of legislation restricting school-busing orders by federal courts, but the proposal only passed after an extensive filibuster by Connecticut Republican Lowell Weicker and died in the House. An attempt by the Judiciary Committee to secure passage of an anti-abortion constitutional amendment failed (with 19 Republicans voting against), and efforts to weaken the extension of the 1965 Voting Rights Act were blocked when Senators Baker and Dole worked with Democrats to fashion a compromise proposal that ran counter to the earlier position of the Reagan administration. In the spring of 1984, a Reagan-backed constitutional amendment (also supported by Majority Leader Baker) permitting organized prayer in public schools fell 11 votes short of the requisite two-thirds majority. Eighteen Republicans were among the 44 who opposed the measure, and the major adversary of the Senate leadership was again Senator Weicker. In brief, the failure of the new right's social agenda to pass the Senate can be attributed to the reluctance of a determined minority of some 15–20 Republican senators to accept fundamentalist positions on these matters.[45]

Even on economic policy Republican unity began to break down as the federal budget deficit increased (an increase due in large part, to Reagan's combination of tax cuts and extensive increases in defense spending in 1981). Deficits in the $200 billion range conflicted with traditional Republican economic doctrine regarding balanced budgets and fiscal responsibility, and Senator Robert Dole of Kansas—the chairman of the Senate Finance Committee and previously regarded as a conservative Republican—crafted a compromise on the budget for fiscal 1983; a compromise that included a tax increase, thus modifying the 1982 budget resolution. Another outspoken critic of the administration's 1983 budget was Budget Committee Chairman "Pete" Domenici, of New Mexico, who piloted the Dole package through his own committee. In the summer of 1984, some half-dozen Senate Republican liberals supported a Democratic alternative budget that was only defeated by the tie-breaking vote of the Vice President. Eight Republicans also broke ranks by failing to support a deficit-reduction package because they sought greater cuts in military, as opposed to domestic, programs. As the deficit increased, the number of Republican dissidents joining with the liberal Republican core began to rise (see Table 5-8).

Although disquiet over Reagan's economic proposals was widely felt among Senate Republicans, it did not lead to the formation of any legislative group like the Gypsy Moths in the House. Liberals in the Senate already held influential positions—Mark Hatfield chaired the Appropriations Committee, Robert Packwood chaired the Commerce Committee, Robert Stafford the Committee

TABLE 5-8.   Leading Republican Dissidents in the Senate, 1981–1983

1981		1982		1983	
Weicker (Conn.)	38%	Weicker (Conn.)	58%	Specter (Pa.)	54%
Specter (Pa.)	34	Mathias (Md.)	55	Andrews (N.D.)	46
Mathias (Md.)	34	Chafee (R.I.)	50	Weicker (Conn.)	45
Heinz (Pa.)	33	Specter (Pa.)	49	Mathias (Md.)	41
Pressler (S.D.)	32	Heinz (Pa.)	43	Stafford (Vt.)	41
		Durenberger (Mn.)	41	Heinz (Pa.)	38
		Cohen (Me.)	36	Packwood (Ore.)	35
		Stafford (Vt.)	36	Chafee (R.I.)	33
		Packwood (Ore.)	32	Hatfield (Ore.)	33
				Boschwitz (Mn.)	32
				Pressler (S.D.)	31

Source: Congressional Quarterly Almanacs 1981–3.

on the Environment and Public Works, and Charles Percy, Foreign Relations. The Senate has always been a more individualistic chamber than the House, and has thus been more tolerant of party defectors. While, in the lower chamber, ideological or issue groups have frequently been necessary in order for junior members to be heard above the throng, a senator has only to rise from his desk to be heard. In the Senate the formation of permanent and tightly organized groups has traditionally been regarded as unnecessary and unseemly.[46] Nevertheless, some of the former members of the House Wednesday Group—particularly Charles Mathias and Richard Schweiker—tried to form a similar group in the Senate when they were elected to that body in 1968. The notion of a "club within a club" was not particularly well received in the Senate, but the Wednesday Club was established and ultimately developed into a typical Senate group, with little discipline and few commitments:

> Although the club was in no way a tightly organized unit, it did provide a means by which views could be exchanged, positions confirmed and strategies planned.[47]

The Wednesday Club did not attempt to provide comprehensive information or voting cues, nor did it ever have a staff. In the end it became little more than the somewhat derisively named "Wednesday Lunch Bunch."

Relations between Senate liberals and the Reagan administration were generally amicable in spite of disagreements on policy. In contrast to the cold and sometimes abrasive behavior of the Nixon White House, the Reagan administration went out of its way not to alienate potential supporters in Congress. Mark Andrews, a stalwart House Republican who moved toward the center after entering the Senate in 1980 explained,

> I have a pleasant relationship with the administration. On the other hand I'm unwilling to go along with their current policy as regards the deficit and the economy. I'm appalled at their failure to pursue energy independence, and I'm concerned about their attitude to world trade. . . . On defense matters we've got an increasing commitment to NATO, at a rate faster than we can afford. It costs three times as much for us to maintain troops in Western Europe as it does back here. We've got to move towards a more efficient defense with greater firepower. I've been trying to make defense more cost-efficient by pursuing issues like warranties on defense procurement.[48]

Other Republicans with stalwart credentials, such as Charles Grassley and Nancy Kassebaum, also gravitated toward the center because of the deficit question and the constitutional issues raised by the right.

As mentioned previously, the liberals' greatest success in overturning administration policy was on the so-called social issues. With the combative Senator Lowell Weicker taking the lead, they prevented the new right from implementing any part of their social program. Weicker was the administration's most persistent opponent on the Republican side of the Senate in 1981–4, and he delighted in his role as a gadfly and self-appointed guardian of the Constitution. In addition to his opposition on the moral questions, the Connecticut senator also criticized Reagan for the use of American troops in Lebanon and Grenada. Moreover, he used his position as Chairman of the Labor and Human Services subcommittee on Appropriations to oppose the administration on domestic spending reductions.[49] Although commonly regarded as a maverick, Weicker's activities in the Senate were generally popular with his Connecticut constituency.[50] According to his special counsel, Steve Moore,

Weicker celebrates his independence—"He's nobody's man but yours" is his election slogan. He thinks that is the reason for his political success. Nobody can count on him on any issue, and he's never a sure vote for any measure. In some ways this is helpful, because people are less likely to take a shot at one of his own programs for fear of alienating him on another vote. He's very good on the floor, and he's a master of procedure—filibustering, creative amendments and so forth. Weicker is widely regarded as a valuable man to have on your side.[51]

Weicker's strident independence and guerrilla tactics constitute one means of exerting influence in the present-day Senate, although it seems to be primarily a negative approach. Another effort to coordinate the activities of the liberal Republicans in the Senate was the formation of the previously mentioned Gang of Six (originally Gang of Five) at the instigation of the veteran liberal Republican from Maryland, Charles Mathias:

Last year [1983] we had the so-called Gang of Five, who presented a budget plan that was ultimately adopted by the whole Senate. The group consisted of Chafee, Hatfield, Weicker, Stafford, and myself. We were later joined by Mark Andrews. We were able to prevail because the Democrats held solidly together with 46 votes, and the other Republicans accounted for 48. By holding the balance of power in the middle we were ultimately able to get enough Republicans and Democrats to get 51 votes.[52]

In 1983 the liberals forced the Senate to drop the Reagan budget plan, substituting a plan with greater reductions in defense spending. In May 1984, however, their strength was diluted when they offered three different amendments rather than one budget package. All three proposals contained reductions in defense spending and a reduced deficit, but none attracted more than 14 Republican votes.[53]

The subsequent failure of the Gang of Six to coordinate their efforts and pass a budget in 1984 left one wondering whether liberal Republicans were not taking their belief in individualism too seriously. This belief made them wary of blocs—reminiscent of Labor, the Democrats, and the new right—and went against the Independent image that had proved to be so useful for them electorally. Rhode Island Senator Chafee expressed the liberal Republicans' almost endemic suspicion of organization:

I'm not strong for blocs in the Senate. We're not here to throw our weight around.[54]

Another leading Republican liberal, Arlen Specter of Pennsylvania (who opposed his party's majority 54% of the time in 1983, more than any other Republican), stated his dissension from the administration in terms of having to meet the needs of his eastern, industrial, recession-affected state. Like Chafee, he found the idea of a liberal bloc "unnecessary and unpleasant."[55]

On the surface, the 1980 election results appeared to usher in a right-wing era in the Senate, but it soon became evident that this was not the case. The desire to take full advantage of the opportunity of having a Senate majority, the priority given to economics by the Reagan administration—an area in which Republicans were fundamentally united—and the personal abilities of Howard Baker enabled the Republican senators to achieve remarkable levels of unity in 1981. After that the growth in the budget deficit brought about a move away from the administration and forced the Senate toward the center on economic policy. The re-emergence of Democratic control in the House after 1982 was also a moderating influence:

> The change has . . . forced Senate Republican Chairmen to deal more directly with their Democratic counterparts in the House to reach agreement on legislation.[56]

The dynamics of Senate elections, which involve appeals to large, heterogeneous constituencies on the basis of personal, rather than ideological or partisan, characteristics, make it likely that liberal Republicans will continue to survive there. The genuinely liberal Republicans—the Javitses, Cases, and Brookes—may have gone for good, but a mainly northeastern liberal element will probably persist as long as the Republicans wish to win enough seats to gain control of the Senate.

The House

> There's still a place for the moderates, liberals and progressives. I don't want to drum anybody out of the party. One of the Democrats' greatest strengths is their ability to encompass a broad range of views within the party. We

> can't become the majority party by trying to read people
> out.
> Congressman Richard Cheney.[57]

Despite the Democrats' numerical advantage in the Ninety-seventh
Congress, House Minority Leader Robert Michel was able to
achieve an astonishing level of success for Reagan administration
proposals in 1981. Even after gaining 33 House seats in 1980, the
Republicans still trailed the Democrats by 243 votes to 192 in
1981; however, by holding his Republicans together on the key
votes on Reagan's spending and tax-cut packages, Michel was able
to secure enough southern Democratic defections to pass the legislation. On the three key budget votes of 1981, Republican rebels
numbered 0, 2, and 1, and in the first session of the Ninety-seventh
Congress, Republican party unity in the House averaged 80%, as
compared to 75% for the Democrats (see Table 5-6).[58] At times
it looked as though Michel had become the *de facto* Speaker of
the House.

Michel had several problems, however, even in the largely successful 1981 session. In his budget proposals of March 10, 1981,
Reagan protected funding for large southern public works projects, such as the Clinch River Tennessee Reactor and the Tennes-
see-Tombigbee waterway, in order to entice southern Democratic
members of the Conservative Democratic Forum to vote for his
proposals. The administration also provided tax concessions for oil
producers and changes in estate taxes for farmers. The price for
these concessions was cuts in programs that were more important
to the Frostbelt states of the Northeast and Midwest.[59] In response, a group of Frostbelt Republicans began to organize in opposition to the southerners. The full impact of this Gypsy Moth
insurgency will be considered shortly, but it will suffice to say here
that the Frostbelt Republicans were able to restore more than $4
billion to the budget for programs such as Medicaid, energy con-
servation, Conrail, Amtrak, mass-transit funding, guaranteed student loans, and vocational training.[60] In addition, some 31 Republicans voted on October 6, 1981 against a Reagan-backed
motion imposing further cuts in appropriations for Labor, Health
and Education.[61] Iowa Republican Tom Tauke summarizes the
achievements of the dissidents as follows:

I think that we were successful, although we probably lost more than we won. But we won more than we would have if we hadn't gotten together. One way in which we hoped that it would be successful was that we hoped it would provide political protection for northeastern incumbents in 1982. Maybe it's impossible to tell how successful we were, but a number of people in the Gypsy Moths didn't make it through the last election.[62]

More an old-fashioned fiscal conservative than a new rightist, Michel was drawn toward adopting a more conciliatory stance vis à vis the Democratic majority in 1982 as the Republican coalition began to suffer from regional strains. These were mainly due to the 1981–2 recession, which had a bitter effect on the minority leader's own congressional district in Peoria, Illinois. Eventually Michel supported a 1982 tax increase to attack the deficit, as it became apparent that the Reagan administration's grip on the House was weakening. Michel was further frustrated by the administration's (and particularly Budget Director David Stockman's) negotiating with leading "Boll Weevils," such as Phil Gramm of Texas, over the head of the House Republican leadership.[63] After the loss of 26 Republican seats in the 1982 midterm elections, the minority leader's position became even more difficult. It was no longer arithmetically possible to control the House through alliances with the Conservative Democratic Forum, and the legislative initiative passed once more to House Speaker O'Neill. Michel found himself with the almost endemic dilemma of Republican minority leaders in the House: he had to try to be a partisan-leader while also attempting to make sure that the business of the House got done with the cooperation of the Democrats. It was the dilemma that had created problems for all his immediate predecessors—Martin, Halleck, Ford, and John Rhodes.

After the beginning of the Ninety-eighth Congress in January 1983, frustration among the younger, more conservative House Republicans led to demands for a more effective partisan assault on the Democrats. A dozen relatively junior House Republican members formed the Conservative Opportunity Society (COS), the most prominent members being Representatives Newt Gingrich (Georgia), Vin Weber (Minnesota), and Robert Walker (Pennsylvania). Their essential protest was against what they regarded as the liberal domination of the House's legislative agenda by the Democratic leadership:

> By contrast, they said, they have been unable to get House votes on such conservative bills as the balanced budget, line-item veto, and prayer in school constitutional amendments, and immigration and anti-crime bills.[64]

The COS spent hours on the House floor harassing the Democrats and engaging in partisan speeches. They used the Special Orders provision of the House to make vehement attacks on Speaker O'Neill before an empty chamber after the conclusion of normal daily business, all for the benefit of cable television viewers who watched C-SPAN programs (which broadcast congressional events).[65] The COS did not find universal favor with other House Republicans. Ranking Republicans on major committees, such as Barber Conable of New York (ranking Republican on Ways and Means in the Ninety-seventh and Ninety-eighth Congresses), who had to try to work with Democrats on a day-to-day basis, did not find the antics of the COS so congenial:

> The Conservative Opportunity Society does a lot of posturing but they have no sense of responsibility. They are junior members concerned about their futures. Part of the process of party renewal takes place when people like me get out and then we get these younger folks to assume responsibility. Then they'll get more interested in government than in confrontation.[66]

The leadership was generally encouraging, however—particularly Conference Chairman Jack Kemp, who was in ideological sympathy with the younger conservatives' demand for an "opportunity society" based on supply-side economics, social conservatism, and an aggressive foreign policy. Policy Committee Chairman Richard Cheney was also in general sympathy with the goals of the COS:

> We have to try something. The problem that we face is that the majority of Americans—61%—either think that we control the House or don't know who controls it. We have found an institutional conflict here between what the President wants to do and what we want to do. The President needs Democratic votes to pass his programs. We want confrontation, not cooperation.[67]

In the Ninety-seventh Congress the locus of liberal Republican activity in the House lay with the Gypsy Moth group, formed in the summer of 1981 out of a desire to protect federal programs of vital importance to the districts of northeastern and midwestern Republicans. The Northeast had been the traditional base of liberal Republicanism, but Republican strength in that region had long been in decline, and by the beginning of the Ninety-seventh Congress there were only about thirty liberal Republicans in the House. The primary aim of the Gypsy Moths was to enhance their re-election chances by protecting programs dear to their districts. With the Reagan administration offering concessions to the Boll Weevils, it became essential for northern Republicans to organize in defense of their own interests.[68] According to the Gypsy Moths' co-chair, Congressman William Green of New York City,

> We saw what the Boll Weevils were doing. They asked for $5 billion in budget reductions and got it. If it had come out of the Tennessee-Tombigbee Waterway, I guess it wouldn't have worried us. But because it came out of mass transit and low-income weatherization, that certainly drove home to us that we had an important regional interest at stake.[69]

In the early months of 1981, the Gypsy Moths consisted of a handful of members who met from time to time to discuss a common interest. In June these members decided to hold an organizational meeting. They had no staff, dues, or officers, although a steering committee was appointed in September when the group began to adopt a higher public profile. The membership stabilized at around twenty, mostly from the New England, mid-Atlantic, and upper midwestern states, which were suffering under the 1981–2 economic downturn.[70]

From the start, a conscious decision was made by the Moths to base their opposition to the administration on regional, rather than ideological, concerns. According to Congressman Tom Tauke,

> When we began to address the budget and tax questions in the early days of the last Congress, it was clear that the southern Democrats held the balance of power. They went from the Democratic leadership to the Republicans attempting to strike the best deal for the areas they represented. Their interests were very contrary to our interests. Republicans who wanted to hold down defense spending

and water projects, change the farm-subsidy program and maintain social programs—particularly in the education field—had to have some counterbalance to the conservative southern Democrats.[71]

Congressman James Jeffords of Vermont concurs:

> The goal of the Gypsy Moths was to point out to the administration that if they had a coalition with the southern conservative Democrats, they couldn't count on the northeastern Republicans to accept their proposals unless they took our needs into consideration. In our area we have to be cognizant of issues like low-income fuel assistance and high energy costs. Many of our districts have a substantial number of poor people, and programs like food stamps are vital to our constituents. The administration had to be made aware of that.[72]

The decision to focus on regional-pork barrel issues, while making good strategic sense and following the mores of the House, did not meet with universal approval. Some Moths, such as Iowa Congressman James Leach, sought a more ideological approach:

> There was division among the Gypsy Moths. Carl Pursell wanted the group to be exclusively regional. People like myself saw the major issues as philosophical rather than regional, although we recognized that there were some regional implications.[73]

Nevertheless the adoption of a primarily regional orientation accorded better with the modern House of Representatives' prevailing norm that a member should vote his district first. Such an orientation, moreover, made Gypsy Moth activity more tolerable for the House Republican leadership and the Reagan administration. According to Congressman Green,

> After Reagan's strong victory we felt that it would be a mistake to pose our opposition on ideological grounds, and we preferred to base it on regional grounds. We were concerned about the hard feelings that might have arisen had we based our opposition on ideological grounds. The regional aspect made it easier for some members, like Chris Smith of New Jersey, who is conservative on social issues, to join us. Unfortunately, however, it also meant that we couldn't bring people like Joel Pritchard, who is an outstanding leader of progressive Republicans in the House.[74]

In the first eight months of 1981, while voting for the Reagan tax cuts, the Moths bargained unobtrusively to protect their programs. They appeared to have convinced the administration to restore $4 billion to the programs mentioned above. Their escalation into the political limelight after the August recess was brought about, according to the Moths, by Reagan himself, when a second round of spending cuts was announced in September. This placed in jeopardy the same programs that the Moths had saved in June. In addition to rebelling against the Labor-Health and Human Services (HHS) appropriation in October 1981, the Moths also proposed a $9 billion cut in defense expenditures. In the end, however, they failed to pass a budget package congenial to their own interests. Perhaps as a consequence of increasing restiveness in the Republican ranks, the House leadership supported a 1982 tax increase, and the Moths were able to save Medicaid reimbursement, the guaranteed student loan program, and mass-transit subsidies. The 1982 midterm elections saw several Moths lose their seats because of the recession, but others, such as Chris Smith of New Jersey, survived in heavily Democratic districts.[75] The reassertion of Democratic authority in the House after 1982, with 26 Democratic gains, neutralized the effectiveness of the Gypsy Moths as the key swing group that they had been to some extent in 1981–2. As a result, their flimsy organization fell into desuetude.

Many of the Gypsy Moths were junior House Republicans and, given the small number of Republican liberals in the House, they found it increasingly difficult to attain senior positions in the House Republican hierarchy. According to the National Journal,

> None of the 39 Republicans who voted against [Representative Ralph] Regula's proposal to send the Spending Bill for the Labor, HHS and Education Departments back to the Appropriations Committee for further cuts sits on the Budget, Rules or Ways and Means Committee.[76]

Junior liberal Republicans in the House persistently complained that the more conservative House Republican Conference and the leadership had tried to keep them off the more important committees:

> A moderate Republican has only a very limited prospect of advancement in the House. When the choicest committee assignments are

given out, party loyalty is the major factor considered. I served as a staff person for 15 years, and I've learned that it doesn't matter which committees you have, you can succeed if you work hard and are innovative and aggressive.[77]

In fact, senior liberals such as Hamilton Fish (Judiciary) and Silvio Conte (Appropriations) were able to achieve positions as ranking members on committees, but the younger liberals seemed to have a more difficult time. There were four liberals on the Appropriations Committee in the Ninety-eighth Congress—Conte, McDade (Pennsylvania), Green (New York), and Pursell (Michigan)—but there were none on Budget, Rules, or Ways and Means. On the Judiciary Committee there was one liberal—Fish, the ranking member—and on Foreign Affairs there were four—Leach, Pritchard, Gilman, and Snowe.[78] One can only conclude that Republican liberals were not encouraged to join the key Rules, Ways and Means, and Budget Committees, which were so important in the 1981–4 period. The changing demographics of the party also damaged the prospects of the younger liberals, as the Northeast became less significant in relation to the South and West within the House Republican Conference.

While frustrations about committee assignments and lack of seniority may have been related to the revolt of the Gypsy Moths, the predominant consideration still appears to have been electoral survival. Ways and Means ranking member Barber Conable had little sympathy with the Moths' complaints regarding committee assignments:

> It's a copout. . . . the moderates' problem is that they want to be loved by everybody. They're not willing to stand up and fight for things that they believe in. They're moderate about everything including their own efforts.[79]

Even if Conable's comments were not entirely fair, it does appear to be intrinsic to liberal Republicanism that its adherents are uncomfortable with partisan politics. Liberal Republicans frequently find themselves in a key position on committees, and this often entails their being the members who have to fashion compromises between Republican conservatives and Democratic liberals. According to Tom Tauke,

> I am not comfortable as a partisan. I feel that I have to work out
> compromises and consensus positions. I don't see myself as a parti-
> san, but I see the need for partisans. The legislative technicians have
> to put together compromises which pass and become law.[80]

And Congressman Stewart McKinney said,

> You don't find Stu McKinney on the Budget, Rules, Appropriations,
> or Ways and Means Committees, because I'm not ideologically pure.
> For example: I was one of only two Republicans to vote in favor
> of the federal bailout of New York City. On the other hand, being
> a moderate is often the most powerful way you can be a Republican.
> Often the moderate Democrats come to the moderate Republicans
> saying: "Let's get together and straighten this thing out." I got five
> pieces of legislation through last term because I serve as an agent
> of compromise.[81]

Before concluding this analysis of the liberal Republicans' influence in the House, it is necessary to examine the role of the
Wednesday Group, which has survived for over twenty years since
its foundation in the early 1960s.[82] The thirty-odd members are
preponderantly from the liberal section of the House GOP, and no
new right conservatives have ever been associated with it. Nevertheless, its ideological complexion has changed slightly, as has the
group's conception of its role, which is now seen less as a liberal
caucus and more as a provider of services to its members; these
include information about constructing legislative proposals and
and monitoring proceedings in the various House committees. According to Executive Director Steve Hofman,

> The group's main reason for being is to break down the walls of
> specialization that exist between members and between staffs. The
> members report on what's going on in the various committees, and
> they share political information about what's going on in their
> districts. By serving as an information exchange the group gives
> them a broader view.[83]

The group is funded out of the office accounts of the membership, which, according to Hofman, is limited to "the number of
people you can get into one room."[84] The membership is quite exclusive, unlike that of other House groups, such as the right-wing
Republican Study Committee and the various lunching and dining

societies. Several liberals, such as Representatives Benjamin Gilman (New York), Claudine Schneider (Rhode Island), and Tom Tauke were not members in 1984. The group maintained a staff of five plus interns and a part-time counsel—in 1984, Washington lawyer Martin Gerry. This staff has traditionally been of high quality, and in recent years the group has published reports and ideas on a wide variety of subjects: civil rights, job retraining, defense reform, etc. The Wednesday Group has cultivated an image as a serious, policy-making group, as opposed to being preoccupied with ideological vote-coordinating and extracongressional activities. Most of the group's members in 1984 stressed how valuable they had found it to be. According to Congressman Joel Pritchard,

> The value of the group is that there is no other way of keeping up with everything that's going on. It's a great resource [for] information. The people on the committees report what's going on, and we are like good friends. It's easier to deal with people you wouldn't otherwise know very well. We have retreats and social things and all that makes for very good relations.[85]

The loss of the Wednesday Group's advocacy role and the stress on information, expertise, and other services has resulted in its being a very heavyweight group in terms of seniority and ability. According to the group's counsel Martin Gerry,

> It's gone from being a freshman's group to being the opposite. There are disproportionately high numbers of ranking members and senior members in there, which has led to a change in the political impact of the group. There are at least seven or eight ranking members in the group, and Barber Conable is one of the two or three intellectual leaders of the House. Like Bob Dole in the Senate: he has emerged as a uniquely respected person. Conable's summary of the business in the House Ways and Means Committee is worth all the dues which the members have paid.[86]

The group has also become broader in its ideological outlook, though no new rightists are among its ranks. Caldwell Butler, Richard Cheney, William Whitehurst, Bob Livingston, and Barber Conable have all been members of the Wednesday Group, and none of them could really be designated as liberal Republicans on the basis of their voting records. According to Silvio Conte,

> Originally the group was a haven and a hideaway for people of like thinking. Today you have a wide spectrum, from conservatives to moderates.[87]

Given the high number of ranking members in the group, it is not surprising that most Wednesday Group members have good relations with House Democrats, relationships that become very important once legislation comes to the House floor. As a group of experts, legislators, and ideas it has been a success. The price for that success, however, has been the Wednesday Group's failure to serve as an effective liberal Republican pressure group within the House.

Overall, the relatively small band of liberal Republicans in the House probably attained an importance out of proportion to their numbers in the 1981–4 period. Many were senior Republicans with proven legislative ability, who fought hard and with a certain degree of success in defense of their districts. On the other hand, many of the senior liberals were nearing the end of their careers, and the incentives for younger liberals to remain in the House were not strong, as the House Republican Conference moved further to the right. More ambitious younger liberals may now tend to abandon the House as soon as alternative political means of advancement become available, since their career prospects within the Chamber are not great. Tom Tauke's attitude is typical:

> If I were interested in entering the leadership ranks in the House, I'd have to take a more conservative stance. But I don't see myself as a career House member.[88]

Conclusion

This survey of the post–New Deal development of the Republican party in Congress suggests that, since 1960, the liberal element of the party has been more influential on Capitol Hill than in presidential politics. This is not to deny, however, that extensive changes within the congressional GOP have taken place. Like the presidential Republican party, the congressional party became more southern and western, and lost strength in the traditional Republican strongholds of the Northeast and Midwest. This has reinforced the traditional conservative bias of Republicans in Congress, although the modern conservatives are more likely (in Reichley's terms) to be of a fundamentalist than a stalwart cast. As the fundamentalists gained strength, the party declined in the Northeast, and northeastern Republicans who predominated within the congressional party in the 1930s (and who were the most conservative sector of the party at that time) have now become the deviant liberal minority (see Tables 5-3, 5-4, and 5-9).

While the genuinely liberal Republican does appear to be a figure of the past, there are still self-defined moderate Republicans in both the House and Senate, where the increasingly personalized methods of campaigning and the decline of party allegiances within the electorate have prevented them from being wiped off the political map, as they have been in presidential politics. It is important, however, to return to *the* crucial point with regard to liberal Republicans in Congress over the past two decades: the liberals in the Senate have been much more effective and influential than their House counterparts. During the first Reagan administration, the difference grew as the Senate moved toward the center after the first partisan flush of Republican victory in 1980. In addition, the

TABLE 5-9. Republican Opposition to the Conservative
Coalition (by Region) 1981–1984

Year	All Republi- cans	East	Midwest	South	West
Senate:					
1981	15	35	15	4	10
1982	18	41	19	4	11
1983	18	37	20	8	13
1984	14	34	15	3	9
House:					
1981	17	29	19	9	9
1982	18	31	19	9	9
1983	18	33	19	9	9
1984	15	30	14	8	9

Source: Congressional Quarterly Almanacs 1981–1984.

deficit issue was something of a moderating influence on leading Republicans in both Houses.

In the House, liberal Republicans are relatively few in number, but in 1981–2, owing to unusually effective organization and co-ordination on key votes and a clear set of objectives, they were able to exert more power in the chamber than they had for some time. The redundancy of the Gypsy Moths after 1982 does not preclude a revival of this kind of legislative activity, should congressional arithmetic permit. Moreover, the Wednesday Group, though less exclusively liberal than in the past, has played an important role in formulating legislation and in keeping its mainly liberal membership informed on key issues. For all the publicity generated by the COS and their radical alternatives to Democratic rule in the House, Reagan was able to bring in only 14 new House Republicans in his landslide re-election in 1984—an insufficient number to reassemble the conservative coalition of spring and summer 1981. The immediate outlook for Republican control of the House does not look promising, particularly given that the cumulative effects of "Democrat-biased" redistricting in 1961, 1971, and 1981, together with incumbency protection, have helped the Democratic majority to maintain their position.[89] With the likely continuance of Democratic control in the short term, the pattern of conservative predominance within the House Republican Conference and of cyclical revolts by frustrated junior members against the leadership is likely to persist.

In the Senate, its traditional individualism exacerbated by the decline of the "inner club" and of leadership authority during Mike Mansfield's tenure as majority leader, party management has become much more difficult. Under these circumstances, the levels of partisan cohesion achieved by Reagan and the Senate Republican leadership in 1981–2 were truly remarkable after years of Democratic disarray. By 1983, however, once the debate had moved beyond the area of tax cutting and had become more concerned with spending reductions and defense, liberal voices of dissent began to be raised. To date, however, the liberals have been unable to overcome a personal and institutional dislike of factionalism; and this has precluded maximizing their opportunities for influence in the Senate. Yet, while proving themselves unwilling or unable to alter the direction of the administration on foreign and defense policy, the liberals were of critical importance in defeating the moral agenda of the new right. The election of Senator Dole (by 28 votes to 23) to succeed Howard Baker in December 1984, and the elevation of liberal Republican Senators Chafee and Heinz to become Conference Chairman and Campaign Committee Chairman, respectively, appeared to indicate that the battle for ideological control among Republican senators had been won, at least temporarily, by an alliance of liberals and stalwarts.

Thus, Reagan's perceived success and that of his Republican leaders in Congress in 1981 should not be permitted to obscure the difficulties that faced that leadership in holding their congressional coalition together after that year. As issues concerning foreign policy, social policy, and the budget deficit—which divided Republicans as the tax-reduction issue did not—began to arise, Republicans in Congress were in as much disarray as their Democratic counterparts had been in 1977–81. While Senate and House Republicans were still more ideologically homogeneous than the Democrats (and thus more likely to be highly cohesive on major votes), the changing context of congressional elections, with a diminished role for the party and a greater emphasis on the individual candidate, helped to sustain liberal Republicanism. Certainly, as long as the Republican party is interested in securing congressional seats in the northeastern United States, some kind of liberal Republicanism is likely to persist.

6

Liberal Republicans in the 1980s and Beyond

The Liberal Decline

> The progressives have concentrated too much on ideas and
> less on nuts and bolts politics. This is the general weakness
> which we have exhibited. We have been so eager to get into
> a debate on substance, that we forget the means by which
> the substance is to be attained.
>
> SENATOR CHARLES MATHIAS[1]

Since 1952, where this analysis of liberal Republicanism began,
the New Deal party system has been in a state of flux. The increasing identification of the national Democratic party with liberal positions across the entire policy spectrum offended much of
that party's traditional support in the conservative southern and
western regions. The growth of Republican electoral support in
those regions, which have expanded in terms of economic growth
and population in the 1960–84 period, had a decisive effect on the
balance of ideological forces within the Republican party nationally by strengthening the conservative wing. The support of southern and western conservatives was critical in securing the presidential nomination for Goldwater in 1964, Nixon in 1968, and Reagan
in 1980. Moreover, Republican growth in the Sunbelt made east-
ern-oriented liberals less electorally important to the party. The
erosion of Democratic ties among traditionally Democratic voting

groups such as Roman Catholics, ethnics, and blue-collar workers also aided conservative Republicans. While many of these voters still supported the Democrats on bread-and-butter economic issues as the party of the disadvantaged, they were increasingly cross-pressured by conservative Republican themes emphasizing the importance of religion, the family, and a strong America. The fact that many of these formerly Democratic voters and their children were no longer the "tired, huddled masses" of legend, but socially mobile, suburban homeowners further contributed to this process.

One consequence of these secular changes has been to fatally undermine the traditional liberal Republican argument that the GOP could only succeed electorally by submerging its policy differences with the Democrats. The relative decline in population of the northeastern region and the loss of some of its economic influence to the Sunbelt further undermined the position of the liberal wing of the Republican party. As the Northeast lost influence within the Republican party as a whole, the GOP lost more and more electoral support in the New England and Mid-Atlantic regions. This dynamic process, in which declining Republican support in the industrial Northeast contributed to a conservative upsurge in the national party, which led in turn to a further electoral erosion in the Northeast, was a crucial factor in the collapse of liberal Republicanism within the national party after 1960.

Although there were significant changes in party alignment among the electorate in the 1960–84 period, the decline of the liberal Republicans was also assisted by structural changes within both major political parties, changes in the relationship between parties and voters, and changes in the relationship between the parties and the other major institutions of American government.

The dealignment of the American electorate from both political parties in the 1960–80 period and the concomitant decomposition of traditional party organizations are symptomatic of a broader transformation in the American political universe. The growth in the size of the federal government, bureaucratization, and the advent of the American welfare system—in Weberian terms, America's "political modernization"—subverted the traditional bases of party politics: geographical and ethnic loyalties, patronage, and poor relief. The revolutions in mass communications of the past half-century undermined the parties' traditional functions of political integration, education, and mobilization. The revolt against the political status quo in the 1960s, and the further changes that it brought in its wake, merely confirmed and institutionalized longer-term secular trends in the making since the Progressive era. A better-educated, more prosperous, more socially mobile electorate, receiving its political education through television and motivated politically by ideas and single issues (rather than familial, ethnic, or neighborhood ties) discovered conventional American party politics to be at best irrelevant and, in some cases, inimical to its political aspirations.

One aspect of this revolt was the development of the conservative movement, or (as it later became) the new right, as a mass political organization in the late 1950s. Working outside the established party system, the conservatives developed an interlocking network of intellectuals, think tanks, fund-raisers, and grass roots activists which succeeded in nominating Barry Goldwater for President in 1964. While the electoral circumstances of that year were peculiar, the Goldwater nomination was a precursor of future developments in American party politics. Goldwater enthusiasts were as opposed to the established New Deal political system as were the later followers of McCarthy and McGovern in the Democratic party. They were motivated primarily by ideology, issues, or the personal characteristics of their candidate, rather than by partisanship and the desire for victory at the polls above all else. In their political style they were amateur or purist: disdainful of the unglamorous coalition-building politics of the old-style party professional and lacking in long-term loyalty to the Republican party. The Goldwater conservatives raised their funds from thousands of small contributors through mass mailings, rather than rely on the Republicans' traditional eastern "fat cats" and corporate givers. They used the mass media and extra-party ideological or single-issue groups to communicate with the electorate. The conservative movement turned the Republican party upside down in 1964, and although 1968 represented something of a reversion to traditional party politics within the GOP, the balance of power between the liberal and conservative wings was decisively altered. The growing strength of conservatism within the Republican party from 1964 to 1984 paralleled the decline of its liberal wing.

The regular Republican party collapsed in the face of the purist onslaught. Presidential nominations were no longer decided through bargaining between party leaders at the national convention but instead were won and lost in primary elections. The increasingly important role played by primaries since 1940 in the presidential nominating process was consolidated by the proliferation of primaries in 1968–76 that followed the McGovern-Fraser reforms within the Democratic party. Although the Republicans' reform effort through the Delegate and Organization (DO) and Rule 29 committees was very limited by comparison, they were generally compelled by state laws or by the exigencies of state politics to mirror the Democrats, and by 1980 over 70% of GOP convention delegates were committed to candidates by primary elections. The alliance of stalwart party professionals and moderates, which controlled the national party in the 1932–60 period, lost its influence over party nominations at the national level, and also, to a large extent, at the lower levels of electoral competition at the long-term decay of traditional party structures continued. The virtual monopoly of resources for national elections once held by the eastern, liberal wing of the party diminished as financial power in the United States became more widely dispersed and was no longer confined to the northeastern corporate and financial elite. The campaign finance reforms of the early 1970s severely curbed the largesse of individual donors, while simultaneously enhancing the influence of corporate, single-issue, and ideological Political Action Committees. These reforms placed an emphasis on small-donor fund-raising (an area in which the Republican right was highly competent), and the advent of full public financing for presidential general elections and of federal matching funds for primary campaigns completed the exclusion of the regular party organization from presidential politics.

All of these developments were inimical to the liberals' position within the Republican party. The exclusion of the regular party from the candidate selection process at the national level meant that the criteria for selection no longer focused by electability or the ability to hold together an ideologically broad coalition of supporters. As the traditional professional party organization became increasingly irrelevant in nominating politics, liberal Republicans lost ground in the intraparty ideological conflict for the sim-

ple reason that considerations of electoral viability and possession
of the national party's fund-raising and organizational resources
were no longer decisive factors. The locus of conflict shifted from
convincing party professionals of one's electability to convincing a
mass audience of the virtues of one's ideas or personality—terrain
on which the party right wing had several distinct advantages.

The advent of media-oriented, candidate-centered electoral politics removed the mainsprings of liberal Republican influence within
the party. The moderate approach, based on working inside the
regular party apparatus and with the party's leadership elite in
the hope of forging alliances with electorally oriented regulars, was
insufficient to withstand the popular onslaught from the right in
1964–80. The new politics emphasized ideas and style, rather than
the social, regional, and patronage ties that had held the old-style
party machinery intact, and the liberal Republicans were simply
overwhelmed by the changed electoral environment in which they
had to compete. In the new politics, in which ideas were increasingly important, they could not develop an ideology with sufficient
breadth and depth of appeal to arouse and mobilize an enduring
national constituency (which would serve as a continuing source
of activists, funds, and votes). In this respect liberal Republicans
suffered from a problem endemic to centrist factions in any political party in the modern era, namely, that moderate politics,
although superficially attractive to a broad section of the electorate, cannot arouse the intense commitment and zeal of party activists to anything like the same extent as the rhetoric of the ideologue. In a politics in which effective candidate organizations and
attractive candidates were essential, the liberals failed to develop
an electoral strategy attuned to the new situation. For too long
they adhered to the old moderate strategy, eschewing mass politicking in favor of cultivating the most important members of the
Republican power elite. Unfortunately for the liberals, by the mid-
1970s there no longer existed a durable national party elite that
could deliver the convention for an electable moderate.

By contrast, the secret of the right's success in Republican party
politics after 1960 was the forging of an enduring ideological constituency out of a variety of causes and issues. In a crude form,
their ideology can be stated as follows: Something is rotten in the

American body politic; that rottenness is due to liberalism; and only by returning to the economic, moral, and foreign policy precepts of America's past can the promise of America be redeemed. This ideology, labeled "conservatism," is the adhesive that holds the diverse conservative constituencies together from election to election. Liberal Republicans have found it difficult to develop an alternative doctrine that can compete with this. In the days when professional party politics predominated, this did not matter a great deal. Liberals could always justify their allegiance to the GOP through adherence to the tradition of Lincoln and Roosevelt, or on family, regional, or ethnic grounds, and they could generally appeal as likely winners to the party regulars, in contrast to more committed Republican partisans such as Robert Taft, who had narrow electoral appeal. The moderate strategy of "me-tooism" made strategic sense as long as American party politics were firmly set along New Deal lines. Only by joining in the New Deal, liberal consensus could Republicans win nationally, and thus liberal Republicans made attractive candidates to party regulars who sought victory at the polls above all else. As the New Deal consensus began to unravel, however, and party structures disintegrated in the face of a purist assault from right and left, the accommodationist doctrines of liberal Republicanism no longer made such good strategic sense. Widespread disenchantment with the state of American politics and society in the 1960s led to demands for change in the direction of policy, and a new public philosophy. Liberal Republicanism offered only a continued adherence to politics as usual and the perpetuation of an increasingly fragile consensus. "Me-tooism" offered no alternative vision or challenge to the prevailing political establishment the way the purist style and uncompromising conservatism of the right did.

Liberal Republicans were not short of ideas and policies, of course. What they lacked was a distinctive ideology. Arthur Larson offered a credible defense of Eisenhower Republicanism in the mid-1950s, but the "end of ideology" political consensus that characterized that era had collapsed by the mid-1960s under the weight of Vietnam, race, and the social issue. Jacob Javits offered an intelligent and impassioned defense of liberal Republicanism in *Order of Battle,* but this modern version of Hamiltonianism was barely distinguishable from the "big government" policies of the Democratic Presidents Kennedy and Johnson. The Ripon Society—formed out of an awareness of the ideological vacuum in the liberal wing of the party—turned out detailed and intelligent policy analyses and prescriptions on a wide range of matters, some of which were adopted by the federal government during the 1970s. Yet despite the plaudits it gained from the eastern media, Ripon was perforce an exclusive organization of intellectuals without a mass base of support. Moreover, there appeared to be no coherent body of thought underlying their specific policy proposals. Ripon activists emphasized their belief in free enterprise and the decentralization of power, but the virtues of the free-enterprise system were hardly in question, even in the turbulent 1960s and the decentralization of power was an idea common to both Republican conservatives and the Democrats' new left. Ripon offered dispassionate, pragmatic, and rational solutions to pressing political problems, but this ad hoc pragmatism was incapable of arousing the mass constituency that the new politics required. What the liberal Republicans needed in addition to sensible and moderate policies was some overall vision of the American future that remained Republican and distinct from the liberal solutions of the Democrats, while at the same time repudiating the crude nostalgia that frequently figured in right-wing rhetoric. This said, it must be conceded that the times were more receptive to radical solutions in the 1960s and 1970s, and, as mentioned above, support for moderation in policy, although broad, lacked the depth and durability to attract a zealous activist constituency.

Rigid adherence to ideological stances, although something of an asset in the reformed nominating process, is not a prerequisite for success. Indeed, a decidedly nonideological candidate, Jimmy Carter secured the Democratic presidential nomination in 1976 on the basis of an excellent organization and an attractive personal image. Liberal Republicans have succeeded (to a remarkable extent, considering their virtual absence from recent presidential politics) in getting elected at the congressional and statewide level on a similar basis: attractive candidates plus good organization. Such candidates were not likely to win, as they did in the past, through support from party professionals. Indeed theirs was an amateur style, invariably hostile toward established parties and party politics as such, and emphasizing themes such as good government and so forth. Liberal Republicans have shown themselves capable of defeating conservatives in many states and districts through mounting this kind of candidate-centered nonpartisan campaign. The question remains, Why did they fail to mount a similar challenge to conservative hegemony at the national level?

The reasons for this failure all derived from an inability to comprehend the transformation in the American political arena in the 1960–80 period. The tactics adopted by the liberals in the crucial nomination contests of 1964–76 demonstrate this clearly. In 1964 Republican liberals failed to appreciate the danger from Goldwater, believing that the powers that be would ultimately ensure the Arizona Senator's defeat. As a consequence of this error, they confined their anti-Goldwater activities to elite politicking, which failed even to produce a candidate behind whom they could unite. The only serious overt challenge to Goldwater came in California, from Rockefeller, and by that time it was almost too late, since the Arizonan had already taken the Republican party away from the professionals virtually unnoticed. Although many subsequently dismissed 1964 as a peculiar year, the Goldwater legions did not disband, but instead consolidated their grip on the party at the grass roots, particularly in the electorally important South and West. All the liberal efforts to establish a national counter-organization failed from indifference, a lack of understanding concerning the transformation in the politics behind presidential nominations, and the complacent attitude that somehow the *status quo ante* within the GOP would be restored. In 1968 the liberals again adopted an elite-oriented strategy which attempted to rally party leaders around George Romney. When Romney appeared to have feet of clay in national politics, Rockefeller re-emerged yet again as the liberal standard-bearer. But tactical ineptitude, which led to his entering the campaign at a ridiculously late stage, and lack of enthusiasm within the Republican ranks doomed the liberals to failure.

After 1968 the decline in liberal influence accelerated. The liberals' sole national fund-raising base and rudimentary national organization came from Rockefeller. That organization showed itself to be totally inept politically outside New York State, but it constituted, at least, some kind of national organization for liberal Republicans. With Rockefeller's demise as a national candidate, his money and organization went too, and the liberals were left without any organizational structure for a national campaign. The new fluidity in the nominating process, introduced by the combination of technological advances and the McGovern-Fraser reforms, might have permitted a particularly attractive moderate candidate with a good organization to sweep to the nomination as Jimmy Carter did in 1976. Apart from the difficulties created by the continuing conservative hegemony among Republican activists, there was no liberal of sufficient caliber for the task, and those who contemplated such a campaign (such as Senator Mathias in 1976) were dissuaded by the likelihood that, in dividing the stalwart-to-liberal primary vote with President Ford, they could only enhance the possibility that Goldwater's heir, Ronald Reagan, would secure the nomination. Only John Anderson, of contemporary Republican liberals, has attempted such a new politics campaign, and although he did win considerable national attention, his primary showings only succeeded in taking votes from Reagan's principal challenger, George Bush, in 1980. The conservative movement had succeeded to the point where a genuine liberal Republican presidential campaign simply had no significant base of support at the Republican grass roots (Anderson's support came mainly from Independents and crossover Democrats). Moreover, such campaigns ultimately aided the more cohesive Republican fundamentalists by taking votes from pragmatic stalwart candidates such as Ford and Bush.

The liberal Republicans' inability to adapt to the changing nature of their party and of American electoral politics in general during the 1964–8 period led them to commit a series of tactical blunders, and ultimately to become irrelevant in Republican national politics. Liberals at the state level succeeded in the new politics to some extent by eschewing outmoded professional tactics and resorting to candidate-centered media campaigns with effective statewide personal organizations. At the national level that lesson was never learned until it was too late to make any difference.

Postscript I: Can Liberal Republicanism Survive?

The main center of liberal Republican intellectual activity in the 1980s remains the Ripon Society, which in mid-1984 had some 3,000 members. The national office is in Washington, DC, with a full-time staff of three: executive director, *Forum* editor, and a secretary. Ripon is funded entirely by membership dues ($25), subscriptions to the *Ripon Forum* (the society's journal), and donations. In the early 1970s Ripon had a budget of $300,000 to $400,000 per annum, but by 1984 this had shrunk to about a quarter of that figure.[2] The *Forum* is theoretically bimonthly, but cash-flow difficulties have been a persistent problem, and for this reason the society could only publish five issues in 1983.[3] The journal has changed from the somewhat rudimentary newsletter of the early days to a more glossy magazine format. The society regards it as being a journal of ideas and opinions, and solicits contributions from liberal Republican intellectuals and politicians. In general, the *Forum* is critical of the Reagan administration, particularly in the civil liberties area, and devotes much space to attacks on the ideology and political strategy of the Republican right.

The survival of Ripon is testimony to the dedication of liberal Republican intellectuals, and in the early 1980s the society enjoyed something of a revival after a period in the doldrums, when many of its original members became involved in other activities or lost interest. It no longer receives the national attention that it got in the heyday of the 1960s, however, and, in comparison to the array of well-funded think tanks, consultants, journals, and PACs of the Republican right, Ripon is very much a shoestring operation.

Iowa Congressman James Leach, who became chairman of Ripon in 1981, has been a persistent critic of the Reagan presidency. He sponsored a bipartisan budget initiative in 1982, supported the nuclear freeze, and was an outspoken opponent of the administration's Central America policy as a member of the House Foreign Affairs Committee. Together with Lowell Weicker (although in a far less abrasive manner) he has been the most prominent national spokesman for liberal Republicans in recent times. Further, Leach has been prepared to challenge new right ideas openly, in contrast to other Republican liberals who have been wary of provoking conservative hostility back home. He still sees a positive role for a rejuvenated Ripon Society within the GOP:

> I took on the Ripon chairmanship because there was a void on the moderate side of the party, and because we had got to be more active. I think that Ripon has a couple of responsibilities. We can still have a role in holding together the moderate wing of the party, and the society can serve as place where moderate ideas are promoted in a credible way. We have to show that moderate Republicanism is legitimate and has a life, and Ripon is the center of that. It is the only moderate organization in American politics, in a country which has historically disassociated itself from extremes. The Democratic party is being pushed to the left, so there is a void for us to fill. We have the task of counter-organizing and counter-articulating within the party. In terms of money, the various conservative organizations like Heritage outspend Ripon by a thousand to one.[4]

Despite Leach's enthusiasm and commitment, other Ripon veterans have not been so sanguine about the society's future prospects and are dubious about its purpose in modern Republican politics. One disenchanted liberal, Howard Gillette, left the society after the 1980 Anderson campaign:

> I am not in Ripon now, and I am less optimistic about progressive prospects within the Republican party than the Ripon people. The demographic sources of progressive support, and the social and economic sources have shifted away from the Republican party.[5]

Other former Riponites moved to the right, accommodating themselves to the new Republican politics. The most celebrated of these is probably George Gilder, now known primarily for his impassioned advocacy of free enterprise and supply-side economics. His co-author of *The Party That Lost Its Head*, Bruce Chapman, became an official in the Reagan White House. The view of this group of disaffected Riponites is summarized at length below by Peter Wallison, a former aide to Nelson Rockefeller and general counsel to the U.S. Treasury in the first Reagan administration:

I am a Reagan Republican. There is no difference between his views and mine except on the stridency with which he approaches the social issues. Issues like school prayer don't matter very much to me. The Reagan economic and foreign policy is far more important. In that area I am fully in agreement with everything that Reagan has done. That is not very different from the views of the original Ripon group. We have to give people the opportunities and that is the traditional Republican point of view. Gilder (who is good at spotting trends early) is right when he talks about the need to create an entrepreneurial society. . . .

I thought that for ten years Ripon had a function; now I think that it no longer has. I resigned in 1972–3. Dick Rahn and Bob Beal were going around working hard to raise funds for Ripon. I kept telling them that they were wasting their time, that the purpose of Ripon was past. The society no longer represents anything. We no longer have a tremendous ideological clash within the party. Nixon adopted many of the ideas that Ripon talked about. They were not predominantly liberal ideas but they were ideas. We were spending time keeping this organization alive and raising funds for it, but there was no rationale for it any more. Now we had to work within the GOP, and there was no danger that we would be thrown out. It's been kept alive because organizations very rarely die once they're established. It gives some people a useful platform, I suppose.[6]

Others who were still involved in the society bemoaned the loss of the freewheeling intellectual atmosphere of the early days before the move from Cambridge to Washington in early 1973. According to Congressman Petri,

I felt that Ripon made a mistake in becoming too close to the day-to-day political machinations of Washington. It was a mistake to move to DC. The society was better when it was headquartered in Cambridge. Being there gave Ripon a more detached perspective, and they could more readily separate significant issues from the less significant.[7]

Former Ripon President Josiah Lee Auspitz took a similar view:

Ripon succeeded because we had smart people and a receptivity in the press. Ripon should never have moved to DC. When you go there you have to compete on Washington's terms. Ripon needed a frame of mind to think contemplatively, but it got lured by Washington society in 1973.[8]

Perhaps Ripon survives for no other reason than that it is still the only national organization that tries to link the scattered band of Republican liberals. However, it remains an intellectual rather than a campaigning body.[9]

With Reagan running unopposed for renomination in 1984, the scope for liberal Republican activity in national party politics was extremely limited. Nevertheless the decision (announced in January) of the Republican Platform Committee that four regional platform hearings were to be cancelled aroused some disquiet.[10] This action provoked the remaining Republican liberals in particular, since they had hoped to use the hearings to raise issues, such as the ERA, abortion, and the bias against the major states in the convention's apportionment formula, that they felt to be important. In response to the RNC decision, Leach and the Ripon Society arranged their own series of platform hearings in different parts of the United States in the winter and spring of 1984.

The author attended two of the five Ripon hearings: in Philadelphia on April 14, 1984 and in Hartford on June 23. Both conferences attracted only the hard core of liberal Republican activists from the Boston-Washington corridor, and neither gained a great deal of national media attention. At both gatherings a series of resolutions critical of administration policy on women's rights, the environment, defense spending, and the nuclear freeze were passed. Some conference participants admitted sympathy for the presidential candidacy of neo-liberal Democrat Senator Gary Hart, but the likely presence of Walter Mondale at the head of the Democratic ticket solidified a wavering loyalty to Reagan.[11] The impression gained from both conferences was that despite the enthusiasm of a number of liberals, they were a group working only on the periphery of Republican party politics, utterly without influence among Republican officeholders and the leadership elite of the party. Neither of the two liberal Republican senators in Pennsylvania found time to attend the Philadelphia conference, and indeed the only officeholders in attendance were Congressmen Leach and (very briefly) Green. At the Hartford meeting Leach again presided, but there were no appearances by any of New England's Gypsy Moth congressmen and women, and Connecticut's liberal Republican Senator Lowell P. Weicker was conspicuous by his absence. Indeed, the highest-ranking officeholder present apart from Congressman Leach was the Assistant Minority Leader of the Connecticut House.

In June 1984 the liberals gained some additional media attention through the formation of the Republican Mainstream Committee to lobby for arms control, women's and minority rights, and environmental concerns at the Republican convention in August.[12] Leach was elected chairman of the group, which also included former RNC Chair Mary Louise Smith of Iowa (sacked by Reagan from the U.S. Civil Rights Commission) and former U.S. Representative John Buchanan of Alabama (defeated by the new right in a 1980 primary). The unease created among many prominent Republican women by the anti-ERA and anti-abortion stances adopted by the Reagan White House was reflected by the emphasis on women's rights issues at the Ripon hearings and the presence of former RNC Chair Smith, former co-chair Crisp, and National Women's Political Caucus (NWPC) Chair Kathy Wilson among the Mainstream Committee dissidents. The committee pledged to work closely at Dallas with Common Cause, the National Education Association (NEA), the NWPC, Republicans for Choice, and the Sierra Club. Leach set forth the rationale for the formation of the Mainstream Committee:

> The strength of our party is its diversity. A platform reflecting a narrow ideological approach to the issues of our day jeopardizes President Reagan's re-election efforts. Our concern is that the Republican party will drift even further to the right, if the only focal point for platform dissent is the far right.[13]

The efforts of the Mainstream Committee members and their allies in Dallas went unrewarded in a Republican convention dominated by dedicated Reagan supporters. The party platform emerged as a document that might have been drafted by the Moral Majority and the Conservative Opportunity Society. On the economic front it totally rejected the liberal-stalwart position on the deficit by unequivocally ruling out a tax increase. The platform again condemned the ERA and restated its 1980 position that only opponents of abortion should be appointed to federal judgeships. A commitment to keep the United States militarily stronger than the USSR was also made. Lee Auspitz and the Ripon Society's long-running demand that the Republican convention's apportionment formula be altered to reflect state population as opposed to Republican electoral performance was rejected by the convention's Rules Committee. The threat of a lawsuit by the Freedom Republicans (a black Republican New York-based group) did, however, force the Rules Committee to create a subcommittee with the purpose of reviewing the delegate-allocation rules for 1988.[14] Despite this consolation, the prominence of new right and religious right spokesmen at the 1984 Republican convention, in comparison to the attention given to the Republican liberals, led one to conclude that at the national level, liberal Republicans were a very marginal group within the Republican electoral coalition, with minimal influence over the White House and the national party.

As a national political entity, liberal Republicanism is virtually moribund and has real political influence only in a few scattered states. Nevertheless, the Ripon Society remains in existence, and spokesmen such as Jim Leach, and to some extent Lowell Weicker, have kept some kind of liberal banner aloft within the GOP. It should be made clear, nevertheless, that liberal Republicanism, in the sense of the big government progressivism characteristic of Nelson Rockefeller, is a thing of the past. Most contemporary Republican liberals feel uncomfortable with the liberal label, and reject it in favor of more politically acceptable terms, such as moderate or progressive. According to leading Gypsy Moth Claudine Schneider, "I'm a moderate Republican. If I have to have a label at all, I like to be known as a progressive moderate."[15] Jim Leach has a similar view:

> I think that the terms moderate, liberal, progressive Republican stand for the same things, but the term "liberal" alienates the conservatives more than the term "moderate." Liberal has pejorative implications.[16]

While the old-fashioned liberal Republican welcomed big government programs and a powerful federal government, nearly all the contemporary Republican liberals supported the tax and spending reductions of the Reagan administration, although they stressed that the axe should fall more heavily on defense expenditures than on the domestic programs important to their states. Their liberalism is more evident regarding social-cultural issues, and it is in this area that their dissent has been most vocal. On foreign policy the vigorous internationalism of Rockefeller has been replaced by a cautious attitude toward U.S. intervention overseas, a resentment of the high defense budget, a strong desire for arms control, and a persisting faith in the value of international organizations. The following series of comments from liberals in the U.S. House give some indication of the ideological standpoint of the contemporary Republican liberal:

> I tend to differ from Reagan most strongly on foreign policy issues, and some social issues. I'm particularly concerned about the administration's disregard for international law and organizations.[17]

> I'm a moderate Republican—particularly on social issues like abortion, school prayer and foreign aid. I'm against covert aid to Nicaraguan rebels. But there's not a definitive line, and I shift back and forth according to the issue. I'm fairly conservative on economic and fiscal issues. I'm very tough on debt.[18]

> I share Reagan's view that increasing taxes won't solve the problem. I support Reagan on tax questions. The Reagan administration really lost its opportunities on the government spending issue. He failed to turn the government around because of big increases in defense spending.[19]

The emphasis on fiscal rectitude enabled Republican liberals in the Senate to forge alliances with stalwart Republicans, who, although less sympathetic toward liberal concerns on environmental and civil liberties issues, were increasingly worried by the burgeoning federal budget deficit and were willing to countenance reductions in defense spending. It was this issue, together with the crisis in American farming (which increased the political cost of supporting curbs on domestic farm programs), that brought traditional farm-belt conservatives such as Grassley, of Iowa, Andrews, of North Dakota, Kassebaum, of Kansas, and even Finance Committee Chairman Robert Dole into the liberal camp in 1983–84. This bloc of about 290 liberals and stalwarts was decisive in turning the balance of the Senate toward deficit reduction and in securing the majority leadership for Dole as the successor to Howard Baker.[20]

In the longer term, it is unlikely, given the decentralized nature of congressional elections, that liberal Republicans will be eliminated from either the House or Senate. The fact that the Republicans' wealthy national party committees distribute their financial largesse and deliver services to Republican candidates regardless of ideology works in the liberals' favor, and it seems likely that in states with Yankee-Scandinavian political cultures, weak party systems, and increasingly post-industrial economies (such as Vermont, Connecticut, Oregon, and Washington) liberal Republicans will continue to win elections. The same can be said for states with large urban populations and structural economic problems such as Pennsylvania. The fact that state officeholders are responsible for maintaining large state governments also indicated that Republican governors are likely to incline toward the liberal side. Thus a good year in gubernatorial elections (such as 1986, when the GOP gained 8 governorships) might marginally extend the influence of Republican liberalism within the party.

The election of statewide officeholders, however, does not in itself establish a *party faction* at the national level, and without some revival in presidential politics, liberal Republicanism is likely to continue to wither on the vine. An observer of the 1984 Republican party convention would have had difficulty discovering any vestiges of liberal Republicanism either on the floor or in the platform. And while relatively liberal Republicans can win the odd congressional seat or governorship, the presidency is perceived as the major area of political competition in the United States, and liberal Republicans can recover national influence only by building a constituency at that level. Continued weakness at the national level will eventually undermine liberal Republicanism even in its few remaining electoral strongholds; this has already occurred to some extent in states such as New York, Massachusetts, California, and Michigan. Americans today tend to take their electoral cues from the highly visible national office of the presidency, rather than from particular local or regional factors. Thus the future prospects of liberal Republicanism as a viable political and ideological entity depend on its revival in presidential politics.

For the reasons summarized in earlier chapters, the prospects for such a revival are not particularly bright. There is no reliable national constituency for liberal Republicanism, and there is no national network of think tanks, PACs, or interest groups that might sustain a viable national campaign dedicated to the liberal Republican cause. The problem of campaigning as a "moderate," given modern presidential politics, is also a major impediment to the liberals' aspirations. According to Republican political consultant John Deardourff,

> It is true that the moderates are often what they seem to be: not emotionally committed in the way that people at the poles are. This is true of both parties. Supporters of conservative Republicans and liberal Democrats have more emotional commitment. I see this myself when I attend Republican meetings in my neighborhood. The people like me don't make a lot of noise; we reveal ourselves only in the voting booths, rather than make the fight in the party caucuses.[21]

Similar views are expressed by Senator William S. Cohen:

> Politically it looks very bad on the national level. Moderates find it difficult to generate a lot of support. Those who dominate both parties are those who feel most passionately on issues—the right and the left. Those classified as moderates tend not to have political power or focus. Those who feel passionately on issues tend to deal in absolutes. Moderates, on the other hand, tend to be pragmatic and reflective. I find it hard to deal with absolutes, but it's difficult to mobilize the people who would be classified as moderates.[22]

There are good reasons, then, to doubt the imminence of a liberal Republican resurgence in national politics. Despite the agitation felt by some Republicans over the party's present positions on moral questions, the harsh fact remains that the majority of the voters who feel most strongly about liberal Republican concerns (women's rights, the environment, arms control) are Democratic activists and not Republican partisans. Even given the possible collapse of "Reaganomics," the Republican right can still counterattack by arguing that Reagan had not gone far enough in reducing the size of government and the burden of taxation. Republican liberals are hopelessly outgunned on the ground by the campaign infrastructure of the Republican right, and for any liberal Republican presidential candidate there remains the further obstacle of the adamantine conservatism of the southern and western sections of the GOP. The effects of twenty years of presidential conservatism within the GOP and the disintegration of the professional party structure at the state and local level have so weakened the popular base of support for liberal Republicanism that any future liberal presidential aspirant is likely to find, as Anderson did in 1980, that his electoral base is confined to crossover Democrats and Independents in New England. Finally, the endemic problem of a lack of discipline is inimical to the success of liberal Republicans in presidential politics. John Deardourff saw this as a major barrier to their aspirations in 1988:

> The next major milestone for moderate Republicans will clearly be the 1988 presidential nomination. If Reagan is re-elected this fall, the 1988 race will be between Bush, Baker, Dole, and Kemp. In all there'll probably be 8–10 people. It is not impossible that out of that mix someone perceived as a moderate could prevail. The question is, Can the moderates discipline themselves enough to win? Had the moderates been more disciplined in 1964, they could have won despite Rockefeller's problems. They won't be very disciplined next time either. There'll not be détente between them.[23]

It thus appears that the chances of a liberal Republican revival at the national level are minuscule. Before the liberals realized what was happening to their national constituency, the latter had more or less evaporated, and any future for liberal Republicanism is likely to lie at the congressional, state, and local levels in those scattered states where it still constitutes a winning formula for election. The "reprofessionalization" of the national Republican committees will also encourage the survival of liberal Republicanism in those places where any other brand of Republicanism is likely to be consistently repudiated by the electorate. Although American politics has become more national and ideological in the years since 1960, there remains a sufficiently heterogeneous spectrum of interests and opinions, and a sufficient decentralization of political power in the United States, to ensure that some remnants of the old progressive Republican tradition will persist, although in presidential politics its time has definitely passed.

Postscript II: Parties, Ideology and Realignment in Modern American Politics

Republicans and Democrats have both fallen victim to the changes in the environment of electoral politics discussed earlier in this chapter. Traditional state- and locally based catchall professional politics has been supplanted to a large extent by a process that is more national, ideological, purist, amateur, and nonpartisan. This process first became evident in the 1950s among James Q. Wilson's "amateur Democrats" in their reform clubs and on the Republican right. In 1964, amateur ideologues captured the GOP at the national level even prior to the formal democratization of the nominating process that followed the McGovern-Fraser reforms of 1968–72. The latter proposals merely consolidated a secular trend away from the issueless coalition politics practiced in conventional party structures. The transformation of the party system has had implications for the pattern of American party factionalism, for the role of ideology, and for the theory of critical realignment discussed in Chapter 4. These implications will now be discussed.

Within both major political parties a change in the pattern of intraparty competition has occurred. Because of the erosion of party influence over candidate selection and the enhanced influence of extra-party organizations, the centrist wing in each party has been adversely affected by the rise of the new politics. The fact that both conservative Democrats and liberal Republicans were associated with a crumbling and discredited consensus contributed to their decline. In each party they were overwhelmed by the rise of presidential candidacies based on single issues or charismatic personalities which held little respect for the accommodationist and inclusive politics of the centrists. In the Democratic party the misfit element—the southern conservatives—retained a regional base of support outside the national party apparatus, and the old-style New Deal oblique Cold War liberals were able to rely on organized labor for electoral support in the last resort. The Liberal Republicans, however, did not establish a cohesive mass base of support, and not only lost influence in national politics, but were all but eliminated from the latter. The new politics emphasizes style and ideology; thus, moderation is usually of limited value in primary elections, where the electorate is likely to be considerably less moderate than the general electorate, more involved in politics, and more susceptible to ideological appeals. Moderation, or centrism, in itself is unable to generate sustained activist commitment, and there are thus considerable disadvantages for self-consciously moderate actors in presidential politics. This factor, in combination with the antiestablishment character of American political debate in the 1960–84 period, has strengthened the power of what one may call—for want of a better term—the more purist tendencies in both parties.

The move toward more ideologically based mass politics has led to greater ideological coherence within the ranks of the major parties. The misfits in both parties—racist, reactionary southern Democrats (such as Theodore Bilbo and Eugene Talmadge) and ultraprogressive eastern urban Republicans (such as LaGuardia and Lindsay)—have virtually disappeared at both the national and state level, and in every region of the United States Republicans are invariably more consistently conservative than Democrats. Throughout most of American history the parties have been divided on regional or ethnoreligious grounds, rather than on the basic philosophy of government. With greater ideological emphasis, there is less tolerance of internal diversity by party activists, and tendencies like liberal Republicanism begin to appear rather anachronistic. Yet both parties still seek to win elections, and complete ideological uniformity in a nation as internally heterogeneous as the United States is unlikely to constitute a long-term formula for success. Thus it makes little sense to talk of the "extinction" of liberal Republicans and conservative Democrats, since in America's still diffuse and indisciplined party politics, tendencies diverging from the party mainstream are likely to persist. As the fervor of the antiestablishment revolt of the 1960s recedes, the ideological purists of that era have become the professionals of the 1980s, if only to gain an opportunity to acquire the power to put their ideas into practice. It seems likely that more moderate elements will continue to be important in American party politics (particularly in Congress and among state governors), although they have lost influence at the presidential level.

Finally, we must consider the troublesome question of realignment. There can be little doubt that some kind of realignment has taken place in American politics since 1960. Both political parties have been internally transformed; there has been an extensive change in party loyalties; and the center of the American ideological spectrum has moved somewhat to the right, particularly on the issues of taxation and the size of government. This shift has not been reflected in a durable shift in party identification toward the GOP, however. In the 1980–84 period, most polls found a plurality of Americans still identifying themselves as Democrats, and while the Republicans have dominated presidential elections since 1968, the Democrats have held a firm grip on the U.S. House, most governorships, and most state legislatures. The more conservative shift in the electorate has been channeled through ideologies, interest groups (such as the tax-cutting movement), and candidate preferences rather than through the parties. While repudiating the Democrats at the national level because of fears of fiscal irresponsibility, inflation, and overextended government, the electorate has not been disposed to give the Republicans a totally free hand in government, and has yet to demonstrate overwhelming enthusiasm for the Republicans as a party, as opposed to individual Republican candidates. Although the electorate has moved marginally to the right in its overall ideological preferences, there are important differences on specific issues, and the typical voter exhibits a great predisposition toward ticket-splitting and antipartisanship than a reliance on the party identification characteristic of past eras of American electoral history. The increasing sophistication and volatility of mass electoral preferences permit liberal Republicans and conservative Democrats to survive at the congressional level, where they have both adapted to the new politics on an individual basis. At the national level, where ideology is more important, both groups have lost power, and, in the Republican case, almost vanished from sight.

The distinction between the congressional and presidential parties remains important. Whereas presidential parties were traditionally inclusive and coalitional, and congressional parties the guardians of party orthodoxy, the presidential party in recent times has become more ideological and exclusive, while Congress, as a less partisan institution, has become even more state- and district-oriented. The congressional party, therefore, contains a wider range of ideologies and interests, since there are no effective sanctions that the national party can impose on recalcitrant congressmen or senators, who generally win re-election independent of party support. Liberal Republicans and conservative Democrats survive better in Congress and in the states because congressional and state politics are less ideologically focused than are modern presidential politics, and because the national party still has no effective means of bringing them to heel.

Having considered the above discussion, one is led to question the utility of the Key-Burnham-Sundquist theory of critical realignment in the study of modern American electoral politics. The durable partisan attachments beloved of realignment theorists and essential to the operation of realignment have become less important in American politics as the electorate has become more volatile and fluid. Realignments in public opinion do, of course, occur, but they are not necessarily reflected in consistent party preferences. The increasing velocity with which political information is transmitted, brought about by the communications revolution, results in realignments of public opinion that are likely to be of shorter duration and to occur more frequently than in the past, as a wider spectrum of issues is brought to public attention. The consequence in electoral politics is likely to be strong swings in support between two, more ideologically distinctive, parties at each different level of party competition, in contrast to the rigid, long-term voter alignments with cohesive but doctrinally indistinguishable parties that prevailed throughout much of American history.

Notes

Introduction

1. Samuel Lubell, *The Future of American Politics,* 3rd ed. (New York: Harper & Row, 1965), pp. 191–192.

2. The best (and virtually only) recent analysis of American party factionalism is Howard L. Reiter, "Intra-Party Cleavages in the United States Today," *Western Political Quarterly* 34 (1981): 287–300.

3. Richard Rose, *The Problem of Party Government* (London: Macmillan, 1974), pp. 320–321.

4. Reiter prefers to use a third term, "cluster," to describe American intraparty groups, since this term "expresses the identifiability of individuals without implying organizational coherence." See Reiter, *Western Political Quarterly* 34 (1981): 287.

5. For a further explication and discussion of this terminology see Chapter 4, p. 126.

6. Gary R. Orren, "The Changing Styles of American Party Politics," in *The Future of American Political Parties: The Challenge of Governance,* ed. Joel L. Fleishman (Englewood Cliffs, N.J.: Prentice-Hall, 1982), p. 6.

7. A. James Reichley, *Conservatives in an Age of Change: The Nixon and Ford Administrations* (Washington, D.C.: Brookings Institution, 1981), pp. 287–300.

8. Reiter, *Western Political Quarterly* 34 (1981): 287.

Chapter 1

1. Milton Viorst, *Fall from Grace: The Republican Party and the Puritan Ethic* (New York: New American Library, 1968), p. 37.

2. Malcolm Moos, *The Republicans* (New York: Random House, 1956), p. 30.

3. Ibid., pp. 31–33.

4. Ibid., p. 30.

5. Paul Kleppner et al., *The Evolution of American Electoral Systems* (Westport, Conn.: Greenwood Press, 1982), p. 124.

6. George H. Mayer, *The Republican Party: 1856–1964* (New York: Oxford University Press, 1964), p. 171.

7. James L. Sundquist, *Dynamics of the Party System: Alignment and Realignment of Political Parties in the United States,* revised ed. (Washington, D.C.: Brookings Institution, 1983), p. 109.

8. The Radicals led by Thaddeus Stevens, Charles Sumner, and Benjamin Wade had sought to enforce a harsher settlement on the South and promote black voting rights. They succeeded in passing the Thirteenth, Fourteenth, and Fifteenth Amendments to the Constitution, and in placing one of their own—General Ulysses S. Grant—in the White House. Disenchanted by the response of the liberated southern blacks to their reforms, however, the Radicals' impetus petered out by the end of Reconstruction in 1876. See Mayer, *The Republican Party*, pp. 126–170.

9. For an account of the Liberal Republican revolt see John G. Sproat, *The Best Men: Liberal Reformers in the Gilded Age* (New York: Oxford University Press, 1968), pp. 74–88.

10. Ibid., pp. 13–23.

11. On the Mugwumps, see Sproat, ibid., pp. 112–141.

12. Richard A. Hofstadter, *The Age of Reform: From Bryan to FDR* (New York: Alfred A. Knopf, 1955), p. 140.

13. Sundquist, *Dynamics of the Party System,* p. 163.

14. Ibid., p. 165.

15. For a description of the grievances of the western farmers against the East, see Russel B. Nye, *Midwestern Progressive Politics* (East Lansing: Michigan State University Press, 1959), pp. 10–15.

16. John Morton Blum, *The Republican Roosevelt,* 2nd ed. (Cambridge, Mass.: Harvard University Press, 1977), p. 35.

17. On Roosevelt's "imperialist" policy and the difficulties it presented for some of his progressive allies in Congress, see Barton J. Bernstein and Franklin A. Leib, "Progressive Republican Senators and American Imperialism 1898–1916: A Reappraisal," *Mid-America* 50 (1968): 163–205.

18. On the urban, middle-class dimension of progressivism, see Hofstadter, *The Age of Reform*, pp. 148–163.

19. Herbert Croly, *The Promise of American Life* (New York: E. P. Dutton, 1963), p. 17.

20. Quoted in Hofstadter, *The Age of Reform*, pp. 262–263.

21. See Nye, *Midwestern Progressive Politics,* p. 14.

22. On the influence of the railroads in California and the resentment they engendered, see George E. Mowry, *The California Progressives* (Berkeley, Calif.: University of California Press, 1951), pp. 1–22.

23. Nye, *Midwestern Progressive Politics,* pp. 257–275.

24. Richard C. Bain and Judith H. Parris, *Convention Decisions and Voting Records* (Washington, D.C.: Brookings Institution, 1973), p. 179.

25. Moos, *The Republicans,* p. 158.

26. For contrasting views on the cohesiveness and influence of the Republican Senate progressives in the 1920s, see Darrel A. Ashby, "Progressivism Against Itself: the Senate Western Bloc in the 1920s," *Mid-America* 50 (1968): 291–304, and Erik Olssen, "The Progressive Group in Congress 1922–1929," *The Historian* 42 (1980): 244–263.

27. On the relationship between the western progressives and the farm bloc, see Ashby, ibid., and Patrick G. O'Brien, "A Reexamination of the Senate Farm Bloc 1921–33," *Agricultural History* 47 (1973): 248–264.

28. See Mayer, *The Republican Party,* p. 386.

29. See Moos, *The Republicans,* pp. 330–331.

30. Mayer, *The Republican Party,* p. 349.

31. See Sundquist, *Dynamics of the Party System,* p. 187.

32. On Hoover's political position in the 1920s, see David Burner, *Herbert Hoover: A Public Life* (New York: Atheneum, 1984), pp. 138–158.

33. On the relationship between FDR and the progressive Republicans in this period, see Ronald A. Feinman, *The Twilight of Progressivism: The Western Republican Senators and the New Deal* (Baltimore: Johns Hopkins University Press, 1981), pp. 48–90; and Ronald A. Mulder, "The Progressive Insurgents in the United States Senate, 1935–36: Was There a Second New Deal?," *Mid-America* 57 (1975): 106–125.

34. Feinman, ibid., p. 204.

35. Cross-filing permitted candidates to enter the primaries of both parties and possibly capture both nominations, as did Governor Earl Warren in 1948.

36. See James T. Patterson, *Congressional Conservatism and the New Deal: The Growth of the Conservative Coalition in Congress 1933–39* (Lexington: University of Kentucky Press, 1967), p. 7.

37. Ibid., p. 16.

38. James T. Patterson, *Mr. Republican: A Biography of Robert A. Taft* (Boston: Houghton Mifflin Co., 1972), p. 192.

39. Henry Cabot Lodge, *The Storm Has Many Eyes: A Personal Narrative* (New York: W. W. Norton & Co., 1973), p. 27.

40. E. J. Kahn, *Jock: The Life and Times of John Hay Whitney* (Garden City, N.Y.: Doubleday & Co., 1981), p. xiv.

41. On government-business relationships during the war years, see John Morton Blum, *V was for Victory: Politics and Culture During World War II* (New York: Harvest, 1976), pp. 105–146.

42. On Wall Street's influence over the GOP in the 1940–50 period, see Michael W. Miles, *The Odyssey of the American Right* (New York: Oxford University Press, 1980), pp. 42–43.

43. Donald Bruce Johnson, *The Republican Party and Wendell Willkie* (Urbana: University of Illinois Press, 1960), pp. 63–67. On Willkie's campaign for the Republican nomination in 1940, see also Steve Neal, *Dark Horse: A Biography of Wendell Willkie* (Garden City, N.Y.: Doubleday & Co., 1984), pp. 66–121.

44. See Johnson, ibid., p. 67.

45. On Dewey's control of the New York GOP, see Neal R. Peirce, *The Megastates of America: People, Politics and Power in the Ten Great States* (New York: W. W. Norton & Co., 1972), p. 48.

46. Interview with Senator Scott, May 16, 1984.

47. Jacob K. Javits (with Rafael Steinberg), *Javits: The Autobiography of a Public Man* (Boston: Houghton Mifflin Co., 1980), p. 320.

48. Interview with Herbert Brownell, February 10, 1984.

49. Patterson, *Mr. Republican,* p. 425.

50. The liberals were able to prevail at Republican conventions in the 1940–52 period because of their solid support in the eastern states, which accounted for approximately one-third of the total convention vote. To this they were usually able to add the midwestern and western progressive strongholds: Michigan, Minnesota, Oregon, and California. If this was still insufficient for a majority, the vital margin of victory could be found through credentials challenges or patronage inducements with regard to some of the southern delegates (see Tables 1-4 and 2-2).

51. Miles, *The Odyssey of the American Right,* p. 182. On Nixon's foreign policy views at this time, see Stephen A. Ambrose, *Nixon: The Education of a Politician 1913–62* (London: Simon & Schuster, 1987).

52. Dewey, quoted in Leonard Lurie, *The King-Makers* (New York: Coward, McCann & Geohegan, 1971), p. 85.

53. Dwight D. Eisenhower, *Mandate for Change: Memoirs 1953–6* (London: Heinemann, 1963), p. 18.

54. Regarding Eisenhower's fears of Taft's isolationism and its impact on his decision to run in 1952, see Stephen A. Ambrose, *Eisenhower: Soldier, General of the Army, President-Elect* (London: Allen & Unwin, 1984), pp. 495–499, 515–523.

55. Paul T. David, Malcolm Moos, and Ralph M. Goldman, *Presidential Nominating Politics in 1952: The National Story* (Baltimore: Johns Hopkins University Press, 1954), p. 49.

56. Patterson, *Mr. Republican,* p. 560.

57. On Eisenhower's Republican background, see Ambrose, *Eisenhower: Soldier, General of the Army, President-Elect,* pp. 24–26.

58. Gary W. Reichard, *The Reaffirmation of Republicanism: Eisenhower and the 83rd Congress* (Knoxville: University of Tennessee Press, 1975), p. VIII.

59. See, for example, Henry Fairlie, *The Parties: Republicans and Democrats in this Century* (New York: Pocket Books, 1979), p. 52; George F. Gilder and Bruce K. Chapman, *The Party that Lost its Head* (New York: Alfred A. Knopf, 1966), p. 45. On Eisenhower's resentment at Republican demands for patronage, see Stephen A. Ambrose, *Eisenhower: The President 1952–69* (New York: Pocket Books, 1979), pp. 152–153.

60. See especially Ambrose, ibid., and Fred I. Greenstein, *The Hidden Hand Presidency: Eisenhower as Leader* (New York: Basic Books, 1982).

61. Cornelius P. Cotter, "Eisenhower as Party Leader," *Political Science Quarterly* 98 (1983): 256.

62. Quoted in Sherman Adams, *Firsthand Report: The Story of the*

Eisenhower Administration (New York: Harper & Brothers, 1961), p. 299.

63. David W. Reinhard, *The Republican Right Since 1945* (Lexington: University of Kentucky Press, 1983), pp. 157–158. For a more sympathetic account of Eisenhower's personal political philosophy see Robert Griffith, "Dwight D. Eisenhower and the Corporate Commonwealth," *American Historical Review* 87 (1982): 87–122.

64. Stewart Alsop, *Nixon and Rockefeller: A Double Portrait* (Garden City, N.Y.: Doubleday & Co., 1960), p. 26.

65. On Rockefeller's 1959–60 effort, see Theodore H. White, *The Making of the President: 1960* (London: Jonathan Cape, 1962), pp. 66–77.

66. Ibid., p. 183.

67. Ibid., pp. 183–184.

69. On the Treaty of Fifth Avenue, see Ambrose, *Nixon,* pp. 550–553.

70. T. H. White, *The Making of the President: 1960,* p. 22.

Chapter 2

1. On the relationship between Eisenhower and Taft, see Patterson, *Mr. Republican,* pp. 577–606.

2. Richard Rovere, *The Goldwater Caper* (London: Methuen, 1966), p. 61.

3. On the growth of Republicanism in the South, see Jack Bass and Walter DeVries, *The Transformation of Southern Politics: Social Change and Political Consequence Since 1945* (New York: New American Library, 1977), esp. pp. 23–40; Alexander P. Lamis, *The Two-Party South* (New York: Oxford University Press, 1984), pp. 20–43; Raymond Wolfinger and Robert B. Arsenau, "Partisan Change in the South 1952–76," in *Political Parties: Development and Decay,* ed. Louis Maisel and Joseph Cooper (Beverley Hills: Sage Publications, 1978), Chap. 6; Paul Allen Beck, "Partisan Dealignment in the Postwar South," *American Political Science Review* 71 (1977): 477–496.

4. On the formation of the core group that later developed into the Conservative movement, see William A. Rusher, *The Rise of the Right* (New York: William Morrow & Co., 1984), pp. 55–86.

5. On McCarthy's appeal to Roman Catholics, see Seymour Martin Lipset, "Three Decades of the Radical Right: Coughlinites, McCarthyites, And Birchers," in *The Radical Right,* ed. Daniel Bell (Garden City, N.Y.: Doubleday & Co., 1962), pp. 391–421, and Miles, *The Odyssey of the American Right,* pp. 142–145.

6. Miles, *The Odyssey of the American Right,* p. 257.

7. Ibid., p. 257.

8. On Buckley's contribution to the growth of the conservative intellectual movement, see George H. Nash, *The Conservative Intellectual Movement in America Since 1945* (New York: Basic Books, 1976), pp. 123–127.

9. Miles, *The Odyssey of the American Right,* p. 265.

10. Ibid., p. 265.

11. Robert D. Novak, *The Agony of the GOP: 1964* (New York: Macmillan, 1965), p. 86. The John Birch Society, founded by Robert Welch in 1958, was the most notorious of the post-McCarthy conservative organizations of the 1950s. Believing in the all-pervasive nature of the "international communist conspiracy" (which even included President Eisenhower), the society was conducted on a strict hierarchical and clandestine basis. At its peak, the John Birch Society had 75,000 members and achieved its greatest political impact in southern California, where it became very influential within the weak and disaggregated state Republican party. See Alan F. Westin, "The John Birch Society," in Bell, *The Radical Right*, pp. 239–268, and Seymour Martin Lipset, "Three Decades of the Radical Right," ibid., pp. 421–439.

12. Ibid., p. 86. See also Ambrose, *Nixon: The Education of a Politician*, pp. 656–660.

13. Stephen Hess and David S. Broder, *The Republican Establishment: The Present and Future of the GOP* (New York: Harper & Row, 1967), pp. 59–60.

14. On the early days of the Goldwater movement, see F. Clifton White, *Suite 3505* (New Rochelle, N.Y.: Arlington House, 1967), esp. pp. 20–98, and Rusher, *The Rise of the Right*, pp. 87–127.

15. John H. Kessel, *The Goldwater Coalition: Republican Strategies in 1964* (Indianapolis, Ind.: Bobbs-Merrill, 1968), p. 70.

16. Barry M. Goldwater, *The Conscience of a Conservative* (New York: Hillman Books, 1960).

17. Novak, *The Agony of the GOP: 1964*, p. 22.

18. Ibid., p. 44.

19. Barry M. Goldwater, *With No Apologies: The Personal and Political Memoirs of United States Senator Barry M. Goldwater* (New York: William Morrow & Co., 1979), p. 110.

20. F. C. White, *Suite 3505*, pp. 48–50.

21. Theodore H. White, *The Making of the Presidency: 1964* (New York: Atheneum, 1965), p. 132.

22. Kessel, *The Goldwater Coalition*, p. 71.

23. Ibid., pp. 39–40.

24. Interview with F. Clifton White, April 5, 1984.

25. Hess and Broder, *The Republican Establishment*, p. 337.

26. Reinhard, *The Republican Right Since 1945*, p. 197.

27. On Goldwater's poor primary showings, see James W. Davis, *Presidential Primaries: Road to the White House* (Westport, Conn.: Greenwood Press, 1980), pp. 330–334.

28. See Kessel, *The Goldwater Coalition*, p. 87.

29. Ibid., p. 87.

30. Ibid., p. 88.

31. See Hess and Broder, *The Republican Establishment*, pp. 58–59.

32. Ibid., p. 51.

33. See George Thayer, *Who Shakes the Money Tree: American Cam-*

paign Financing Practices from 1789 to the Present (New York: Simon & Schuster, 1973), p. 84.

34. Hess and Broder, *The Republican Establishment,* p. 61.

35. Rovere, *The Goldwater Caper,* p. 88. On the purist attitudes of the Goldwater delegates, see also Richard A. Hofstadter, *The Paranoid Style in American Politics,* 2nd ed. (Chicago: Phoenix Press, 1979), Chapter 4, esp. pp. 101–14.

36. Arthur Larson, *A Republican Looks at His Party* (New York: Harper & Brothers, 1956), p. 10.

37. See Novak, *The Agony of the GOP: 1964,* pp. 46–48.

38. Ibid., p. 219.

39. On the collapse of Rockefeller's support, see ibid., pp. 143–157.

40. Ibid., p. 157.

41. On Eisenhower's reluctance to get involved in the 1964 struggle. See T. H. White, *The Making of the President: 1964,* pp. 69–72.

42. Interview with A. James Reichley, April 17, 1984.

43. Hugh Scott, *Come to the Party* (Englewood Cliffs, N.J.: Prentice-Hall, 1968), p. 183.

44. The Republican liberals might, for instance, have emphasized the civil rights tradition of the southern 'mountain' Republicans. Indeed, southern Republicans at the state level, such as Ted Dalton and Linwood Holton in Virginia, Winthrop Rockefeller in Arkansas, and James Holshouser in North Carolina, had some success with this approach in the 1960s. Given the approaching enfranchisement of southern blacks and the party's general identification with modernizing forces in the region, this policy might have made more electoral sense than attempting to conciliate the segregationists.

45. Rovere, *The Goldwater Caper,* p. 52.

46. For a more detailed account of the events at Cleveland, see T. H. White. *The Making of the President: 1964,* pp. 130–161.

47. Novak, *The Agony of the GOP: 1964,* p. 441.

48. Ibid., p. 441.

49. See Aaron Wildavsky, *The Revolt Against the Masses and Other Essays in Public Policy* (London: Basic Books, 1971), pp. 246–69.

50. Gilder and Chapman, *The Party that Lost its Head,* p. 97.

51. On the Citizens' Committee and the part played by Eisenhower, see Ambrose, *Eisenhower: The President,* pp. 98–103.

52. On the failure of the RGA, see The Ripon Society, *From Disaster to Distinction* (New York: Pocket Books, 1966), pp. 78–79.

53. On Miller, Goldwater, and Operation Dixie, see Gilder and Chapman, *The Party that Lost its Head,* pp. 58–62. On the significance of the Alabama Senate race that the Republicans almost won, see Walter Dean Burnham, "The Alabama Senatorial Election of 1962: Return of Inter-Party Competition," *Journal of Politics* 26 (1964): 798–829.

54. At the 1963 YR convention in San Francisco, 75% of the delegates endorsed Goldwater for the presidency. They also passed a "Liberty Amendment" demanding abolition of the federal income tax, and there was a

segregationist slant to the entire gathering, which was widely reported in the press. See Novak, *The Agony of the GOP: 1964*, pp. 195–200.

55. On Morhouse's proposals, see Novak, *The Agony of the GOP: 1964*, pp. 53–60.

56. The success of the very amateurish Henry Cabot Lodge campaign in New Hampshire perhaps serves as an indication of what might have been had the liberals seriously attempted to challenge Goldwater in a grass roots campaign. See T. H. White, *The Making of the President: 1964*, pp. 108–111.

57. See Novak, *The Agony of the GOP: 1964*, pp. 449–455.

58. Kessel, *The Goldwater Coalition*, p. 119.

59. T. H. White, *The Making of the President: 1964*, p. 217.

60. Wildavsky, *The Revolt Against the Masses*, p. 258.

61. On the "hidden conservative vote," see Philip E. Converse, Aage R. Clausen, and Warren E. Miller, "Electoral Myth and Reality: The 1964 Election," *American Political Science Review* 59 (1965): 321–336.

62. On the 1964 Republican general election campaign, see T. H. White, *The Making of the President: 1964*, pp. 315–346.

63. On the impact of Goldwater's candidacy on Republican House candidates, see Robert A. Schoenberger, "Campaign Strategy and Party Loyalty: The Electoral Relevance of Candidate Decision-Making in the 1964 Congressional Elections," *American Political Science Review* 63 (1969): 515–520.

64. From the Gallup poll cited in *Election '64: A Ripon Society Report*, ed. Thomas E. Petri (Cambridge, Mass.: The Ripon Society, 1964), p. 38. On the long-term effects of the 1964 elections on Republican support among blacks, see Robert Axelrod, "Where the Votes Come From: An Analysis of Electoral Coalitions, 1952–1968," *American Political Science Review* 66 (1972): 11–20; "Presidential Elections Coalitions in 1984," *American Political Science Review* 80 (1986): 281–284; and Norman H. Nie, Sidney Verba, and John R. Petrocik, *The Changing American Voter*, enlarged ed. (Cambridge, Mass.: Harvard University Press, 1979), pp. 226–229.

65. See Kevin P. Phillips, *Post-Conservative America* (New York: Vintage Books, 1983), p. 233.

66. See T. H. White, *The Making of the President: 1964*, p. 382.

67. Ibid., p. 382.

68. Petri, *Election '64*, p. 23.

69. See F. C. White, *Suite 3505*, pp. 49–50, and Stephen A. Shadegg, *What Happened to Goldwater? The Inside Story of the 1964 Republican Campaign* (New York: Holt, Rinehart & Winston, 1965), p. 92.

Chapter 3

1. See The Ripon Society, *From Disaster to Distinction*, p. 86.

2. The position of the liberal Republicans in Congress, and the background to the Ford-Halleck contest are discussed at greater length in Chapter 5.

3. Jacob K. Javits, *Order of Battle: A Republican's Call to Reason* (New York: Pocket Books, 1966), p. 63.

4. Ibid., p. 63.

5. The Ripon Society, Preface to *The Lessons of Victory* (New York: Dial Press, 1969).

6. "The Ripon Role as Ripon Sees It," in *The Ripon Papers, 1963–68,* ed. Thomas E. Petri and Lee W. Heubner (Washington, D.C.: The National Press, 1968), pp. 225–230. See also Hess & Broder, *The Republican Establishment,* pp. 68–75; and interviews with Thomas Petri, April 13, 1984, and Josiah Lee Auspitz, March 19, 1984.

7. On Ripon's alternative electoral strategy, see The Ripon Society, *From Disaster to Distinction,* pp. 112–122.

8. *The Ripon Papers 1963–68,* ed. Petri and Heubner, pp. 25–45.

9. Ibid., p. 5.

10. Ibid., p. 12.

11. Ibid., p. 227, and interview with Walter N. Thayer, February 16, 1984.

12. Howard L. Reiter, "Ripon: Left Spur to the GOP," *The Nation,* February 17, 1964, 202–205.

13. *The Ripon Forum* (Newsletter of the Ripon Society), November 1967, 6–7. See also The Ripon Society, *From Disaster to Distinction,* pp. 90–94, and Petri and Heubner, *The Ripon Papers,* pp. 25–45.

14. The Ripon Society, *From Disaster to Distinction,* p. 92.

15. On Lindsay's campaign, see Hess and Broder, *The Republican Establishment,* pp. 318–320, and Nick Thimmesch, *The Condition of Republicanism* (New York: Norton, 1968), pp. 194–221.

16. See Hess and Broder, ibid., p. 320, and Thimmesch, ibid., p. 212.

17. See, for example, an editorial urging Lindsay to remain in the Republican party: *Ripon Forum,* February 1971.

18. Lindsay interview, July 11, 1984. On Lindsay's personal differences with Rockefeller, see Joseph E. Persico, *The Imperial Rockefeller: A Biography of Nelson Rockefeller* (New York: Pocket Books, 1982), pp. 232–236.

19. On the decline in Republican support among "high-status," college educated voters in the 1960s, see Everett Carll Ladd (with Charles D. Hadley), *Transformations of the Party System,* 2nd ed. (New York: Norton, 1978), pp. 239–261.

20. *The Republican Governors' Association: The Case for a Third Force* (Ripon Society Report), December 1964.

21. The Ripon Society, *From Disaster to Distinction,* p. 88. The 1966 RGA meeting at Colorado Springs did nevertheless decide to hire the association's first full-time executive director.

22. On the events at Colorado Springs see *Ripon Forum,* January 1967, 4–8.

23. *Ripon Forum,* January 1969, 7–8. Also Melvin H. Bernstein, "GOP Governors: The Illusion of Power," *The Nation,* January 6, 1969.

24. On the CRO see The Ripon Society, *From Disaster to Distinction,* p. 87.

25. Hess and Broder, *The Republican Establishment,* p. 261.

26. On RFP see ibid., pp. 71–72, and The Ripon Society, *From Disaster to Distinction,* p. 87. See also Edward L. Schapsmeier and Frederick N. Schapsmeier, *The Greenwood Encyclopaedia of American Institutions: Political Parties* (Westport, Conn.: Greenwood Press, 1981), pp. 398–399.

27. On Bliss's revitalization of the Republican national organization for the 1966 campaign, see Hess and Broder, *The Republican Establishment,* pp. 45–54.

28. See *Ripon Forum,* November 1967, 8.

29. On Romney's assets and liabilities see Hess and Broder, *The Republican Establishment,* pp. 117–139.

30. In this election Romney secured an estimated 34% of the black vote in Michigan; see ibid., p. 107.

31. See Theodore H. White, *The Making of the President: 1968* (London: Jonathan Cape, 1969), p. 38.

32. Ibid., pp. 36–38.

33. In a Christmas 1967 poll, Nixon led Romney among Republicans by 64% to 12%. See T. H. White, *The Making of the President: 1968,* p. 57.

34. Lewis Chester, Godfrey Hodgson, and Bruce Page, *An American Melodrama: The Presidential Campaign of 1968* (London: Andre Deutsch, 1969), pp. 100–101.

35. Ibid., p. 100.

36. Richard M. Nixon, *RN: The Memoirs of Richard Nixon* (London: Arrow Books, 1979), p. 264.

37. On the movement of some conservatives towards Nixon, see Rusher, *The Rise of the Right,* pp. 194–202.

38. Garry Wills, *Nixon Agonistes: The Crisis of a Self-Made Man* (New York: New American Library, 1979), p. 240.

39. See Jules Witcover, *The Resurrection of Richard Nixon* (New York: G. P. Putnam's Sons, 1970), p. 183.

40. Ibid., p. 147.

41. A poll of Republican County Chairmen in April 1966 had Nixon leading by 4 to 1 over Romney. In Romney's supposed stronghold in the East, Nixon led by 260 to 177, and in the South he led by 663 to 53. See Witcover, *The Resurrection of Richard Nixon,* p. 184.

42. On Reagan's baptism in presidential politics, see Rusher, *The Rise of the Right,* pp. 202–207; Chester et al., *An American Melodrama,* pp. 190–208; and Lou Cannon, *Reagan* (New York: Perigree Books, 1982), pp. 157–160.

43. Chester et al., *An American Melodrama,* pp. 217–220; and The Ripon Society, *The Lessons of Victory,* pp. 69–71.

44. Chester et al., ibid., pp. 220–223.

45. T. H. White, *The Making of the President: 1968,* p. 231.

46. Interview with Senator Javits, November 25, 1983.

47. Interview with Meade Alcorn, January 25, 1984.

48. R. Connery and G. Benjamin, *Rockefeller of New York: Executive*

Power in the Statehouse (Ithaca, N.Y.: Cornell University Press, 1979), p. 76.

49. Thayer interview, February 16, 1984.

50. Chester et al., *An American Melodrama,* p. 380.

51. T. H. White, *The Making of the President: 1968,* pp. 137–138.

52. Connery and Benjamin, *Rockefeller of New York,* p. 72.

53. Herbert E. Alexander, *Money in Politics* (Washington, D.C.: Public Affairs Press, 1972), p. 61.

54. Chester et al., *An American Melodrama,* p. 392.

55. Ibid., pp. 457–458.

56. Ibid., pp. 459–475, and interview with F. Clifton White, April 5, 1984.

57. Ibid., p. 483. Some liberals did attempt to organize a revolt on the convention floor against Agnew, with John Lindsay as their alternative candidate. Governor John Chafee of Rhode Island and Congressman Charles Goodell of New York attempted to organize the revolt, but Lindsay was eager to retain some credibility as a genuine Republican and Nixon had already requested that he nominate Agnew from the platform of the convention. Thus, in a fashion similar to that of so many attempted liberal counterattacks, the insurgency petered out in a derisory effort to nominate the unfortunate George Romney for the vice presidency.

58. Joe McGinnis, *The Selling of the President 1968* (New York: Washington Square Press, 1969).

59. On the "southern strategy," see Chester et al., *An American Melodrama,* pp. 620–621.

60. Ibid., p. 763.

61. Richard Norton Smith, *Thomas E. Dewey and His Times* (New York: Simon and Schuster, 1982), pp. 595–97, and interview with Herbert Brownell, February 10, 1984. Indeed, in the 1964–68 period, Nixon had probably taken more interest in Ripon's activities than any other leading Republican had; see Reiter, "Ripon: Left Spur to the GOP," *The Nation,* February 17, 1969, and interview with Congressman Petri, April 13, 1984.

62. Nixon, *RN,* p. 23.

63. On the Nixon team, see A. James Reichley, *Conservatives in an Age of Change: The Nixon and Ford Administrations,* pp. 59–78; and Rowland Evans, Jr. and Robert A. Novak, *Nixon in the White House: The Frustration of Power* (New York: Vintage Books, 1972), pp. 38–74.

64. Evans and Novak, ibid., p. 34.

65. Kevin P. Phillips, *The Emerging Republican Majority* (Garden City, N.Y.: Anchor Books, 1970), p. 471.

66. *Ripon Forum,* July/August 1970.

67. See Ripon's attack on Phillips, ibid., pp. 9–20.

68. The concept of a guaranteed income (originally based on economist Milton Friedman's idea of a "negative income tax") appealed to Moynihan and Nixon as a means of alleviating poverty without creating a massive welfare bureaucracy. They also hoped that it would give more incentives to

recipients to get off welfare and look for work. The plan was too reminiscent of Great Society–style social engineering for both Republican and Democratic conservatives, while many liberals regarded it as an underhanded means of dismantling the welfare system. Although the House passed FAP in 1970 and 1971, the plan died each time in the Senate Finance Committee. See Reichley, *Conservatives in an Age of Change,* pp. 138–151.

69. In fact, school integration proceeded at a rapid pace during the Nixon years, with the number of black children in all-black schools falling from 68% to 8% during his time in office. However, this was due more to court orders and congressional threats to cut off funds to segregated school districts than to the administration's efforts. See Nixon, *RN,* p. 443.

70. See Evans and Novak, *Nixon in the White House,* pp. 133–176.

71. Evans and Novak, *Nixon in the White House,* pp. 159–172.

72. Quoted in Evans and Novak, ibid., p. 316.

73. On the 1970 campaign, see Evans and Novak, ibid., pp. 303–346, and William Safire, *Before the Fall: An Inside View of the Pre-Watergate White House* (New York: Belmont Tower Books, 1975), pp. 316–340.

74. Nixon, *RN,* p. 491. The term "social issue" was devised by Scammon and Wattenberg to refer to a series of related issues that cut across the traditional New Deal socioeconomic cleavage: "These situations have been described variously as law and order, backlash, antiyouth, malaise, change or alienation. These situations, we believe, constitute a new and potent political issue." This should be distinguished from the term "social issues," as used by the new right in the 1980s to refer more specifically to issues related to religion and the family, e.g., abortion, school prayer, premarital sex. See Richard M. Scammon and Ben J. Wattenberg, *The Real Majority* (New York: Coward, McCann & Geohegan, 1971), p. 20.

75. On Nixon's relations with the liberal Republicans in Congress, see Reichley, *Conservatives in an Age of Change,* pp. 89–97.

76. Interview with Charles Goodell, April 6, 1984.

77. The New York Conservative party had been formed in 1961 by J. Daniel Mahoney and Kieran O'Doherty in reaction to Rockefeller and Javits's control of the state Republican party, and to the influence of the Liberal party on elections in New York. In 1965, William F. Buckley, Jr. had run on the Conservative line for Mayor of New York City against John Lindsay. In 1966 the Conservatives outpolled the Liberals and won the coveted "third line" on the New York ballot. On the origins and development of the Conservative party in New York, see J. Daniel Mahoney, *Actions Speak Louder* (New Rochelle, N.Y.: Arlington House, 1968).

78. Safire, *Before the Fall,* p. 318.

79. Goodell interview.

80. On the change in economic policy, see Reichley, *Conservatives in an Age of Change,* pp. 217–230.

81. Evans and Novak, *Nixon in the White House,* pp. 364–367.

82. I am using the terms moderate and progressive in the sense used in the Introduction and in Reichley's *Conservatives in an Age of Change,* pp. 217–230.

83. Ibid., pp. 85–86.
84. Ibid., p. 91.
85. Interview with Senator Scott, May 16, 1984.
86. Senator Scott, who voted against Haynsworth and for Carswell, later described this as "the worst damn mistake I ever made. The charges against Haynsworth were probably insufficient to warrant the vote I cast against him. There was only one Senator who cast the right vote. Marlow Cook knew both nominees, and he voted for Haynsworth and against Carswell." Scott interview.
87. Reichley, *Conservatives in an Age of Change,* p. 119, pp. 195–197.
88. On FAP it was the conservatives who deserted the Republican fold and defeated the administration; see ibid., p. 151.
89. Interview with Mr. Gude, April 30, 1984.
90. Donald Riegle (with Trevor Armbister), *O Congress* (New York: Popular Library, 1972), p. 55.
91. On Ashbrook's campaign, see Rusher, *The Rise of the Right,* pp. 244–246.
92. On Rockefeller's move to the right, see Robert D. Behn, "The New Rockefeller," *Ripon Forum,* January 1974, 5–7.
93. On the negative character of the Nixon vote in 1972, see Stanley Kelley, Jr., *Interpreting Elections* (Princeton, N.J.: Princeton University Press, 1983), pp. 99–125.
94. Nixon, *RN,* pp. 761–770.
95. The passage of the 1973 War Powers Act over Nixon's veto was one indication of the distance between Nixon and the Republican liberals in the final phase of his presidency. The act was drawn up in large part by Jacob Javits and had heavy liberal Republican support.
96. This appointment infuriated conservatives and turned many of them decisively against the Ford administration. See Rusher, *The Rise of the Right,* pp. 263–264.
97. On Ford's conservative philosophy of government, see Reichley, *Conservatives in an Age of Change,* p. 287.
98. Ibid., pp. 299–300.
99. Ibid., pp. 392–394.
100. Ibid., pp. 322–332.
101. Persico, *The Imperial Rockefeller,* pp. 284–294, and interview with Rockefeller's counsel as Vice President, Peter Wallison, April 20, 1984.
102. Persico, ibid., p. 285.
103. On the right's disenchantment with Nixon, see Rusher, *The Rise of the Right,* pp. 239–261.
104. William A. Rusher, *The Making of the New Majority Party* (New York: Sheed & Ward, 1975), p. xxii.
105. On the genesis of the Reagan campaign, see Jules Witcover, *Marathon: The Pursuit of the Presidency 1972–76* (New York: Viking Press, 1977), pp. 65–76, and Cannon, *Reagan,* pp. 192–201.
106. Interview with Mr. Sears, April 27, 1984.
107. Interview with Senator Mathias, May 7, 1984.

108. Interview with Mr. Wallison, April 20, 1984.

109. On Ripon's move to Washington, see Chapter 6.

110. On liberal Republicans in Congress, see Chapter 5.

111. Robert D. Behn, "The Plight of Progressive Republicans," *Ripon Quarterly* 3 (1977): 11.

112. Ibid., p. 13.

113. For an example of bad relations between liberal Republicans and state party activists, see the section on Connecticut and Massachusetts in Chapter 4.

114. For an account of the Ford-Reagan primary campaign, see Jules Witcover, *Marathon*, pp. 373–432.

115. Ibid., pp. 456–471.

116. Nie et al., *The Changing American Voter*, p. 364.

117. On the rise of the South and West, see Kirkpatrick Sale, *Power Shift: The Rise of the Southern Rim and Its Challenge to the Eastern Establishment* (New York: Vintage Books, 1976); also Peter Wiley and Robert Gottlieb, *Empires in the Sun: The Rise of the New American West* (New York:' G. P. Putnam's Sons, 1982), esp. Part I, pp. 3–74; and Philips, *Post-Conservative America*, esp. pp. 88–104.

118. See Scammon and Wattenberg, *The Real Majority;* Jeane J. Kirkpatrick, *The New Presidential Elite: Men and Women in National Politics* (New York: The Russell Sage Foundation and The 20th Century Fund, 1976), esp. pp. 239–328; Ladd and Hadley, *Transformations of the Party System,* pp. 181–274; William Schneider, "Democrats and Republicans, Liberals and Conservatives," in *Emerging Coalitions in American Politics*, ed. Seymour Martin Lipset (San Francisco Institute for Contemporary Studies, 1978), pp. 183–254; Phillips, *Post-Conservative America*, pp. 220–233.

119. *Ripon Forum*, May 1968, 4.

120. Ibid., p. 4.

121. Nie et al., *The Changing American Voter*, pp. 223–226; John R. Petrocik, "Realignment: New Party Coalitions and the Nationalization of the South," *Journal of Politics* 49 (1987): 347–375.

Chapter 4

1. Nie et al., *The Changing American Voter;* Jeane J. Kirkpatrick, "Changing Patterns of Electoral Competition," in *The New American Political System,* ed. Anthony King (Washington, D.C.: American Enterprise Institute, 1978); Ladd and Hadley, *Transformations of the Party System;* Walter Dean Burnham, *The Current Crisis in American Politics* (New York: Oxford University Press, 1982).

2. On party identification in the 1950s see Angus Campbell, Philip E. Converse, Warren E. Miller, and Donald E. Stokes, *The American Voter— An Abridgement* (New York: John Wiley & Sons, 1964), pp. 67–96.

3. Burnham, *The Current Crisis,* pp. 121–161; Nie et al., *The Changing American Voter,* pp. 53–54, 57–59. See also Martin P. Wattenberg, *The*

Decline of American Political Parties 1952–80 (Cambridge, Mass.: Harvard University Press, 1984); and William Schneider, "Antipartisanship in America," in *Parties and Democracy in Britain and America,* ed. Vernon Bogdanor (New York: Praeger, 1984), pp. 92–123.

4. Nie et al., *The Changing American Voter,* pp. 96–173.

5. On the theory of realignment and critical elections see V. O. Key, Jr., "A Theory of Critical Elections," *Journal of Politics* 17 (1955): 3–18; "Secular Realignment and the Party System," *Journal of Politics* 21 (1959): 198–210; Walter Dean Burnham, *Critical Elections and the Mainsprings of American Politics* (New York: Norton, 1970), pp. 1–33; and Sundquist, *Dynamics of the Party System,* pp. 1–18, 35–49.

6. Burnham, *The Current Crisis in American Politics,* pp. 121–161; Nie et al., *The Changing American Voter,* pp. 47–73; Kirkpatrick, in King, *The New American Political System,* pp. 249–285.

7. Nie et al., ibid., pp. 47–73.

8. See Larry Sabato, *The Rise of Political Consultants: New Ways of Winning Elections* (New York: Basic Books, 1984).

9. Nelson W. Polsby, *Consequences of Party Reform* (New York: Oxford University Press, 1983); Jeane J. Kirkpatrick, *Dismantling the Parties: Reflections on Party Decline and Party Decomposition* (Washington, D.C.: American Enterprise Institute, 1978); and Austin Ranney, "The Political Parties: Reform and Decline," in King, *The New American Political System,* pp. 213–247.

10. Burnham, *Critical Elections,* pp. 134–174; Ladd and Hadley, *Transformations of the American Party System,* pp. 181–275; and Howard L. Reiter, *Selecting the President: The Nominating Process in Transition* (Philadelphia: University of Pennsylvania Press, 1985), esp. pp. 24–83.

11. Nie et al., pp. 96–173.

12. James Q. Wilson, *The Amateur Democrat: Club Politics in Three Cities* (Chicago: University of Chicago Press, 1962), p. 17.

13. Ibid., p. 18.

14. Wildavsky, *The Revolt Against the Masses,* p. 258.

15. Kirkpatrick, *The New Presidential Elite;* Polsby, *Consequences of Party Reform;* Ranney, "The Political Parties Reform and Decline," in King, *The New American Political System,* pp. 213–247; and Byron E. Shafer, *Quiet Revolution: The Struggle for the Democratic Party and the Shaping of Post-Reform Politics* (New York: Russell Sage Foundation, 1983).

16. Burnham, *The Current Crisis.* See also Wattenberg, *The Decline of American Political Parties 1952–84.*

17. Cornelius P. Cotter and John F. Bibby, "The Institutional Development of Parties and the Thesis of Party Decline," *Political Science Quarterly* 95 (1980): 1–27; Cornelius Cotter, James L. Gibson, John F. Bibby, and Robert J. Huckshorn, *Party Organizations in American Politics* (New York: Praeger, 1984); Xandra Kayden and Eddie Mahe, Jr., *The Party Goes On: The Persistence of the Two-Party System in the United States* (New York:

Basic Books, 1985); and A. James Reichley, "The Rise of National Parties," in *The New Direction in American Politics,* ed. John E. Chubb and Paul E. Peterson (Washington, D.C.: Brookings Institution, 1985), pp. 175–200.

18. I generally agree with Epstein's argument that party organizations in the contemporary United States are neither declining nor reaching new heights of organizational strength, but instead are adapting to a transformation in the wider political system that negates their role as candidate selection mechanisms while simultaneously enhancing their importance as providers of campaign services to candidates. See Leon D. Epstein, *Political Parties in the American Mold* (Madison: University of Wisconsin Press, 1986).

19. See Polsby, *Consequences of Party Reform,* pp. 53–64; also Byron E. Shafer, *Quiet Revolution: The Struggle for the Democratic Party and the Shaping of Post-Reform Politics* (New York: Russell Sage Foundation, 1983), pp. 269–294, 320–366, 492–522.

20. See D. Tony Stewart, "American Political Parties: Self-Reform or Oblivion," *Ripon Forum,* October 1970, 21–23, and Daniel J. Swillinger, "Proposals for Party Reform," *Ripon Forum,* August 1972, 21–27.

21. For the effects of the Democratic changes on the GOP, see Polsby, *Consequences of Party Reform,* p. 54.

22. Sears interviews, April 24 and 27, 1984.

23. See John S. Saloma and Frederick H. Sontag, *Parties: The Real Opportunity for Effective Citizen Politics* (New York: Vintage Books, 1973), pp. 176–178.

24. Jo Freeman attributes the lack of procedural reform within the GOP in the 1968–80 period to the party's social homogeneity and leadership-oriented political culture. Jo Freeman, "The Political Culture of the Democratic and Republican Parties," *Political Science Quarterly* 101 (1986): 327–356.

25. John F. Bibby, "Party Renewal in the Republican Party," in *Party Renewal in America,* ed. Gerald Pomper (New York: Praeger, 1982), p. 104. Bibby may be exaggerating the force of the original McGovern-Fraser guidelines. The relevant guideline A-1 on Discrimination on The Basis of Race, Color, Creed, or National Origin stated, ". . . requires affirmative steps to overcome past discrimination, including minority presence in the state delegation in reasonable relationship to group presence in the state as a whole." See Shafer, *Quiet Revolution,* p. 541 (Appendix A).

26. On the DO and Rule 29 committees see Bibby, ibid., pp. 103–107; Cotter and Bibby, "The Institutional Development of Parties and the Thesis of Party Decline," *Political Science Quarterly* 95 (1980): 17–19; Charles Longley, "Party Nationalization in America," in *Paths to Political Reform,* ed. William J. Crotty (Lexington, Mass.: Lexington Books, 1980), pp. 176–178; Daniel J. Swillinger, To DO or not to DO," *Ripon Forum,* September 1972; Richard Behn, "We got 'em, but we didn't get 'em good enough," *Ripon Forum,* March 1975.

27. Josiah Lee Auspitz, "Republican Party Rules: The Mandate for Change," *Ripon Forum,* April 1983, 18.

28. *Ripon Society, Inc. v. National Republican Party,* 74–1337 and 74–1338, 1975. On the Ripon suit see *Ripon Forum,* October 1975, 1–3.
29. Sears interview.
30. Sears interview. Sears's views were corroborated by a study of delegates to the 1976 Republican convention undertaken by Denis G. Sullivan. Classifying a sample of Ford and Reagan delegates as "purists" or "professionals" by virtue of their answers to a series of questions concerning party unity, nominating a winner, the platform and so forth, he found that only 20% of Ford's delegates were purists, compared to 51% of Reagan's. See Denis G. Sullivan, "Party Unity: Appearance and Reality," *Political Science Quarterly* 92 (1977–8): 635–645. On the rightward shift among GOP activists in the 1972–80 period, see also Warren E. Miller and M. Kent Jennings, *Parties in Transition: A Longitudinal Study of Party Elites and Party Supporters* (New York: Russell Sage Foundation, 1986), pp. 40–53, 133–139, 145–150.
31. Sears interview.
32. On FECA and the proliferation of right-wing PACs, see Gillian Peele, *Revival and Reaction: The Right in Contemporary America* (Oxford: Clarendon Press, 1984), pp. 55–65.
33. For the traditional view of the activities and significance of the national party committees in American politics, see Cornelius P. Cotter and Bernard C. Hennessey, *Politics Without Power: The National Party Committees* (New York: Atherton Press, 1964).
34. On Bliss as RNC Chairman, see Hess and Broder, *The Republican Establishment,* pp. 42–54; Kayden and Mahe, *The Party Goes On,* pp. 70–71.
35. Epstein, *Political Parties in the American Mold,* Appendix C, p. 351.
36. On the impact of Brock and his reforms, see Reichley, "The Rise of National Parties," in *The New Direction in American Politics,* ed. Chubb and Peterson, pp. 175–200, and Bibby, "Party Renewal in the Republican Party," in Pomper, *Party Renewal in America,* pp. 107–108.
37. For a discussion of the neutral nature of the Brock reforms and their potential for enhancing national party control, see F. Christopher Arterton, "Political Money and Political Strength," in *The Future of American Political Parties: The Challenge of Governance,* ed. Joel L. Fleishman (Englewood Cliffs, N.J.: Prentice-Hall, 1982), esp. pp. 129–130.
38. On the neoconservatives, see Peele, *Revival and Reaction,* pp. 19–50, and Peter Steinfels, *The Neo-Conservatives: The Men Who Are Changing America's Politics* (New York: Touchstone Books, 1979).
39. Richard A. Viguerie, *The New Right: We're Ready to Lead,* revised ed. (Falls Church, Va.: The Viguerie Company, 1981), p. 70.
40. Peele, *Revival and Reaction,* pp. 80–179; Alan Crawford, *Thunder on the Right: The New Right and the Politics of Resentment* (New York: Pantheon, 1980), pp. 144–164; A. James Reichley, *Religion in American Public Life* (Washington, D.C.: The Brookings Institution, 1985), pp. 311–331; also *The New Christian Right: Mobilization and Legitimation,* eds. Robert C. Leibman and Robert Wuthnow (New York: Aldine Publishing Company, 1983).

236   NOTES

41. On Helms, see "Senator Helms Builds a Machine of Interlinked Organizations to Shape Both Politics, Policy," *National Journal,* March 6,
1982, 449–505, and Ernest B. Furguson, *Hard Right: The Rise of Jesse
Helms* (New York: Norton, 1986).

42. Peele, *Revival and Reaction,* pp. 101–116; Viguerie, *The New Right,*
pp. 123–126; and Robert C. Leibman, "Mobilizing the Moral Majority," in
Leibman and Wuthnow, *The New Christian Right.* pp. 49–73.

43. Peele, ibid., pp. 53–54, and John S. Saloma III, *Ominous Politics: The
New Conservative Labyrinth* (New York: Hill & Wang, 1984), pp. 7–23.

44. Peele, ibid., pp. 65–70; Crawford, *Thunder on the Right,* pp. 225–244.

45. Quoted in Phillips, *Post-Conservative America,* p. 48n.

46. Behn, *Ripon Quarterly* 3 (1977): 13.

47. *Congressional Quarterly Weekly Report,* 10, June 1978, 1446.

48. Ibid., p. 1446.

49. Charles O. Jones, "Nominating Carter's Favorite Opponent: The Republicans in 1980," in Ranney, *The American Elections of 1980* (Washington, D.C., American Enterprise Institute, 1981), pp. 86–87.

50. Interview with Mr. Anderson May 7, 1984.

51. See Crawford, *Thunder on the Right,* pp. 286–287, for an account
of the new right's campaign against Anderson in 1978.

52. Interviews with John Topping, April 12, 1984, and Howard Gillette,
April 19, 1984.

53. Gillette interview.

54. Charles O. Jones, in Ranney, *The American Elections of 1980,* pp.
81–87.

55. Ibid., p. 85.

56. Gillette interview.

57. Topping interview.

58. Anderson interview.

59. Ibid.

60. On the pattern of Anderson's support in the general election, see
Phillips, *Post-Conservative America,* pp. 230–231. After 1980 Mr. Anderson
was preoccupied with founding a National Unity party as a vehicle for his
ideas, and, he hoped, to tap his middle-class professional constituency. In
1984 he endorsed the Democratic candidate Walter Mondale for President.

61. Jones, in Ranney, *The American Elections of 1980,* pp. 88–96.

62. Rusher, *The Rise of the Right,* pp. 302–304.

63. Jones, in Ranney, *The American Election of 1980,* pp. 92–93.

64. Interview with Mary Dent Crisp, May 10, 1984.

65. Adamany, in Bogdanor, *Parties and Democracy in Britain and
America,* pp. 165–180.

66. On the Javits-D'Amato race, see *Congressional Quarterly Weekly
Report,* August 30, 1980, 2578–2579; September 13, 1980, 2675–2676;
October 11, 1980, 3044.

67. On the Republican tradition in Massachusetts, see Peirce, *The Megastates of America,* pp. 139–141, and Duane Lockard, *New England State
Politics* (Princeton, NJ: Princeton University Press, 1959), pp. 136–156.

68. Telephone interview with Eunice Howe, March 19, 1984.

69. On the changing ethnic and social balance within Massachusetts, see John Kenneth White, *The Fractured Electorate: Political Parties and Social Change in Southern New England* (Hanover, NH: University Press of New England, 1983), p. 41.

70. Interview with Andrew Natsios, March 19, 1984.

71. Howe interview.

72. Interview with Gordon Luciano of the "Ray Shamie For U.S. Senate Campaign," July 10, 1984.

73. *Boston Globe,* August 22, 1984.

74. *National Journal,* September 22, 1984.

75. *New Republic,* October 8, 1984.

76. On the Republican tradition in Connecticut, see Lockard, *New England State Politics,* pp. 136–156, and Neal R. Peirce, *The New England States: People, Politics and Power in the Six New England States* (New York: Norton, 1977), pp. 188–202.

77. Interview with Mr. Alsop, June 12, 1984.

78. Peirce, op. cit., pp. 200–202.

79. Alsop interview.

80. On the Bush-Weicker contest see *Politics in America: Members of Congress in Washington and At Home,* ed. Alan Ehrenhalt (Washington, D.C.: CQ Press, 1983), p. 251.

81. Interview with Stephen Moore, April 6, 1984.

82. *New Haven Register,* January 15, 1984.

83. Ibid.

84. Connecticut Committee for Party Renewal, "Statement on The Recent Proposal Regarding Republican Party Rules," Hartford, Conn.: December 19, 1983. These arguments were employed by the Connecticut Democrats when they challenged the constitutionality of the Republicans' open primary in the courts. In the landmark decision of *Tashjian v. Republican Party of Connecticut,* however, the Supreme Court found in favor of the Connecticut GOP. See *Election Administration Reports* 16 (20, 24) (1986); also *Congressional Quarterly Weekly Report,* December 13, 1986, 3064–3065.

85. J. K. White, *The Fractured Electorate,* p. 41.

Chapter 5

1. See Moos, *The Republicans,* pp. 324–387, and Charles O. Jones, *The Minority Party in Congress* (Boston: Little, Brown & Co., 1970), p. 50.

2. Jones, ibid., p. 64.

3. Mayer, *The Republican Party 1854–1964,* pp. 431–432.

4. Patterson, *Congressional Conservatism and the Neal Deal,* pp. 16–17.

5. On the origins of the conservative coalition, see Patterson, *Congressional Conservatism and the New Deal,* pp. 101–126.

6. The official position of Majority Leader was held by Senator White of Maine in the Eightieth Congress, but he only performed his duties in a ceremonial fashion and the real leadership came from Taft and Vandenberg.

Taft finally became *de jure* as well as *de facto* Majority Leader in 1953, but he died within a few months, being succeeded by the conservative California Republican William Knowland.

7. Reichard, *The Reaffirmation of Republicanism,* p. 188.

8. The Policy Committees—created in the Senate in 1947 and in the House in 1949—were unique to the Republicans at this time and had two main functions: to conduct research on policy and to develop party stands on legislation. On the Policy Committees, see Jones, *The Minority Party in Congress,* pp. 30–50.

9. Ibid., p. 153.

10. Barbara Sinclair, *Congressional Realignment 1925–78* (Austin: University of Texas Press, 1982).

11. Ibid., pp. 23, 29–31.

12. Interview with Congressman Conte, May 7, 1984.

13. Interview with Mr. Lindsay, July 11, 1984.

14. Hess and Broder, *The Republican Establishment,* p. 72.

15. The Wednesday Group membership comprised fifteen northeasterners, eleven midwesterners, no southerners, and four westerners. See ibid., p. 73.

16. The leading Young Turks were Charles Goodell (New York), Melvin Laird (Wisconsin), Robert Griffin (Michigan), Thomas Curtis (Missouri), John Anderson (Illinois), Albert Quie (Minnesota), and Donald Rumsfeld (Illinois). See Robert Peabody, *Leadership in Congress: Stability, Succession and Change* (Boston: Little, Brown & Co., 1976), p. 307.

17. Halleck's old-fashioned brand of midwestern conservatism and his political style were ill-suited to the modern age. A joint television venture with Senate Minority Leader Dirksen, intended to illustrate Republican positions on the issues of the day and to highlight the quality of the leadership, soon became an object of press ridicule. The program was derisively dubbed "the Ev and Charlie Show."

18. Interview with Mr. Goodell, April 6, 1984.

19. Ibid. "Quie-dell" is a conflation of the names of Congressman Goodell and Congressman Albert Quie, the sponsors of these bills.

20. Peabody, *Leadership in Congress,* p. 103.

21. Goodell interview. Ford got the best part of the 30-odd Wednesday Group votes, although 6–8 of them (including Lindsay's and Bradford Morse's) were for Halleck; these men trusted the devil they knew in a contest between two ideologically indistinguishable candidates. See also ibid., p. 136.

22. Peabody, *Leadership in Congress,* p. 307. In referring to the Wednesday Club in the House, Peabody is in error. This was the name given to the equivalent grouping in the Senate.

23. Peabody, *Leadership in Congress,* p. 427.

24. Ibid., p. 426.

25. On the Scott-Baker contest, see ibid., pp. 432–440.

26. In attempting to quantify the strength of the various Republican ideological clusters in both the House and Senate since 1970, the most useful classification is probably that used by Reichley and referred to in Chapter 1.

On a scale from right to left, Reichley divides the Republicans in Congress into four main categories: fundamentalists, stalwarts, moderates, and progressives. As the numbers of both moderates and progressives have tended to dwindle since 1970, I shall continue to use the term liberal to refer to both groups, and conservative to refer to stalwarts and fundamentalists. See A. James Reichley, *Conservatives in an Age of Change*, pp. 22–37.

27. Lindsay interview.
28. Ibid., p. 329.
29. Sinclair, *Congressional Realignment*, p. 128.
30. Sinclair, *Congressional Realignment*, p. 174.
31. William Shaffer, *Party and Ideology in the United States Congress* (Washington, D.C.: University Press of America, 1980), p. 339.
32. On the revolt against FAP and the formation of the RSC, see Edwin J. Feulner, *Conservatives Stalk the House: The Republican Study Committee 1970–82* (Ottawa, Ill.: George Hill Publishers, 1983), pp. 41–57.
33. Ibid., pp. 3–11.
34. Ibid., p. 7.
35. *National Journal*, March 6, 1982, 522.
36. Interview with Senator Lugar, May 17, 1984.
37. *Congressional Quarterly Weekly Report*, September 12, 1981, 1743.
38. Interview with Senator Andrews, May 3, 1984.
39. Interview with Senator Cohen, May 1, 1984.
40. Interview with Senator Mathias, May 7, 1984.
41. *Congressional Quarterly Weekly Report*, September 2, 1981, 1747.
42. Ibid., September 12, 1981, 1743.
43. *National Journal*, January 21, 1984, 102.
44. *National Journal*, September 10, 1983, 1827.
45. The social issues became less salient in Congress during Reagan's second term until the battle over the nomination of Judge Robert Bork to the Supreme Court in October 1987. Six Republican Senators—Chafee (R.I.), Packwood (Ore.), Specter (Pa.), Stafford (Vt.), Warner (Va.), and (inevitably) Weicker (Conn.)—voted with 52 Democrats to reject the nomination. See *Congressional Quarterly Weekly Report*, October 24, 1987.
46. Michael Foley, *The New Senate* (London: Yale University Press, 1980), p. 174.
47. Ibid., p. 182.
48. Interview with Senator Andrews, May 3, 1984.
49. Howard Kurtz, "How Lowell Weicker Gets Even—He Raises Reagan's Budgets," *Washington Post National Weekly Edition*, May 6, 1985.
50. See Chapter 4, pp. 188–93.
51. Interview with Mr. Moore, April 24, 1984.
52. Mathias interview.
53. *Congressional Quarterly Weekly Report*, May 25, 1984, 1287.
54. Ibid., 1287.
55. Ibid., 1287.
56. *National Journal*, September 10, 1983, 1284.
57. Interview with Congressman Cheney, May 2, 1984.

58. The figures on the 1981 budget votes are from Philip M. Williams, "Power and the Parties," in Bogdanor, *Parties and Democracy in Britain and America,* p. 26.

59. *Congressional Quarterly,* October 10, 1981, 1950.

60. After the southern Democrats had chosen the name "Boll Weevil" (a cotton pest prevalent in the southern United States), Representative Lawrence J. DeNardis of Connecticut used the term "Gypsy Moth," (after an insect that attacks trees in New England) to describe the Republican insurgents.

61. *National Journal,* October 31, 1981, 1948.

62. Interview with Congressman Tauke, May 4, 1984.

63. On Michel's difficulties, see *National Journal,* February 20, 1982, 316–319.

64. *National Journal,* January 21, 1984, 413.

65. A decision by Speaker O'Neill to change the television camera angles so that the viewer would see the Republicans talking to an empty chamber created a furious row in the spring of 1984, with O'Neill taking the floor of the House to defend his position. On the COS see *National Journal,* January 21, 1984, p. 413.

66. Interview with Congressman Conable, May 7, 1984.

67. Interview with Congressman Cheney, May 2, 1984.

68. On the Gypsy Moths, see *Congressional Quarterly Weekly Report,* October 10, 1981, 1950–1952, and *National Journal,* October 31, 1981, 1946–1949.

69. Ibid., p. 1950.

70. There were twenty-six Moths in all: seventeen from the Northeast, nine from the Midwest. The members of the Gypsy Moths' Steering Committee were Green, Pursell, DeNardis, Hollenbeck, Horton, Jeffords, Schneider, Snowe, and Tauke.

71. Tauke interview.

72. Interview with Congressman Jeffords, May 2, 1984.

73. Interview with Congressman Leach, April 25, 1984.

74. Interview with Congressman Green, April 12, 1984.

75. Representatives DeNardis, Dougherty, Dunn, Erdahl, Heckler, and Hollenbeck were all defeated in the 1982 midterm elections. Fenwick lost a bid for the Senate and Marks retired. The Moths lost eight members in all.

76. *National Journal,* October 31, 1981, 1947.

77. Interview with Congressman Sherwood Boehlert, May 2, 1984.

78. Ehrenhalt, *Politics in America,* pp. 1699–1724.

79. Conable interview.

80. Tauke interview.

81. Interview with Congressman McKinney, April 26, 1984.

82. For a recent account of the House Wednesday Group, see also "There's Still Life on the GOP Left," *New York Times,* August 23, 1986.

83. Interview with Mr. Hofman, May 7, 1984.

84. Ibid.

85. Interview with Congressman Pritchard, May 7, 1984.

86. Interview with Mr. Gerry, April 26, 1984.

87. Conte interview.

88. Tauke interview.

89. "Incumbency protection" refers to the increasing tendency of incumbent congressmen to be re-elected in recent years. This has been attributed to the decline of party in the electorate and the development of technological advantages for incumbents in House races, e.g., mass mailing, access to local and national media, access to PAC funds. See David R. Mayhew, *Congress: The Electoral Connection* (New Haven and London: Yale University Press, 1974), and "Congressional Elections: The Case of the Vanishing Marginals," *Polity* 6 (1974): 295–315; Thomas E. Mann, *Unsafe at Any Margin: Interpreting Congressional Elections* (Washington, DC: American Enterprise Institute, 1978); and Gary C. Jacobson, "The Marginals Never Vanished: Incumbency and Competition in Elections to the U.S. House of Representatives 1952–82," *American Journal of Political Science* 31 (1987): 126–141.

Chapter 6

1. Mathias interview.

2. Interview with Jayne Hart, Executive Director of the Ripon Society, April 23, 1984.

3. Ibid.

4. Leach interview.

5. Gillette interview.

6. Wallison interview.

7. Interview with Congressman Petri, April 13, 1984.

8. Interview with Josiah Lee Auspitz, March 19, 1984.

9. In 1983 a new organization was formed to raise funds, publicize, and campaign for liberal GOP candidates. In deciding to establish MODRN PAC New York Congressman S. William Green showed the kind of initiative that has been lacking among liberal Republicans in recent years. It is doubtful, however, that moderate pragmatic politics that deemphasize ideology can arouse the depth of commitment necessary to sustain extensive direct-mail fund-raising. Green's initiative, finally, may have come too late in the day to instigate a liberal revival within the GOP.

10. This decision was taken at the behest of the Reagan administration, which hoped to avoid any appearance of divisions within Republican ranks. See *Congressional Quarterly Weekly Report,* March 17, 1983, 630.

11. "Ripon Seeks Impact on GOP Platform," *Washington Times,* April 16, 1984.

12. *New York Times,* June 21, 1984.

13. Ibid.

14. *National Journal,* September 1, 1984, 1610–1611.

15. Interview with Congresswoman Schneider, May 2, 1984.

16. Leach interview.

17. Ibid.

18. Interview with Congressman Pritchard, May 7, 1984.

19. Tauke interview. In early January 1985, the liberal Republicans in the House formed yet another group to increase their visibility and leverage. The group was named the '92 Committee (so-called because 1992 is the year in which Republican campaign experts believe that their party has the best prospect of gaining control of the House), and it consisted of some thirty Republican congressmen and women, with a fourteen-member Steering Committee. Many of the members of the Steering Committee—Green, Tauke, Snowe, Johnson, McKinney, Schneider, and Leach—had been prominent Gypsy Moths, although the new group was intended to have a broader ideological focus than its regionally oriented predecessor. The activities of the COS provided an incentive for the formation of the '92 Group, and its members also found the budget crisis a powerful mobilizing issue. On the '92 Committee, see *National Journal,* January 5, 1985, 27, May 4, 1985, 998, and May 11, 1985, 1038; and David S. Broder, "Here Come Republican Moderates," *International Herald Tribune,* April 5, 1985.

20. In the November 1984 election, Dole triumphed by 28 votes to 25 over Baker's deputy, Ted Stevens of Alaska. Conservative Reagan loyalist James A. McClure came out at the bottom of the first ballot, with only 8 votes out of 53. See *Congressional Quarterly Weekly Report,* December 1, 1984, 3020.

21. Interview with John Deardourff, May 16, 1984.

22. Interview with Senator Cohen, May 1, 1984.

23. Deardourff interview.

Bibliography

Manuscript Sources

The John V. Lindsay Papers, Sterling Memorial Library, Yale University, New Haven, CT.
Series V, Box 59.
Series XI, Box 28.
Series XIII, Boxes 32, 101.

List of Persons Interviewed

Alcorn, H. Meade, Jr. Former Chairman of the Republican National Committee. January 25, 1984.

Alsop, John. Former member of the Republican National Committee from Connecticut. June 12, 1984.

Anderson, John B. Former congressman and presidential candidate. May 7, 1984.

Senator Andrews, Mark. May 3, 1984.

Auspitz, Josiah Lee. Former President of the Ripon Society. March 19, 1984.

Bixby, R. Burdell. Former aide to Thomas E. Dewey and campaign manager for Nelson Rockefeller. June 7, 1984.

Block, Barbara. Aide to Senator Charles Percy. April 19, 1984.

Congressman Boehlert, Sherwood. May 2, 1984.

Judge Breitel, Charles. Former Dewey aide. February 21, 1984.

Broder, David S. *Washington Post*. April 20, 1984.

Brownell, Herbert. Former U.S. Attorney General and Dewey campaign manager. February 10, 1984.

Sheriff Buckley, John. Telephone conversation, March 20, 1984.

Congressman Cheney, Richard. May 2, 1984.

Senator Cohen, William S. May 1, 1984.

Cole, Ceci. Communications Director, National Republican Senatorial Committee. May 3, 1984.

Congressman Conable, Barber. May 7, 1984.

Congressman Conte, Silvio O. May 7, 1984.

Crisp, Mary Dent. Former Co-chair, Republican National Committee. May 10, 1984.

Cuttell, John. Chief of Staff to Congresswoman Marge Roukema. May 16, 1984.

Deardourff, John. Bailey, Deardourff & Co. May 16, 1984.

Dudley, Christine. Member, National Republican Congressional Committee. May 2, 1984.

Elis, Mark. Legislative aide to Senator Arlen Specter. May 9, 1984.

New York Assemblyman Flanigan, Peter. February 14, 1984.

Frank, Gerald, Chief of Staff for Senator Mark Hatfield. May 1, 1984.

Gerry, Martin. Special Counsel to the House Republican Wednesday Group. April 26, 1984.

Gillette, Howard F., Jr. Former campaign aide to John Anderson. April 19, 1984.

Congressman Green, S. William. April 12, 1984.

Gude, Gilbert. Former congressman and Director of the Congressional Research Service. April 30, 1984.

Hannahan, Michael. Assistant to Massachusetts Republican Chairman Andrew Natsios. March 19, 1984.

New York Assemblyman Hannon, Kemp. Deputy Minority Leader. February 14, 1984.

Hess, Stephen. Former Eisenhower aide, now Senior Fellow at The Brookings Institution. April 4, 1984.

Hofman, Steve. Executive Director, House Republican Wednesday Group. May 7, 1984.

Holton, Linwood. Former Governor of Virginia. April 17, 1984.

Houston, Neal. Administrative Assistant to Senator Robert Stafford of Vermont. April 17, 1984.

Howe, Eunice. Former member from Massachusetts, Republican National Committee. Telephone conversation, April 20, 1984.

Hughes, Larry. Director of Communications, Connecticut Republicans. June 13, 1984.

Jacobs, William. Administrative Assistant to Senator Daniel Evans. April 11, 1984.

Senator Javits, Jacob K. November 25, 1983.

Congressman Jeffords, James. May 2, 1984.

Congresswoman Johnson, Nancy. April 25, 1984.

Kellogg, Frederick Rogers. President of the Ripon Society. April 30, 1984.

Congressman Leach, James. April 25, 1984.

Lindsay, John V. July 11, 1984.

Lovell, Malcolm. Under Secretary of Labor 1981–82, and former aide to George Romney. April 19, 1984.

Luciano, Gordon. Staff member, "Ray Shamie for U.S. Senate" campaign. July 10, 1984.

Senator Lugar, Richard. May 17, 1984.

Marans, J. Eugene. Founder-member of the Ripon Society. April 11, 1984.

Senator Mathias, Charles. May 7, 1984.

Mattarazzo, Mike. Member of "Ray Shamie for U.S. Senate" campaign. July 10, 1984.

McKenzie, William. Editor, *Ripon Forum*. April 27, 1984.

Congressman McKernan, John. May 3, 1984.

Congressman McKinney, Stewart. April 2, 1984.

Melich, Tanya. Former aid to Nelson Rockefeller, and former President of the Ripon Society. June 22, 1984.

Moore, Stephen. Special Counsel to Senator Lowell Weicker. April 24, 1984.

Nathan, Donald. Research Director, "Richardson for Senate" campaign. July 10, 1984.

Olsen, Michael. Press Secretary to Senator Mark Andrews. April 5, 1984.

Congressman Petri, Thomas E. April 13, 1984.

Congressman Pritchard, Joel. May 7, 1984.

Reichley, A. James. Former aide to William Scranton, now Senior Fellow at The Brookings Institution. April 17, 1984.

Richards, Richard. Chairman of the Republican National Committee 1981–83. April 20, 1984.

Congressman Ridge, Tom. May 16, 1984.

Rooney, Maureen. Assistant to the Massachusetts House Minority Leader. March 20, 1984.

Rusher, William. Publisher, *National Review*. June 29, 1984.

Sears, John P. Reagan presidential campaign manager 1975–76, and 1979 to March 1980. April 24, 1984 and April 27, 1984.

Congresswoman Schneider, Claudine. May 2, 1984.

Senator Scott, Hugh. May 16, 1984.

Steers, Newton. Former congressman. Telephone conversation, May 11, 1984.

New York Assemblyman Straniere, Robert. February 14, 1984.

Congressman Tauke, Tom. May 4, 1984.

Thayer, Walter Nelson. Former Publisher, *New York Herald Tribune.* February 16, 1984.

Topping, John C., Jr. Former President of the Ripon Society. April 12, 1974.

Wallison, Peter, Former Counsel to Nelson Rockefeller, April 20, 1984.

White, F. Clifton, Jr. Manager of the Goldwater prenomination campaign 1961–64, and of the Reagan campaign 1968. April 5, 1984.

Whitney, Carol. Executive Director, Republican Governors' Association. April 30, 1984.

Zagame, John. Deputy White House Liaison, Republican National Committee. May 11, 1984.

Printed Sources

Newspapers and Periodicals

Congressional Quarterly Weekly Report
The Economist
International Herald Tribune
The Nation
The National Journal
The New Republic
The New York Times
Public Opinion
Ripon Forum
Ripon Quarterly
The Washington Post

Memoirs and Personal Statements

Adams, Sherman. *Firsthand Report: The Story of the Eisenhower Administration.* New York: Harper & Brothers, 1961.

Bain, Richard C., and Judith H. Parris. *Convention Decisions and Voting Records.* Washington, D.C.: Brookings Institution, 1973.

Connecticut Committee for Party Renewal. "Statement on the Recent Proposal Regarding Republican Party Rules." Hartford, Conn., 1983.

Croly, Herbert. *The Promise of American Life.* New York: E. P. Dutton & Co., 1963.

Davis, James W. *Presidential Primaries: Road to the White House.* Westport, Conn.: Greenwood Press, 1980.

Dewey, Thomas E. *Thomas E. Dewey on the Two-Party System.* Edited by John A. Wells. Garden City, N.Y.: Doubleday, 1966.

Eisenhower, Dwight D. *The Eisenhower Diaries.* Edited by Robert H. Ferrell. New York: Norton, 1981.

———. *Mandate for Change: 1953–56.* London: Heinemann, 1963.

———. *Waging Peace: Memoirs 1957–61.* London: Heinemann, 1963.

Goldwater, Barry M. *The Conscience of a Conservative.* New York: Hillman Books, 1960.

———. *With No Apologies: The Personal and Political Memoirs of U.S. Senator Barry M. Goldwater.* New York: William Morrow & Co., 1979.

Javits, Jacob K. *Order of Battle: A Republican's Call to Reason.* New York: Pocket Books, 1966.

———. *Javits: The Autobiography of a Public Man.* With Rafael Steinberg. Boston: Houghton, Mifflin Co., 1981.

Larson, Arthur. *A Republican Looks at his Party.* New York: Harper & Brothers, 1956.

Lodge, Henry Cabot. *The Storm Has Many Eyes: A Personal Narrative.* New York: Norton, 1973.

Mahoney, J. Daniel. *Actions Speak Louder.* New Rochelle, N.Y.: Arlington House, 1968.

Nixon, Richard M. *RN: The Memoirs of Richard Nixon.* London: Arrow Books, 1979.

Reiter, Howard L. "Nominating Process Briefing Paper." Unpublished paper, Department of Political Science, University of Connecticut, 1984.

Riegle, Donald. *O Congress.* With Trevor Armbister. New York: Popular Library, 1976.

Ripon Society. *From Disaster to Distinction: A Republican Rebirth.* New York: Pocket Books, 1966.

———. *Election '64: A Ripon Society Report.* Cambridge, Mass.: Ripon Society, 1964.

———. *Jaws of Victory: The Game Plan Politics of 1972, the Crisis of the Republican Party, and the Future of the Constitution.* With Clifford W. Brown. Boston: Little, Brown & Co., 1974.

———. *The Lessons of Victory.* New York: The Dial Press, 1969.

———. *The Ripon Papers 1963–1968.* Washington, D.C.: The National Press, 1968.

Rusher, William A. *The Making of the New Majority Party.* New York: Sheed & Ward, 1975.

Rusher, William A. *The Rise of the Right.* New York: William Morrow & Co., 1984.

Safire, William. *Before the Fall: An Inside View of the Pre-Watergate White House.* New York: Belmont Tower Books, 1975.

Scott, Hugh. *Come to the Party.* Englewood Cliffs, N.J.: Prentice-Hall, 1968.

Viguerie, Richard A. *The Establishment vs. The People: Is a New Populist Revolt on the Way?* Chicago: The American Populist Institute, 1983.

———. *The New Right: We're Ready to Lead.* Falls Church, Va.: The Viguerie Company, 1981.

Warren, Earl. *The Memoirs of Earl Warren.* Garden City, N.Y.: Doubleday, 1977.

Welch, Robert. *The Politician.* Published privately by Welch, 1963.

White, F. Clifton. *Suite 3505.* New Rochelle, N.Y. Arlington House, 1967.

Other Secondary Sources

Adamany, David. "Financing Political Parties in the United States." *Parties and Democracy in Britain and America.* Edited by Vernon Bogdanor. New York: Praeger, 1984.

Alexander, Herbert E. *Money in Politics.* Washington, D.C.: Public Affairs Press, 1972.

Alsop, Stewart. *Nixon and Rockefeller: A Double Portrait.* Garden City, N.Y.: Doubleday, 1960.

Ambrose, Stephen E. *Eisenhower: Soldier, General of the Army, President-Elect 1890–1952.* London: Allen & Unwin, 1984.

———. *Eisenhower: The President 1952–1969.* London: Allen & Unwin, 1984.

———. *Nixon: The Education of a Politician 1913–62.* London: Simon & Schuster, 1987.

Ashby, Darrel A. "Progressivism Against Itself: The Senate Western Bloc in the 1920s." *Mid-America* 50 (1968): 291–304.

Auspitz, Josiah Lee. "Republican Party Rules: The Mandate for Change." *Ripon Forum,* April 1983.

Axelrod, Robert. "Presidential Election Coalitions in 1984." *American Political Science Review* 80 (1986): 281–284.

———. "Where the Votes Come From: An Analysis of Electoral Coalitions 1952–1968." *American Political Science Review* 66 (1972): 11–20.

———. "Where the Votes . . ."

Barone, Michael, and Grant Ujifusa. *The Almanac of American Politics 1984.* Washington, D.C.: National Journal, 1983.

Bartley, N. V., and H. D. Graham. *Southern Politics and the Second*

Reconstruction. Baltimore: Johns Hopkins University Press, 1975.

Bass, Jack, and Walter DeVries. *The Transformation of Southern Politics: Social Change and Political Consequence Since 1945.* New York: New American Library, 1976.

Beck, Paul Allen. "Partisan Dealignment in the Post-War South." *American Political Science Review* 71 (1977): 477–496.

Behn, Robert D. "The Plight of Progressive Republicans." *Ripon Quarterly* 3 (1977): 10–19.

Bell, Daniel, ed. *The Radical Right.* Garden City, N.Y.: Anchor Books, 1964.

Bernstein, Barton J., and Franklin A. Leib. "Progressive Republican Senators and American Imperialism 1898–1916: A Reappraisal." *Mid-America* 50 (1968): 163–205.

Bernstein, Melvin H. "GOP Governors: The Illusion of Power." *The Nation,* January 6, 1969.

Bibby, John F. "Party Renewal in the Republican Party." In *Party Renewal in America: Theory and Practice.* Edited by Gerald M. Pomper, 102–115. New York: Praeger, 1980.

Bisnow, Mark. *Diary of a Dark Horse: The 1980 Anderson Presidential Campaign.* Carbondale: Southern Illinois University Press, 1983.

Binkley, Wilfred E. *American Political Parties: Their Natural History.* New York: Alfred A. Knopf, 1961.

Blum, John Morton. *The Republican Roosevelt,* 2nd ed. Cambridge, Mass.: Harvard University Press, 1977.

———. *V was for Victory: Politics and American Culture During World War II.* Chicago: Harvest/HBJ, 1977.

Blumenthal, Sidney. "The Republican Undead." *New Republic,* January 7 and 14, 1984.

Bogdanor, Vernon, ed. *Parties and Democracy in Britain and America.* New York: Praeger, 1984.

Burner, David. *Herbert Hoover: A Public Life.* New York: Atheneum, 1984.

Burnham, Walter Dean. *Critical Elections and the Mainsprings of American Politics.* New York: Norton, 1970.

———. *The Current Crisis in American Politics.* Oxford: Oxford University Press, 1982.

———. "The Alabama Senatorial Election of 1962: Return of Inter-Party Competition." *Journal of Politics* 26 (1964): 798–829.

Burns, James MacGregor. *The Deadlock of Democracy: Four Party Politics in America.* Englewood Cliffs, N.J.: Prentice-Hall, 1963.

———. *The Power to Lead: The Crisis of the American Presidency.* New York: Simon & Schuster, 1984.

Campbell, Angus, Philip E. Converse, Warren E. Miller, and Donald E.

Stokes. *The American Voter: An Abridgement*. New York: John Wiley & Sons, 1964.

Cannon, Lou. *Reagan*. New York: Perigree, 1984.

Ceaser, James W. *Reforming the Reforms: A Critical Analysis of the Presidential Selection Process*. Cambridge, Mass.: Ballinger Publishing Co., 1982.

Chambers, William Nisbet, and Walter Dean Burnham, eds. *The American Party Systems*. New York: Oxford University Press, 1975.

Chester, Edward W. *A Guide to Political Platforms*. Hamden, Conn.: Anchor Books, 1972.

Chester, Lewis, Godfrey Hodgson, Bruce Page. *An American Melodrama: The Presidential Campaign of 1968*. London: Andre Deutsch, 1969.

Clubb, Jerome E., William H. Flanigan, and Nancy H. Zingale. *Partisan Realignment: Voters, Parties and Government in American History*. Beverly Hills, Calif.: Sage Publications, 1980.

Collier, Peter, and David Horowitz. *The Rockefellers: An American Dynasty*. London: Jonathan Cape, 1976.

Connery, Robert H., and Gerald Benjamin. *Rockefeller of New York: Executive Power in the Statehouse*. Ithaca, N.Y.: Cornell University Press, 1979.

Converse, Philip E., Aage R. Clausen, and Warren E. Miller. "Electoral Myth and Reality: The 1964 Election." *American Political Science Review* 59 (1965): 321–336.

Cotter, Cornelius P. "Eisenhower as Party Leader." *Political Science Quarterly* 98 (1983): 255–283.

Cotter, Cornelius P., John F. Bibby. "Institutional Development and the Thesis of Party Decline." *Political Science Quarterly* 95 (1980): 1–27.

Cotter, Cornelius P., and Bernard C. Hennessey. *Politics Without Power: The National Party Committees*. New York: Atherton Press, 1964.

Cotter, Cornelius P., James L. Gibson, John F. Bibby, and Robert J. Huckshorn. *Party Organizations in American Politics*. New York: Praeger, 1984.

Crawford, Alan. *Thunder on the Right: The New Right and the Politics of Resentment*. New York: Pantheon, 1980.

Cresnap, Dean R. *Party Politics in the Golden State*. Los Angeles: Hayes Foundation, 1954.

Crotty, William. *Paths to Political Reform*. Lexington, Mass.: Lexington Books, 1980.

David, Paul T., ed. *The Presidential Election and Transition 1960*. Washington, D.C.: Brookings Institution, 1961.

David, Paul T., Ralph M. Goldman, and Richard C. Bain. *The Politics of National Party Conventions.* Washington, D.C.: Brookings Institution, 1960.

David, Paul T., Malcolm Moos, and Ralph M. Goldman. *Presidential Nominating Politics in 1952.* 5 vols. Baltimore: Johns Hopkins University Press, 1954.

Drew, Elizabeth. *Portrait of an Election.* London: Routledge & Kegan Paul, 1981.

Ehrenhalt, Alan, ed. *Politics in America: Members of Congress in Washington and at Home.* Washington, D.C.: CQ Press, 1983.

Epstein, Leon. *Political Parties in the American Mold.* Madison: University of Wisconsin Press, 1986.

Evans, M. Stanton. *The Future of Conservatism.* New York: Holt, Rinehart & Winston, 1968.

Evans, Rowland, and Robert D. Novak. *Nixon in the White House: The Frustration of Power.* New York: Vintage Books, 1972.

Fairlie, Henry. *The Parties: Republicans and Democrats in this Century.* New York: Pocket Books, 1979.

Feinman, Ronald A. *The Twilight of Progressivism: The Western Republican Senators and the New Deal.* Baltimore: Johns Hopkins University Press, 1981.

Feulner, Edwin J. *Conservatives Stalk the House: The Republican Study Committee 1970–82.* Ottawa, Ill.: Green Hill, 1983.

Fleishman, Joel L., ed. *The Future of American Political Parties: The Challenge of Governance.* Englewood Cliffs, N.J.: Prentice-Hall, 1982.

Foley, Michael. *The New Senate: Liberal Influence on a Conservative Institution 1959–72.* London: Yale University Press, 1980.

Freeman, Jo. "The Political Culture of American Political Parties." *Political Science Quarterly* 101 (1986): 327–356.

Furgurson, Ernest B. *Hard Right: The Rise of Jesse Helms.* New York: Norton, 1986.

Gilder, George F., and Bruce K. Chapman. *The Party that Lost its Head.* New York: Alfred A. Knopf, 1966.

Graebner, Norman A. *The New Isolationism: A Study in Politics and Foreign Policy Since 1950.* New York: The Ronald Press, 1956.

Greenstein, Fred I. *The Hidden Hand Presidency: Eisenhower as Leader.* New York: Basic Books, 1982.

———. ed. *The Reagan Presidency: An Early Assessment.* Baltimore: Johns Hopkins University Press, 1983.

Griffith, Robert. "Dwight D. Eisenhower and the Corporate Commonwealth." *American Historical Review* 87 (1982): 87–122.

BIBLIOGRAPHY

Harris, Louis. *Is There a Republican Majority? Political Trends 1952–56.* New York: Harper & Brothers, 1954.

Havard, William C., ed. *The Changing Politics of the South.* Baton Rouge: Louisiana State University Press, 1972.

Hess, Stephen, and David S. Broder. *The Republican Establishment: The Past, Present and Future of the GOP.* New York: Harper & Row, 1967.

Hodgson, Godfrey. *In Our Time: America from World War II to Nixon.* London: Macmillan, 1976.

Hofstadter, Richard. *The Age of Reform: From Bryan to FDR.* New York: Alfred A. Knopf, 1955.

———. *The American Political Tradition and the Men Who Made It.* New York: Random House, 1974.

———. *The Paranoid Style in American Politics.* Chicago: Phoenix Press, 1979.

Huntington, Samuel P. *American Politics: The Promise of Disharmony.* Cambridge, Mass.: Belknap Press, 1960.

Jacobson, Gary C. "The Republican Advantage in Campaign Finance." In *The New Direction in American Politics.* Edited by John E. Chubb and Paul Peterson, 143–175. Washington, D.C.: Brookings Institution, 1985.

———. "Party Organization and Distribution of Campaign Resources: Republicans and Democrats in 1982." *Political Science Quarterly* 100 (1985–6); 603–625.

———. "The Marginals Never Vanished: Incumbency and Competition in Elections to the US House of Representatives, 1952." *American Journal of Political Science* 31 (1987): 126–141.

Johnson, Donald Bruce. *The Republican Party and Wendell Willkie.* Urbana: University of Illinois Press, 1960.

Jones, Charles O. *The Republican Party in American Politics.* New York: Collier/Macmillan, 1965.

———: *The Minority Party in Congress.* Boston: Little, Brown & Co., 1970.

Joyner, Conrad. *The Republican Dilemma: Conservatism or Progressivism.* Tucson: University of Arizona, 1963.

Kahn, E. J. *Jock: The Life and Times of John Hay Whitney.* Garden City, N.Y.: Doubleday, 1981.

Kayden, Xandra, and Eddie Mahe. *The Party Goes On: The Persistence of the Two-Party System in the United States.* New York: Basic Books, 1985.

Kelley, Stanley. *Interpreting Elections.* Princeton, N.J.: Princeton University Press, 1983.

Kessel, John H. *The Goldwater Coalition: Republican Strategies in 1964*. Indianapolis: Bobbs-Merrill, 1968.

King, Anthony, ed. *The New American Political System*. Washington, D.C.: American Enterprise Institute, 1978.

Kirkpatrick, Jeane J. *The New Presidential Elite: Men and Women in National Politics*. New York: Sage Foundation and 20th Century Fund, 1976.

———. *Dismantling the Parties: Reflections on Party Reform and Party Decomposition*. Washington, D.C.: American Enterprise Institute, 1978.

Kleppner, Paul et al. *The Evolution of American Electoral Systems*. Westport, Conn.: Greenwood Press, 1982.

Ladd, Everett Carll. *Transformations of the Party System: Political Coalitions from the New Deal to the 1970s*. 2nd ed. With Charles D. Hadley. New York: Norton, 1978.

———. *Where Have All the Voters Gone? The Fracturing of America's Political Parties*. 2nd ed. New York: Norton, 1982.

Lamis, Alexander P. *The Two-Party South*. New York: Oxford University Press, 1984.

Liebman, Robert C., and Robert Wuthnow, eds. *The New Christian Right: Mobilization and Legitimation*. New York: Aldine Publishing Co., 1983.

Lipset, Seymour Martin, ed. *Emerging Coalitions in American Politics*. San Francisco: Institute for Contemporary Studies, 1978.

———. Three Decades of the Radical Right: Coughlinites, McCarthyites, and Birchers." In *The Radical Right*. Edited by Daniel Bell, 307–446. Garden City, N.Y.: Anchor Books, 1964.

Lipset, Seymour Martin, and Earl Raab. *The Politics of Unreason: Right Wing Extremism in America*. London: Heinemann, 1971.

Lockard, Duane. *New England State Politics*. Princeton, N.J.: Princeton University Press, 1959.

Lubell, Samuel. *The Future of American Politics*. 3rd ed. New York: Harper-Colophon Books, 1965.

———. *The Revolt of the Moderates*. New York: Harper & Brothers, 1965.

Lurie, Leonard. *The King-Makers*. New York: Coward, McCann & Geoghegan, 1971.

Mann, Thomas E., and Norman J. Ornstein, eds. *The American Elections of 1982*. Washington, D.C.: American Enterprise Institute, 1983.

Marcus, Robert D. *Grand Old Party: Political Structure in the Gilded Age 1880–1896*. New York: Oxford University Press, 1971.

Mayer, George H., *The Republican Party 1854–1964*. New York: Oxford University Press, 1964.

Mayhew, David R. *Party Loyalty Among Congressmen: The Difference Between Democrats and Republicans*. Cambridge, Mass.: Harvard University Press, 1966.

———. *Congress: The Electoral Connection*. London: Yale University Press, 1974.

———. "Congressional Elections: The Case of the Vanishing Marginals." *Polity* 6 (1974): 295–315.

McClosky, Herbert, Paul Hoffman, and Rosemary O'Hara. "Issue Conflict and Consensus Among Party Leaders and Followers." *American Political Science Review* 54 (1960): 406–427.

McCormick, Richard L. "The Discovery that Business Corrupts Politics: A Reappraisal of the Origins of Progressivism." *American Historical Review* 86 (1981): 247–275.

McGinnis, Joe. *The Selling of the President 1968*. New York: Washington Square Press, 1970.

Miles, Michael W. *The Odyssey of the American Right*. New York: Oxford University Press, 1980.

Miller, Warren E., and M. Kent Jennings. *Parties in Transition: A Longitudinal Study of Party Elites and Party Supporters*. New York: Russell Sage Foundation, 1986.

Moos, Malcolm. *The Republicans*. New York: Random House, 1956.

Mowry, George E. *Theodore Roosevelt and the Progressive Movement*. New York: Hill & Wang, 1946.

———. *The California Progressives*. Berkeley: University of California Press, 1951.

Mulder, Ronald A. "The Progressive Insurgents in the United States Senate: Was There a Second New Deal?" *Mid-America* 57 (1975): 106–125.

Munger, Frank, and James Blackhurst. "Factionalism in National Party Conventions, 1940–1964: An Analysis of Ideological Consistency in State Delegation Voting." *Journal of Politics* 27 (1965): 375–394.

Nash, George H. *The Conservative Intellectual Movement in America Since 1945*. New York: Basic Books, 1976.

Nice, David. "Ideological Stability and Change at the Presidential Nominating Conventions." *Journal of Politics* 42 (1980): 846–853.

———. "Polarization in the American Party System." *Presidential Studies Quarterly* 14 (1984): 109–116.

Nie, Norman H., Sidney Verba, and John R. Petrocik. *The Changing American Voter*. Enlarged ed. London: Harvard University Press, 1979.

Novak, Robert D. *The Agony of the GOP 1964*. New York: Macmillan, 1965.

Nye, Russel B. *Midwestern Progressive Politics*. East Lansing: Michigan State University Press, 1959.

O'Brien, Patrick J. "A Re-Examination of the Senate Farm Bloc 1921–33." *Agricultural History* 47 (1973): 248–264.

Olssen, Erik. "The Progressive Group in Congress 1922–1929." *The Historian* 42 (1980): 244–263.

Ornstein, Norman J., Thomas E. Mann, Michael J. Malbin, Allen Schick, and John F. Bibby. *Vital Statistics on Congress 1984–1985*. Washington, D.C.: American Enterprise Institute, 1984.

Orren, Gary R. "The Changing Styles of American Party Politics." In *The Future of American Political Parties: The Challenge of Governance*. Edited by Joel L. Fleishman, 4–41. Englewood Cliffs, N.J.: Prentice-Hall, 1982.

Patterson, James T. *Congressional Conservatism and the New Deal*. Lexington: University of Kentucky Press, 1967.

————. *Mr. Republican: A Biography of Robert A. Taft*. Boston: Houghton, Mifflin Co., 1972.

Peabody, Robert L. *Leadership in Congress: Stability, Succession and Change*. Boston: Little, Brown & Co., 1976.

Peele, Gillian. *Revival and Reaction: The Right in Contemporary America*. Oxford: Clarendon Press, 1984.

Peirce, Neal R. *The Megastates of America: People, Politics and Power in the Ten Great States*. New York: Norton, 1972.

————. *The Border South States: People, Politics and Power in the Five Border South States*. New York: Norton, 1975.

————. *The New England States: People, Politics, and Power in the Six New England States*. New York: Norton, 1976.

Persico, Joseph E. *The Imperial Rockefeller: A Biography of Nelson A. Rockefeller*. New York: Washington Square Press, 1982.

Petrocik, John R. "Realignment: New Party Coalitions and the Nationalization of the South." *Journal of Politics* 49 (1987): 347–375.

Petrocik, John R., and Dwaine Marvick. Explaining Party Elite Transformation: Institutional Changes and Insurgent Politics." *Western Political Quarterly* 36 (1983): 345–363.

Phillips, Kevin P. *The Emerging Republican Majority*. New York: Anchor Books, 1970.

————. *Post-Conservative America: People, Politics and Ideology in a Time of Crisis*. New York: Vintage Books, 1983.

Polsby, Nelson W. *Consequences of Party Reform*. New York: Oxford University Press, 1983.

Pomper, Gerald M. *Party Renewal in America: Theory and Practice.* New York: Praeger, 1980.

———. Ed. *The Election of 1984: Reports and Interpretations.* Chatham, N.J.: Chatham House, 1985.

Ranney, Austin. *Curing the Mischiefs of Faction: Party Reform in America.* Berkeley: University of California Press, 1975.

———. Ed. *The American Elections of 1980.* Washington, D.C.: American Enterprise Institute, 1981.

Reichard, Gary W. *The Reaffirmation of Republicanism: Eisenhower and the 83rd Congress.* Knoxville: University of Tennessee Press, 1975.

Reichley, A. James. *Conservatives in an Age of Change: The Nixon and Ford Administrations.* Washington, D.C.: Brookings Institution, 1981.

Reichley, A. James. "The Rise of National Parties." In *The New Direction in American Politics.* Edited by John E. Chubb and Paul E. Peterson, 175–200. Washington, D.C.: Brookings Institution, 1985.

Reinhard, David W. *The Republican Right Since 1945.* Lexington: University Press of Kentucky, 1983.

Reiter, Howard L. *Selecting the President: The Nominating Process in Transition.* Philadelphia: University of Pennsylvania Press, 1985.

———. "Ripon: Left Spur to the GOP." *The Nation,* February 17, 1969.

———. "Purging the GOP." *The Nation,* January 18, 1971.

———. "Parties Have Come Back Before." *The Nation,* December 7, 1974.

———. "Winter Book on the GOP." *The Nation,* February 7, 1976.

———. "Party Factionalism: National Conventions in the New Era." *American Politics Quarterly* 8 (1980): 303–318.

———. "Intra-party Cleavages in the United States Today." *Western Political Quarterly* 34 (1981): 287–300.

———. "The Limitations of Reform: Changes in the Nominating Process." *British Journal of Political Science* 15 (1985): 399–423.

Rogin, Michael Paul. *The Intellectuals and McCarthy: The Radical Specter.* Cambridge, Mass.: MIT Press, 1967.

Rovere, Richard. *The Goldwater Phenomenon.* London: Methuen, 1966.

Sale, Kirkpatrick. *Power Shift: The Rise of the Southern Rim and Its Challenge to the Eastern Establishment.* New York: Random House, 1976.

Saloma, John S. *Parties: The Real Opportunity for Effective Citizen Politics.* With Frederick H. Sontag. New York: Vintage Books, 1973.

————. *Ominous Politics: The New Conservative Labyrinth.* New York: Hill & Wang, 1984.

Scammon, Richard M., and Ben J. Wattenberg. *The Real Majority.* New York: Coward, McCann & Geoghegan, 1971.

Schapsmeier, Edward L., and Frederick N. Schapsmeier. *The Greenwood Encyclopedia of American Institutions: Political Parties and Civic Action Groups.* Westport, Conn.: Greenwood Press, 1981.

Schoenberger, Robert A. "Campaign Strategy and Party Loyalty: The Electoral Relevance of Candidate Decision-Making in the 1964 Congressional Elections." *American Political Science Review* 63 (1969): 515–520.

Shaffer, William R. *Party and Ideology in the United States Congress.* Washington, D.C.: University Press of America, 1980.

Sinclair, Barbara. *Congressional Realignment: 1925–1978.* Austin: University of Texas Press, 1982.

Smith, Richard Norton. *Thomas E. Dewey and His Times.* New York: Simon & Schuster, 1982.

Soule, John W., and J. W. Clarke, "Issue Conflict and Consensus: A Comparative Study of Democratic and Republican Delegates to the 1968 National Conventions." *Journal of Politics* 33 (1971): 72–91.

Sproat, John G. *The Best Men: Liberal Reformers in the Gilded Age.* New York: Oxford University Press, 1968.

Steinfels, Peter. *The Neoconservatives: The Men Who Are Changing America's Politics.* New York: Touchstone, 1980.

Sundquist, James L. *Dynamics of the Party System: Alignments and Realignment of Political Parties in the United States.* Revised ed. Washington, D.C.: Brookings Institution, 1983.

————. "Whither the American Party System?—Revisited." *Political Science Quarterly* 98 (1984–85): 573–593.

Sullivan, Denis G., Robert T. Nakamura, Martha Wagner Weinberg, Christopher F. Arterton, and Jeffrey L. Pressman. "Exploring the 1976 Republican Convention: Five Perspectives." *Political Science Quarterly* 92 (1977–78): 633–682.

Thayer, George. *Who Shakes the Money Tree? American Campaign Financing Practices from 1789 to the Present.* New York: Touchstone, 1973.

Thimmesch, Nick. *The Condition of Republicanism.* New York: Norton, 1968.

Thomson, Charles A., and Frances M. Shattuck. *The 1956 Presidential Campaign.* Washington, D.C.: Brookings Institution, 1960.

Turner, Michael. *The Vice-President as Policy-Maker: Rockefeller in the Ford White House.* Westport, Conn.: Greenwood Press, 1982.

Underwood, James F., and William J. Daniels. *Governor Rockefeller in New York: The Apex of Pragmatic Liberalism in the United States.* Westport, Conn.: Greenwood Press, 1982.

Viorst, Milton. *Fall from Grace: The Republican Party and the Puritan Ethic.* New York: New American Library, 1968.

Wattenberg, Martin P. *The Decline of American Political Parties 1952–80.* Cambridge, Mass.: Harvard University Press, 1984.

Weiss, Nancy J. *Farewell to the Party of Lincoln: Black Politics in the Age of FDR.* Princeton, N.J.: Princeton University Press, 1983.

White, G. Edward. *Earl Warren: A Public Life.* New York: Oxford University Press, 1982.

White, John Kenneth. *The Fractured Electorate: Political Parties and Social Change in Southern New England.* Hanover, N.H.: University Press of New England, 1983.

White, Theodore H. *The Making of the President: 1960.* London: Jonathan Cape, 1962.

———. *The Making of the President: 1964.* New York: Atheneum, 1965.

———. *The Making of the President: 1968.* London: Jonathan Cape, 1969.

Wildavsky, Aaron. *The Revolt Against the Masses: And Other Essays on Politics and Public Policy.* New York: Basic Books, 1971.

Wiley, Peter, and Robert Gottlieb. *Empires in the Sun: The Rise of the New American West.* New York: G. P. Putnam's Sons, 1982.

Williams, Philip M. "Power and the Parties: The United States." In *Parties and Democracy in Britain and America.* Edited by Vernon Bogdanor, 7–37. New York: Praeger, 1984.

Wills, Garry. *Nixon Agonistes: The Crisis of a Self-Made Man.* New York: New American Library, 1979.

Wilson, James Q. *The Amateur Democrat: Club Politics in Three Cities.* Chicago: University of Chicago Press, 1962.

Witcover, Jules. *The Resurrection of Richard Nixon.* New York: G. P. Putnam's Sons, 1970.

———. *Marathon: The Pursuit of the Presidency 1972–76.* New York: The Viking Press, 1977.

Wolfinger, Raymond, and Robert B. Arsenau. "Partisan Change in the South 1952–76." In *Political Parties: Development and Decay.* Edited by Louis Maisel and Joseph Cooper, 179–208. Beverly Hills: Sage Publications, 1978.

Index